Oh, Yuck!

THE ENCYCLOPEDIA OF EVERYTHING NASTY

BY JOY MASOFF

Illustrated by Terry Sirrell

WORKMAN PUBLISHING · NEW YORK

Library of Congress Cataloging-in-Publication Data

Masoff, Joy, 1951–
    Oh yuck!: the encyclopedia of everything nasty/ by Joy Masoff; illustrations by Terry Sirrell.
        p. cm.
    Includes bibliographical references (p.) and index.
    Summary: An alphabetical collection of articles about disgusting things, from acne, ants, and bacteria to worms, x-periments, and zits.
    ISBN-13: 978-0-7611-0771-2; ISBN-10: 0-7611-0771-1
        1. Handbooks, vade-mecums, etc.–Juvenile literature.2. Aversion–Miscellaneous–Encyclopedias, Juvenile. 3. Aversion–Encyclopedias, Juvenile. [1. Curiosities and wonders.] I. Title: Encyclopedia of everything nasty. II. Sirrell, Terry, ill. III. Title

AG105 .M428 2000
031.02—dc21   99-043603

Front cover and spine photography by Graham French, www.grahamfrench.com

Photo research and editing: Alexandra Truitt and Jerry Marshall

Illustrations by Terry Sirrell

Workman Publishing Company, Inc.
225 Varick Street
New York, NY 10014–4381
workman.com

Manufactured in the United States of America

First printing September 2000
40 39 38 37 36 35 34

This Is Dedicated to the Ones I Love...

For many years, as a den leader and packmaster of Cub Scout Troop 154, I had the pleasure of listening to a nonstop barrage of belching accompanied by the fragrant aroma of farting. I heard endless discussions about who had lost their lunch at lunch and other delicate subjects. It became painfully obvious to me that these items were of actual interest to kids. And is not just a "guy" thing, as I discovered when I became the leader of Girl Scout Troop 2340. The girls can belch with the best of them!

So I dedicate this compendium of crud to all those sweet boys and girls... and especially to my own children, Alex and Natasha (Tish) Scolnik, who never cease to amaze me with their appetite for knowledge of the bizarre. Thanks also to my husband, Lou, who endured countless gross dinner conversations that sometimes made eating tricky.

ACKNOWLEDGMENTS

I could not have written this book without the help of Pamela Adler Golden, a tireless and zealous researcher, who uncovered an awesome pile of putrid facts and made this book such great fun to work on. She was truly my partner in slime!

Also, a thousand pats on the back to Dr. Peter Richel, wacky, wild, and completely body savvy when it comes to medical matters.

Kudos as well to Margot Herrera and Tim Prairie, my editors at Workman, for their patience and their ability to discuss the ins-and-outs of fungus with complete aplomb. Thanks also to designers Lisa Hollander and Kristen Nobles for bringing the grisly side of life so vividly to the page.

And now, I think I'll go clean my ears and pick the lint out of my belly button!

CONTENTS

INTRODUCTION

What's more fun than farting, burping, and picking your nose? *Reading* about farting, burping, and picking your nose—plus a few hundred other truly disgusting things. In fact, if it's mushy, squishy, or just plain revolting, you'll find it in these pages.

Let's face it. The world is brimming over with truly gnarly, nasty things. Acne and ants. Barf and bats. Cannibals and cockroaches. And that's just the A, B, and C of it. There's a whole alphabet of nastiness out there and it's all in here. Best of all, this book will teach you all the scientific facts about this nastiness so you can dazzle your friends and relatives when having a conversation about, say, pooping or maggots.

WARNING THIS BOOK IS DOWNRIGHT DISGUSTING

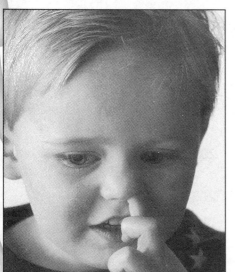

Chances are that this child will follow his nose mining with nose dining. Crusty snot—yum!

TAKE YOUR BODY FOR STARTERS

Is that dandruff flaking down onto your shoulders? And how about those ears? What is that yellow-brown gunk caught in the folds? Nose? Well, who hasn't poked around in there with the tip of a finger. Mouth? Handy to have as long as you don't breathe on someone first thing in the morning. And elsewhere . . . your belly button is full of lint, your toes have all this strange stuff lurking between them, and we haven't even *begun* to talk about the funky things that happen between your waist and your knees.

But you'll discover that some of the most disgusting things in and on your body are really just doing their job to keep you healthy. That gross greenish pus oozing out from under the scab on your knee means that your body is fighting off infection. That snot dripping from your nose is escorting some unwelcome guests—viruses or bacteria—right out through your nostrils. Strange little machine your body is. But totally awesome when you begin to understand the ways it keeps you ticking. It's cooler than a sleek racing car, more powerful than the mightiest computer. If only it didn't itch and leak!

AND HOW ABOUT THE WORLD AROUND US?

Nature is full of strange creatures—behemoth beetles, loathsome leeches, slimy slugs, and fungi the size of hippos, not to mention poop eaters, bloodsuckers, and skin shedders. It's enough to make a person say "eeek!"

Those animal-world nasties aren't all that bad, though. For instance, if those sickening vultures, maggots, and beetles weren't around to chow down on their favorite animal carcasses, we'd be living side by side with huge

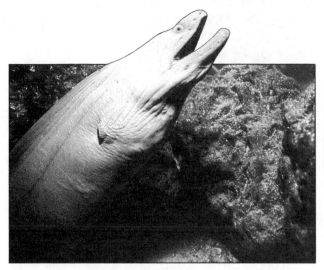

When a moray eel bites, it won't let go—you have to chop off its head and break its jaws to get it off.

piles of stinking, rotting corpses! Once you begin to understand the amazing things some of these obnoxious critters can do, you won't think they're quite so gross after all.

EVEN HISTORY IS PACKED WITH PUTRID MOMENTS

You might think that a stopped-up, overflowing toilet in the school bathroom is pretty disgusting. And you'd be right! But think about what it was like to live a few hundred years ago. No indoor toilets. (Uh-oh! Watch where you walk!) No bathing. (Did something die in here or is that just my armpits?) No refrigerators. (But Mom, I don't *like* to eat food that's moving!) Imagine wearing powder that poisoned you while it made you paler. Or following the medical advice of a doctor who tells you to drink a glass of goat pee every three hours! Trust me—the history you find in this book won't be boring. Watch for the words "The Putrid Past" for your sickening history lessons.

YOU WON'T WANT THESE IN YOUR FRIDGE

I bet you sometimes look down at your dinner plate and think, "Oh, no. Not lima beans *again.*" Well, just wait until you read about some dinnertime delicacies from around the world. Insects, worms, and monkey brains— they're all on the menu. I'll tell you one thing, though: someone somewhere in the world sitting down to a plate of fried grasshoppers would probably blow chunks if you served him a ballpark frank with all the fixin's.

Fried grasshoppers—mmm, mmm good!

So, here's the bottom line. Even some of the most revolting things in the world have an important job to do and serve a worthwhile purpose. In fact, many of the very things that make us gag form an important part of the gentle balance of our planet. Some gross things can actually bring people pleasure. (Surely you know someone who has a pet tarantula or boa constrictor, right? And those people eating fried grasshoppers actually *like* them!) So read on to discover all the good things about some of the baddest stuff on earth!

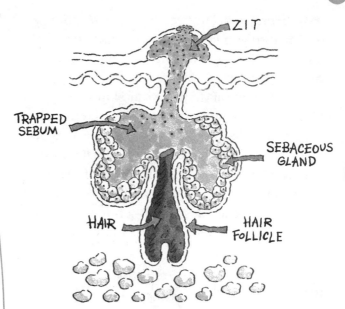

A

ACNE

Of all the cruel jokes that life plays on us—sweaty armpits, stinky breath, and gym class—pimples rank right up there on the "not fair" chart. Just when you realize that the opposite sex is actually an okay thing, you wake up one morning looking like something out of a Japanese horror movie.

GLAND-LAND

The trouble starts when you hit puberty. At teen time, your body releases a whole mess of ANDROGENS

I WISH I COULD STAY HOME, MOTHER— MY FACE LOOKS SO AWFUL

(*an-drow-ginz*), which is a fancy word for sex hormones. (They're the ones that turn your voice deep and help you grow a cool goatee if you're a guy, and that give you curves in all sorts of places if you're a girl!) But they also make the SEBACEOUS (*si-bay-shuss*) glands in your skin go crazy. These glands make SEBUM (*sea-bum*), which is a clumpy-looking fat. (See DANDRUFF, page 35, for more on sebum.)

You need sebum to keep your skin stretchy and soft. (Without it, you'd look like a lizard.) But the recipe for making sebum can get all messed up. Sometimes it becomes too thick and really sticky—kind of like substituting peanut butter for egg whites in a cake. The sebum, which is now gunky, gets stuck and blocks the sweat glands and the hair follicles around them. The follicles have no choice but to stretch outward to make room for all the dead skin cells that would normally have been shed. They're stuck—with no way out! Before you know it, you're staring at a lump the size of a volcano waiting to blow . . . right on the tip of your nose!

When an oil duct in your skin gets blocked off by a thick cap of oil mixed with dead skin cells and hunks of bacteria, you become the proud owner of a COMEDO (*kah-meh-doe*). If that oil plug makes it all the way to the surface of your skin and breaks through, you now have a blackhead—a hunk of sebum that turned dark when the air hit it. Fun, huh? If the sebum simmers just below the surface of the skin and can't get any air, you merely have a whitehead.

Blackheads and whiteheads are both pretty annoying. But on the pain-in-the-rump scale of annoying things, they're about the equivalent of your little brother whining about wanting to watch some stupid cartoon when you want to watch a really cool action flick. On the other hand, PIMPLES, also known as ZITS, are the equivalent of being forced to spend eternity with that geeky kid from homeroom! A major, major bummer!

To Squeeze or Not to Squeeze

Resist the temptation to press, push, pop, or in any way *touch* that poor little pimple. Messing with it damages the surrounding skin, spreads bacteria like crazy, and leaves a yucky mess on your bathroom mirror! Doctors all say No! No! No! And in case you didn't hear me just now . . . NO!

Let's go back to that blocked gland. Suppose it stretches and stretches and the sebum mutates into something called FREE FATTY ACIDS (let's call them FFAs for short). Now, FFAs and your body don't get along well. FFAs are, to put it mildly, irritating. Bacteria, though, love to feast on them. Word gets out that there are good eats at pimple number 23. Crowds of hungry bacteria pile on. Mount Pimple is about to erupt. (To read more about the nasty antics of BACTERIA, turn to page 6.)

That's when you get those mammoth red lumps with the dainty frosting of white-yellow-green on top. That frosting is something called PUS, which is formed by white blood cells coming to the rescue to do what they do best—kill bacteria. (See PUS, page 124, for more on the daring adventures of white blood cells.)

ZITCODES

What to do if you wake up one morning looking like last night's pepperoni pizza? First off, don't panic. Nerves make the hormones kinda . . . nervous. Then they start making even more trouble. So, stay *calm*. Then try the following remedies.

Wash a couple of times a day with an antibacterial soap, but don't wash too often. (If you wash too much, your skin gets faked out, thinks it's too dry, and starts making even more oil!)

Over-the-counter medications can help a little. (They're the ones you don't need a doctor's prescription for.) Some contain stuff that can cover the redness. But they can't make you any older, and in the end that's what needs to happen. You'll find that as you get older your hormones will finally settle down and stop making your skin so oily. And don't give up hope if things get really out of hand. Skin docs, called DERMATOLO-GISTS *(der-ma-tol-o-jists)*, can prescribe super medications that can clear up your skin by calming those ruffled hormones.

Remember . . . zits happen to everyone to some degree. The rare few who escape will probably end up getting wrinkles a lot earlier, and will look like shriveled-up old prunes by the time they're forty. There. Does that make you feel any better?

ANTS

What's worse than ants in your pants? How about stepping on a nest of angry ones that chew on your ankles and bite their way up to your neck, leaving juicy blisters wherever they've gnawed?

ATTACK OF THE KILLER ANTS!

Ants are everywhere. More than 8,800 different types swarm all over the globe. Some like sweets, some like meat, some can kill a person. You may think they're merely annoying. But what could be more disgusting than something like the PHAROAH ANT?

This nuisance loves hospitals, where it feasts on surgical wounds, IV solutions, sealed packs of sterile dressings or, better yet, used bloody bandages that have been tossed in the trash! And then there's the famous ODOROUS HOUSE ANT—it stinks of rotten coconuts when you squish it.

No doubt about it—a swarm of 300,000 ants can ruin a picnic and turn a stomach pretty quickly. Ants can live in burning-hot sand, in bricks, on dead plants, and—a particular favorite—under layers of greasy garbage. One famous ant colony even lived in the biology labs at Harvard University. They were discovered carrying radioactive particles from the petri dishes into the walls of the school. They were completely unharmed by radioactive dosages that could have killed Godzilla!

THE PUTRID PAST

In ancient times, (say, 20 years ago), skin doctors figured that if you ate fried food you'd be adding to your body's oil supply (remember . . . "fried" means cooked in oil). Chocolate—another high-fat food—was also a no-no. So kids were told to stop eating the only things they actually like to eat!

Of course, that advice was nonsense. It's not like kids were taking those french fries and chocolate bars and rubbing them all over their faces! So, unless you're rubbing fried chicken or melted chocolate bars all over your skin, food is rarely a player in this game. The bad guy here is hormones and there's not a lot you can do about them except *grow up!*

SQUISH-A-THON

Start stomping! Where there's one ant, there are hundreds of thousands more right behind it. Ants are social insects that live in colonies ruled over by a queen. But being a queen ant is no great shakes. It's not as if she gets to sit around on a throne all day fussing with her tiara. A queen ant lives only to make babies. She is helped by males that make her egg-laying possible and that form an ant army to protect those eggs. The unluckiest ants are the workers. They will never become mommies, never fall in love with another ant. Many are born blind. Workers are doomed to a life of endless drudgery, spending their whole short lives gathering food for the colony and looking after all of the queen's new babies. And speaking of eating . . .

The most dangerous and strongest part of an ant is its mouth. Powerful MANDIBLES (an ant's jaws) work like scissors—slicing and dicing food *and* foes. Behind the mandibles lie a second set of jaws called the MAXILLAE (*mac-sill-eye*). These grind food into small pieces, so the ant can suck out all the liquid and spit the leftover food onto the ground. That's one reason not to walk barefoot in the summer. Who wants bits of leftover ant spit clinging to the soles of their feet?

There sure are a lot of gross ants to step on. But you might well want to steer clear of these . . .

ALLEGHENY MOUND ANTS You've probably seen an anthill or two in your life—those little mounds of dirt that pile up in the cracks of the pavement. But the ALLEGHENY MOUND ANT likes to think big. Their anthills can measure up to 3 feet high and 6 feet wide. Not exactly something you can muss up with your shoe, is it?

ARMY ANTS These are truly icky. They march neatly along in lines of up to a million bugs, mostly in Central and South America. In Mexico, people move out of their houses when they see the lines approaching. The ants gobble up everything in their path—insects, spiders, even rats and mice. These bugs can team up to dismember a chicken with their fierce mandibles and then devour it. They have even been known to pig out on pigs that happened to be injured or ill. When the ants have finished swarming and eating, they keep on marching. The people can then move

4

back into their de-bugged houses. Free spring cleaning!

CARPENTER ANTS Although these ants don't bite, they do destroy houses. They like to make their nests in wood. To do this, they hollow out all the beams that hold your house up. Before you know it, your walls are caving in and your roof is falling. *Timber!*

DRIVER ANTS If you are a small mammal in Africa, you do not want to be in the path of a DRIVER ANT. Driver ants are closely related to the army ants and they love meat! They kill anything that happens to get in their way—even a wounded lion or crocodile—by using their scissorlike mandibles to slash their unlucky victims who then bleed to death.

In parts of Africa, people use driver ants instead of stitches to close deep cuts. A person will pinch the wound closed and then drop an ant down on the cut. The ant bites down on either side of the wound and the person quickly snaps off the body, leaving the ant's head in place until the wound heals. The mandibles remain in the closed position, locked tight until they eventually fall apart. And speaking of biting. . .

All out of Band-Aids? Try clamping your next cut closed with the mandibles of an army or driver ant.

With a nickname like "the dinosaur ant," you know it's got to be big. Over an inch long, you wouldn't want to find one on your sandwich!

FIRE ANTS Being bitten by a FIRE ANT is like being hit with a blowtorch. Once bitten, your skin literally burns as the ant's poisonous venom seeps into your skin. You'll soon be covered with pus-filled blisters wherever you've been bitten. Fire ant bites are tons of "not-fun." It used to be that fire ants only hung out in South America, but they've snuck into at least 11 southern states. And for those unlucky enough to be allergic to the fire ant's venom, one bite can spell R.I.P.—*rest in peace!*

GREASE ANTS Some ants like sweets, but the GREASE ANT likes guess what? Grease! They also like dead insects and rodents, which makes them the vultures of the ant family. (To learn about the real thing, see VULTURES on page 192.)

So the next time you're at a picnic and an innocent little BLACK ANT (the kind that most of us have squooshed to smithereens) crosses your plate, just be grateful it's not going to make you bleed to death.

B

BACTERIA

You can't see 'em; you can't hear 'em; you can't taste 'em. But, oh boy, can they make you smelly or sick!

THE GOOD, THE BAD, AND THE STINKY

Bacteria are tiny living things (known as microorganisms) that cover the entire earth. They live in the dirt and deep in the sea. They float through the air and thrive in the bodies of every living thing. They are *not* plants, *not* animals, *not* fungi. Instead they belong to a group of living things called MONERA (*moan-air-ah*).

Most bacteria are so small that if you put 10,000 of them in a row, they would measure only about an inch. (And getting your hands on 10,000 bacteria is a snap. One bacterium can divide into a million bacteria in half a day!) Of course, there always has to be an exception to every rule. A monster bacteria has just been discovered lurking in the reeking, sulfurous muck of the ocean bottom near the coast of Namibia in Africa. These are big guys, big enough that you can see them without using a microscope. Each is about the size of the period at the end of this sentence. That may not seem huge, but in the bacteria world, that's a King Kong of a germ.

What do bacteria love to do most of all? Munch! They munch on the oil in our skin and the partially digested dinner in our guts. They'll invade the flesh of a dead cow and the grease in your kitchen drain. They'll even take on a half-mile-wide oil spill!

Most bacteria are totally cool little microbes (another name for microorganisms). Some turn raw sewage into chemicals that help plants grow. Then there are the ones that specialize in devouring grease, eating pond scum, or lapping up those huge oil spills. Good bacteria such as these are actually sold by laboratories around the world. Other good bacteria help break down animal hides so they can be turned into shoes, handbags, briefcases, and those cool motorcycle jackets. Other ones are used to make vaccines, medicines, yogurt, and even tea!

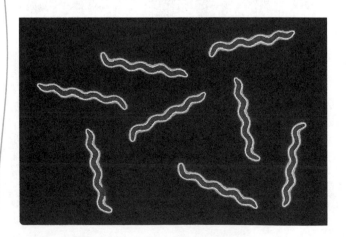

Then there are the "geeky" bacteria, like the ones that create a stink in our armpits. They're not exactly harmful, but they sure are annoying. (See BODY ODOR, page 21, and FOUL FEET, page 63, for more on those icky geeks.)

Finally, there are "bully" bacteria that can make us sick by causing food poisoning, strep throat, pneumonia, diarrhea, and other big-time problems.

Bacteria come in different shapes, just like the bullies at school. There are tall, skinny ones, round, pudgy ones, spiral ones, and curvy ones. And just like the school bullies, they can make your life miserable. Read "Bacteria—Up Close and Personal" to find out their names.

WHERE THE BAD GUYS HIDE

One of the main ways that bully bacteria are spread is through bad hygiene. Translation? Not washing your hands after you go to the bathroom. Remember that half of what your

Back to back bacteria! The squiggly ones at far left are spirochetes just waiting to give someone Lyme disease. The round ones in the middle are cocci that cause pneumonia, and the cheese-doodle-shaped ones below are vibrios, which can give you cholera.

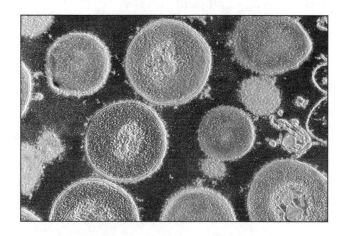

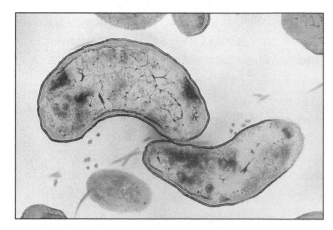

body's getting rid of when you poop is bacteria. Some of it is harmless, but some is not. (See POOP, page 121.) As you wipe, bacteria can leap onto your hands. Once on your hands, the bacteria start to reproduce like crazy. If a person who works at the local burger joint doesn't wash, those bacteria creep into everything he handles—the burgers and fries and milk shakes. And before you can say "I think I'm gonna hurl," you—and anyone else who had the bad luck to eat there that day—will be tossing cookies!

Other times, sickness starts when bacteria that live aboard one animal make the move to another. A perfectly healthy chicken's guts are crawling with salmonella bacteria that help the chicken digest all that chicken feed. But when that same bacteria gets into our intestines, disaster can strike (see "The Baddest Bacteria in Town!"). "But," you say, "it's not like I'm kissing a chicken." True, but chances are you're eating one! Undercooked chicken can give you salmonella. Even eating the uncooked egg that has been beaten into brownie batter can make you pretty sick, so don't lick that spoon!

Some nonliving things, such as air conditioners, can hide bacteria cities. Certain types of these microbes adore the warm wetness that's created by air conditioner motors. And the air blowing from them propels millions of bacteria into the air—*and* the lungs of whoever happens to be in the room! Before you

know what's hit you, you'll be shaking with chills and flushed with a fever from Legionnaires' disease (see the box for more grisly details).

Fortunately, other living creatures, namely FUNGI *(fun-guy),* can beat the bully bacteria up. That's basically what that nasty pink stuff is that your doctor gives you for ear infections or strep throat—a mess of bigger, meaner critters.

Kind of like the principal and the dean of students on the warpath. These ANTIBIOTICS (that's what the pink stuff is called) destroy bacteria. And, boy, are we grateful to them. Their only downside: they wipe out the good bacteria (those that break down food) along with the bad. That's why lots of us end up with the trots when we take antibiotics. But fear not! The good-guy bacteria will be back! And you can even help bring them back faster by eating yogurt that contains active acidophilus cultures (See POOP, page 121, for more on the trots.)

The Baddest Bacteria in Town!

They're deadly, dangerous, and downright disgusting. Here are some of the meanest microbes and how to avoid them.

1. CAMPYLOBACTER (camp-peh-low-back-ter)

Got a bad case of the runs? This critter could be the cause. It invades the intestines through poorly cooked food, then excretes a toxin that destroys the mucus lining of the gut.

2. CLOSTRIDIUM TETANI (klah-stri-dee-yum tet-in-eye)

All of you have had to get a tetanus (tet-nus) shot from time to time. That's to protect you from this nasty bacterium. Down in the dirt, just about everywhere in the world, there are sleeping spores of clostridium. Infection begins when the spores creep into an injury or wound. The spores germinate, just like a seed that grows into a plant, except the spores release active bacteria. These bacteria multiply and produce a neurotoxin that makes muscles go into severe spasms. Your muscles can rip and your bones snap from the power of these contractions, and some very little bacteria can leave you very dead. Suddenly that tetanus shot doesn't seem quite so bad, does it?

3. E. COLI (Ee coe-lie)

Chances are you've heard of this little creep. It's most often found hiding out in cattle doo-doo, and each year over 20,000 Americans end up sick as dogs from eating food tainted with it. At its least, it can give you the nastiest case of diarrhea you've ever had; at its worst, this bug can destroy every organ in your body, turning your heart and liver to mush. How can you avoid this deadly bug? Cook your hamburgers really well. No pink meat for you! Wash forks and knives that have touched raw meat before using them again. And always wash your hands after you shape those hamburger patties!

4. LEGIONELLA (lee-jon-el-ah)

Remember Legionnaires' disease from page 8? Back in the 1970s, a bunch of guys who belonged to an organization called the American Legion went to a convention in Philadelphia. While they were there, a lot of them got really sick with a serious lung infection that came to be known as Legionnaires' disease. The culprit was the hotel's air-conditioning, which was sending airborne bacteria hurtling through the hotel! Scientists named this strain of bacteria after those unlucky folks who got sick.

5. SALMONELLA (sal-muh-nell-uh)

Chickens and eggs, when not cooked enough, harbor this dandy disease-bringer. Even fruit and ice cream can hide this varmint. Got food poisoning? Chances are, if you're puking your guts out, the culprit was salmonella.

6. SHIGELLA (shi-gell-ah)

This breed of bacteria attacks the lining of the small intestines. Cramps, gas, and the "squirts" are the result. And how does the bacteria get there? Contaminated food, fly-infested homes, and bad sanitation. Shigella is especially common in developing countries and refugee camps.

BACTERIA BREAKDOWN

When bacteria eat, they break complex substances, like your half-digested dinner, into smaller, simpler things. Imagine a huge Lego tower. It's made of a thousand little tiny blocks, all snapped together. But the bacteria only want to play with three or four blocks, three rows from the bottom. So they start to unsnap the whole building! When they are done, the tower doesn't look like a tower anymore. It looks like a mess.

Bacteria—Up Close and Personal

Bacteria are tiny but that doesn't mean they all look alike. Here are their four basic shapes.

COCCI (*cock-eye*) As round as marbles, not nearly as much fun. They like to gang up and cause strep throat, pneumonia, and boils (a nasty skin infection).

 **BACILLI** (*ba-sill-eye*) Rod-shaped, and an occasional big-time troublemaker. Bacteria from this group cause the lung disease tuberculosis.

SPIROCHETES (*spy-ra-keets*) Look like a kind of curly pasta. They don't taste like it, though. Some of these bullies are responsible for Lyme disease, which is spread by tick bites and is a real nuisance in the northeastern part of the United States.

VIBRIOS (*vib-ree-ohs*) Curvy and sometimes creepy. They look like miniature commas and can cause all sorts of tummy troubles.

Some bacteria breathe in oxygen just like we do. Some breathe in hydrogen sulfide and exhale sulfur. And where there's sulfur, there's *stinkiness!*

All living things rot . . . sometimes quickly, sometimes very, v-e-r-y slowly. Rotting is, believe it or not, a part of growing—of living. Without rotting, the corpses of everything that has died since life on earth began would be piled up all over the place! Bacteria help makes that rotting happen. Let's say that a caterpillar gets squooshed on the street. A goner, right? No heartbeat. No breathing. But the bacteria living on the caterpillar are still chugging along. They invade the tissue and alter the chemical makeup of that caterpillar, breaking it down into smaller and smaller bits until it disappears and is reabsorbed into the earth.

So let's have a round of applause for those hard-working bacteria. If it weren't for them, you'd be stepping on a mile-high mound of dead bodies on your way to school every day!

BAD BREATH

Just woke up and wondering what that awful stench is? Well, it's probably coming from your mouth. Whether you call it horse breath, moose breath, or just plain morning mouth, to find out more about it see HALITOSIS on page 78.

BARF

What's green and brown and red all over? Barf! Want to know more about that stinky, goopy, altogether nasty stuff? Turn to VOMIT on page 187 to find out what's up with tossed cookies (and why they sure don't smell like chocolate chips!).

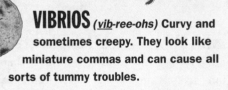

BATS

Are they evil creatures, determined to latch on to your neck and suck every ounce of blood from your body? Are they some disgusting combination of bird and rat? Do you still believe in the Easter Bunny and the Tooth Fairy? If you answered "yes" to all the above questions, you need to wise up and learn a bit about bats.

TALES FROM THE BAT CAVE

Once again, those high-paid Hollywood scriptwriters have gotten it all wrong. Let's get something straight right off the bat. Out of the 850 species of bat, only 3 drink blood. They are called VAMPIRE BATS and they live in Central and South America. But they don't swoop down on their prey (which usually is a cow, not a person, by the way). Instead, they climb up a furry leg to just above the hoof, or slip silently onto the back of an ear. They then make a small incision with their razor-sharp teeth. And, contrary to popular opinion, bats don't suck blood. They lap it up, kind of like a cat drinking milk from a bowl. An ANTICOAGULANT (*an-tee-co-ag-u-lent*) in their saliva keeps the blood from clotting. No one likes lumpy gravy!

As vampire bats drink blood at one end of their bodies, they are busy at the other. While they're busy sipping, they are also busy peeing—all at the same time. This lightens their load, so if they have to take off in a hurry, they'll be ready to fly high, fast.

Vampire bats are very kind creatures when it comes to the way they treat each other. If one is too sick to go out to dinner, a buddy will fly out, drink a blood meal, fly back, and then puke it all up for the sick bat to drink. Sweet, huh?

The exception to this kindly behavior is the FALSE VAMPIRE BAT. These creatures sometimes eat other bats, along with rodents and bugs. They treat their victims like bat-flavored chewing gum, chomping for long periods of time and sucking all the flavor out of them before swallowing.

And in case you're curious about the bathroom habits of food-eating bats, they work a little differently. Instead of peeing constantly, these bats are prolific poopers, and the stuff they produce is called GUANO (*gwa-no*). Which leads us into a truly yucky place.

HOME STINKY HOME

What's it like inside a typical bat cave? Imagine thick piles of powdery guano all over everything. If you were to walk across the floor of a bat cave, you would leave fluffy footprints in the guano. But all that guano is actually useful. During America's Civil War, bat poop was used to make gunpowder. Today, companies actually sell the stuff because it makes great fertilizer.

Don't be afraid! It's just a common vampire bat!

Bat guano is sometimes home to millions of creeping, crawling beetles. If you decided to stop and take a snooze in a pile of beetle-infested bat guano (talk about bats in your belfry!) you would be a skeleton within 24 hours. That's all the time it takes for those beetles to strip a carcass clean! (For the lowdown on other members of this vile group of critters, see BEETLES on page 14.)

By the way, visiting bat caves is a definite no-no. The air inside the caves is filled with toxic levels of ammonia, which is a waste product of the beetles that live in the guano. Another reason to stay out of bat caves is that you can actually catch rabies by breathing in the airborne virus in an infested cave.

Bracken Cave, near San Antonio, Texas, is home to 20 million bats. Every evening, from spring until fall, as the sun sets, great swarms of bats swirl out of the mouth of the cave in a counterclockwise tornado-like formation. In the morning, the bats return, 50,000 at a time, each group

What's hangin' around in Bracken Cave in Texas? Oh, just out one of the world's biggest swarms of bats. Watch out for falling guano!

Bat Stats

Bat "pups" are big babies, weighing in at a quarter of their mom's weight. That's like your mother giving birth to someone the size of a first-grader. Ouch!

Bats are the only true flying mammals. Flying squirrels don't really fly, they glide, and lemurs actually leap.

World's smallest bat? The Bumblebee Bat of Thailand is about the size and weight of a penny. The biggest? That'd be the giant Flying Fox of Indonesia (which, of course, isn't a fox at all) with a 6-foot wingspan.

Bats use up a lot of energy in their pursuit of groceries! And if the bug-and-blood pickings have been slim, they need to conserve that energy. They do this by lowering their body temperature from close to 100°F to just above freezing. Then, they take a snooze. A bat that's shivering is trying to warm and wake himself up again.

Can males make milk? They can if they're male Malaysian fruit bats! They have—pardon me—bosoms, and they really do lactate! (In case you didn't know, "lactate" means to produce milk.)

Bats *do* carry rabies, as do many other warm-blooded animals, but they are not the source of the disease. And unlike other sick critters, sick bats are never aggressive. They just get very sleepy and hang around their caves until they literally drop and become dinner for a hungry beetle or two.

Bats hang upside down because their legs are too weak to support their weight. If a bat tried to stand up, it would topple over.

circling in a mile-high holding pattern, waiting for their turn to call it a day—better make that a *night*. When it is their turn, they dive down at 80 miles an hour, before spreading their wings and gliding in for a landing, each drawn to its exact roosting spot by the sounds of its pups' chirps. It all looks like a giant black waterfall when it's happening!

BLIND AS A BAT?

Actually, bats can see just fine, but they do their dining in the hours of darkness, and their night vision is nothing special (except for some species, like the Asian fruit bat, which has extraordinary night vision). Just the same, a bat can catch 600 mosquitoes in the dark in less than an hour! Finding those tasty morsels takes superpowers! That's where bat ears come into the picture. Now, bat ears may look gross, but they are definitely cool. Using something called ECHOLOCATION *(eck-o-lo-kay-shun)*, a kind of sonar, bats can identify anything in their path. Their superpower ears, each equipped with a tough, pointed piece of skin called a TRAGUS *(tray-gus)*, are perfect for catching those bounced-back sound waves. Think of them as super sound-scoopers.

Here's how echolocation works. If you've ever made an echo, either in a canyon or in a tunnel, you've gone a little "batty." A bat produces ultrasonic, high-frequency sounds through its mouth and nose—about 30 times a second. As the sound waves bounce back, they give the bats information about what's out there. Bats can tell the difference between a rock and a beetle—and can even zero in on tasty moth wings, skipping the moth's crusty middle parts. The bats' ears are so finely tuned that they can detect the ripple in a pond as a minnow's fin breaks the surface—even from a block or two away.

As for bats flying into people's hair and getting all tangled up in it? Come on! If these guys can find a mosquito in the sky, surely they can steer clear of a 90-pound kid!

Gross but Good

On a hot muggy night in midsummer, the average bat will gobble up between 3,000 and 7,000 mosquitoes—averaging about 600 an hour. Think what 600 mosquitoes could do to your skin! Feeling grateful yet? A colony of 500 bats will polish off an amazing quarter of a million insects in just one hour. No bug zappers. No stinky pesticides. Just a bunch of flying mammals with a hearty appetite.

Bats are even protected by the governments of many countries because they are so crucial to the ecology. They spread seeds in forests by eating their meals in-flight and dropping the seeds in barren areas. Bats also pollinate plants that other creatures don't visit. The lesser long-nosed bat below is doing just that to this saguaro cactus while he slurps up its nectar. Bats are also the sworn enemies of a lot of the bugs that damage crops. Best of all, unlike those nasty chemical sprays, bats leave no harmful poisons behind.

BEETLES

They make a disgusting crunch when you step on them. They can grow to be as much as seven inches long (try flattening that with your shoe). They can kill a healthy tree. Others do nothing all day but play with and eat piles of doo-doo. Some have farts so stinky, they make skunks seem sweet-smelling. Others are so aggressive, they can strip a dead animal down to the bones in a matter of hours. And to think, all this foulness comes neatly packed up in one shiny little type of bug—the beetle.

THE BEETLE BEAT

If you think humans are the dominant life form on earth, think again. One out of every five living species is a beetle! There are over 350,000 different kinds! And these little armored-tank bugs have some wild tricks up their wings. Beetles belong to a group of insects called COLEOPTERA (*co-lee-op-ter-a*), which means "sheath-winged." A sheath is a protective covering. (Hunters keep knives in sheaths, for example.) Beetles' steely, strong, outer wings, called ELYTRA (*el-i-trah*), are what give them their hard, shell-like appearance. They keep a second pair of wings tucked inside their sheaths.

These delicate inner wings are the ones they use to fly.

But this isn't a biology book, so let's get down to the good 'n' gross parts.

DINNER AT THE DUNG DINER

Picture a huge pile of elephant poop. Can you see it in your mind? Smell it? Good! Now, be careful not to step in it . . . and picture *this*. A parade of insects has just marched out to that poop pile. Pretend a whistle is blown. The game is on! Within a few hours the entire smelly mound will be gone. Another victory for Africa's DUNG BEETLE.

These beetles adore eating manure. Dung. Poop. Ca-ca. Call it what you want, but know that they love it! (One researcher counted 16,000 beetles snacking happily on a three-pound pile of poop. It was gone in two hours.) And, if you can believe it, some beetles are very picky eaters, feasting on the poop of only one kind of animal.

Poop is the dung beetles' life. Their whole society revolves around it. Lovers present each other with balls of it instead of candy and flowers. Weddings are held when a male and female roll a ball of dung together.

(These are not little balls, either. Some are 50 times the weight of a single beetle.) And the dung beetles are nothing if not fore-sighted. Not only do they burrow into it and roll in it, but they save it and squirrel it away for dungless days. SCARAB BEETLES, which can be found in most tropical climates, are a kind of dung beetle. These crafty beetles roll themselves into a ball of poop, then lay their eggs in it, before crawling out.

Dung beetles don't live on poop alone. They also adore eating horn flies. Now, these varmints attack livestock, especially bulls. Attracted by the bull's "manly" scent, as many as 10,000 flies can creep onto a bull's back and suck the poor boy's blood until he dies. Enter "superbeetle," gobbling up the horn fly eggs and larvae like popcorn at a movie. Dung beetles have actually wiped out these cow-killing flies in a couple of places. So, to ranchers, some dung beetles are heroes!

A Beastly Bit

Ever wonder how animals and plants get those fancy Latin names? If you find a new species that has never been recorded before, you get to name it. Terry Erwin is a beetle researcher, a COLEOPTERIST (*co-lee-op-ter-ist*) for all you Latin-lovers, who works in the Peruvian rain forest. He has discovered thousands of new beetle species, and coming up with Latin names for them can be fun. When Terry discovered two beetles from the family Agra, he called the two new species *Agra sasquatch* and *Agra yeti,* because they had big feet. But he also found one that he had a hard time describing, so he called it *Agra vation.* Say it three times fast. Get it?

BIG. BAD. AND SMELLY.

The world is full of fascinating beetles. Some are cute, like LADYBUGS. But many of them are totally disgusting. Here are just a few of the not-so-charming ones.

BOMBARDIER (bom-ba-deer) BEETLES

These beetles shoot a toxic chemical from their anal glands when they get scared, just like skunks do. These little stink bombs explode into puffy clouds, accompanied by a noisy, whoopee-cushion symphony. The frog who might have been considering this beetle for dinner loses track of it in a noxious fog and has to plug its nose and dive for cover.

BURYING BEETLES

If you're looking for the most ghoulish beetle . . . the BURYING BEETLE takes the bodies of dead birds and mammals and buries them, just the way a dog buries a bone. This beetle has helpers—thousands of little mites that live right on the beetle, waiting to slide off onto the soon-to-be-buried victim. Together they make mincemeat of the corpse. The mites eat maggots off the dead creature so there's more left for the beetles. The beetles lay

Dig those burying beetles doing their ghoulish thing with a dead mouse.

their eggs near the carcass. Then they bite off a hunk of dead flesh, eat it, puke it up, and feed it to their growing babies!

DERMESTID (der-mess-tid) BEETLES One of these can strip the skin off a dead animal in a matter of hours, leaving

nothing but perfect, picked-clean bones. Natural history museums use dermestid larvae to clean up critters that are going to be used in exhibits. Unfortunately, this sometimes-helpful beetle also causes millions of dollars in crop damage each year. They adore eating grain almost as much as rotten animal flesh. If they happen to move indoors, they'll eat your wool carpeting right down to the bare floor.

GOLIATH BEETLES The world's heaviest beetle is the GOLIATH BEETLE. Got a hamster? Now, imagine a beetle that size! But don't worry. Unless you live in a tropical rain forest, such as the Amazon, you don't have to worry about stepping on one. These poop-eating creatures hold the prize for being the heaviest insects in the world. And since dung is the Goliath beetle's primary food source, I'd

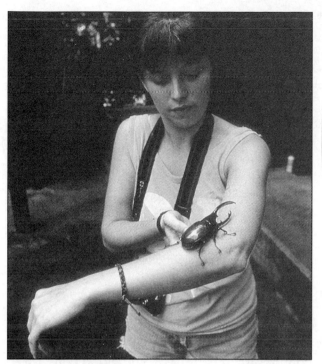

This giant rhinoceros beetle's Latin name is Dymastes hercules, *named for the famous strongman from mythology.*

RHINOCEROS STAG BEETLES

This beetle wins the prize for the ugliest beetle around—a creature with not one but three spiky horns sticking out of its head and chest. Wouldn't want to meet one of them in a dark alley.

STINK BEETLES

These can produce an odor like the stinkiest, rottenest cheese. They ooze a vile-smelling liquid from the tip of their abdomens. Even the hungriest predator will steer clear of the stench. Some female stink beetles even spray pesky male beetles who pay them unwanted attention. One whiff can leave a male stink beetle unconscious for hours.

hate to think what would squoosh out of one if you should happen to step on it.

JAPANESE BEETLES

For sheer peskiness, the award goes to this beetle, which is as shiny as a cheap suit. JAPANESE BEETLES are the ones that devour Mom's prized roses.

THE PUTRID PAST

The ancient Egyptians adored beetles, and their sacred scarab beetle was a symbol of life and rebirth. But how did the scarab beetle get its reputation as a heavenly creature when all it did was roll big balls of doo-doo around all day before burying them? The Egyptians saw the scarab as the symbol of the god KHEPHER, whose job it was to roll the sun across the sky every day before burying it for the night.

Well-dressed Egyptians wore pins that looked like beetles. Mummies had scarabs wrapped in with their bandages. Some corpses even had their hearts replaced with carvings that looked like scarabs.

WATER BEETLES

Folks in Florida are used to finding something else besides shampoo in their showers. WATER BEETLES can be the size of a small hairbrush and love hanging around bathtub drains.

BLISTERS

So you didn't listen to your mom when she told you not to wear your new shoes without socks. Now your heel's sporting a big painful bubble the size of a volcano—and it's about to blow! To find out more about that awful blister (and why Mom always knows best!) see SKIN ERUPTIONS on page 144.

BLOOD

It drips from banged-up noses and oozes from freshly picked scabs. It gushes like a bright red fountain from damaged body parts and the sight of it can make a grown man faint. And, without it, you'd be dead as a doorknob.

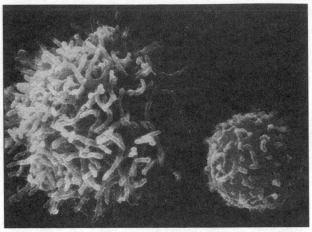

These white blood cells may not look like much, but when an enemy—bacteria, fungi, or viruses—attack, these warrior cells will fight to the finish to keep you healthy.

CITY OF BLOOD

A single drop of your blood is made up of 250 *million* separate cells. Blood is like a huge community in your body. The blood cells are the people that live and work there. Each type of blood cell has a different job to do and there are over 25 billion blood cells swirling around inside you at this very second. If you could string all your blood cells together they would circle the globe four times.

The RED CELLS are sort of a combination of pizza delivery guy and trash hauler all in one. They bring oxygen to your organs (kind of like when the pizza guy brings you a pizza) and carry away the carbon dioxide (like a garbage truck that picks up the crust, the left-over anchovies, and the box when you're through).

The WHITE BLOOD CELLS are the Army, the Navy, and the Air Force. They protect your body against enemy attacks by those nasty invaders—bacteria

and viruses. There are five different types of white blood cells, all with different jobs. Think of them as everything from foot soldiers to experienced generals.

PLASMA, which makes up over half of your blood, is the transportation system in your body—the cars and buses, trains and planes. It transports all the other cells to the places they need to go. The plasma carries all sorts of other things too, like salt, sugars, vitamins, and waste products.

PLATELETS help your blood to clot. Think of them as containers for your blood's Silly String. When you get hurt, the "string" (which is called FIBRIN) gets released, makes a web that traps the other cells, and ties up the wound.

WHAT'S BLACK AND BLUE AND GREEN ALL OVER?

Turning blue and green and purple is kind of cool, and that's what you can look forward to when you have a HEMATOMA *(hee-ma-toe-ma)*, the fancy doctor-word for a big, bad bruise. Trip into the edge of your desk and, before you know it, there's a life-or-death drama going on under your skin.

What you're actually seeing is a blood clot underneath your skin, caused by blood that's leaked out from the blood vessels into the surrounding tissue. How does your body get rid of that bluish/purply splotch? Think white!

White blood cells rush to the rescue! Charging into the injured area, hungry for a meal of red corpuscles (another name for a blood cell), they'll chomp away until those blood cells are small enough to be absorbed back into the bloodstream.

Hematomas start out purple, then fade to brown, then greenish-yellow as the blood is digested. Next time you get one, why not stop to choose a favorite color in the bruise rainbow?

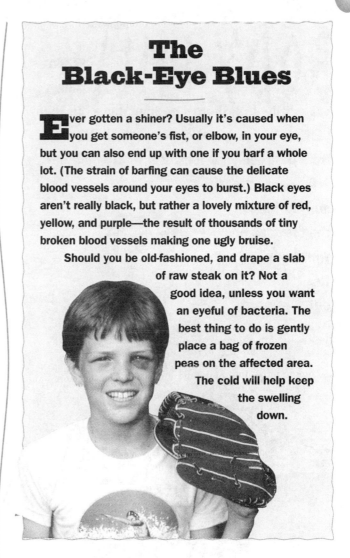

The Black-Eye Blues

Ever gotten a shiner? Usually it's caused when you get someone's fist, or elbow, in your eye, but you can also end up with one if you barf a whole lot. (The strain of barfing can cause the delicate blood vessels around your eyes to burst.) Black eyes aren't really black, but rather a lovely mixture of red, yellow, and purple—the result of thousands of tiny broken blood vessels making one ugly bruise.

Should you be old-fashioned, and drape a slab of raw steak on it? Not a good idea, unless you want an eyeful of bacteria. The best thing to do is gently place a bag of frozen peas on the affected area. The cold will help keep the swelling down.

ROSY NOSIES

The medical word for a nosebleed is EPISTAXIS *(ep-ah-stack-sis)*. It can be caused by dry air, but the number one reason it happens is those picky fingers. Noses are loaded with blood vessels lying just below the thin mucous membranes. They are there to help warm the incoming air. So leave it alone. (See SNOT, page 160, for more on the perils of picking.)

Without blood we wouldn't have all those dandy little things like SCABS (see page 134) and PUS (see page 124). There'd be no MOSQUI-TOES (see page 103), FLEAS (see page 57), LICE (see page 91), or LEECHES (see page 88). And what on earth would Dracula do for dinner?

BODY LINT

When things get a little dull, there's nothing more fun than picking the goop out of your belly button or from between your toes. But what *is* all that yellow-gray greasy stuff lurking in the crevices of your body? Read on!

THE "INNIES" AND "OUTIES" OF YOUR BELLY BUTTON

The word "navel" comes from the word "nave," which means the hub of a wheel. The "el" after "nave" means little. So a navel is a little wheel-hub, probably so called because people used to think the belly button was the center of the body.

Before your belly button was a belly button, it was a thick cord (about 1/2 inch thick and a little longer than an actual baby!). Called the UMBILICAL *(um-bill-uh-cul)* CORD, it connected you to your mother back in the days

before you were born. The cord was a link between the two of you, bringing you oxygen and food and taking away waste.

After you popped out, the umbilical cord was cut, and a 2- to 3-inch stump was left on you and clamped with a special device. After about two weeks, the stump dried up and dropped off. (But don't worry: There are no nerve endings in the cord. You didn't feel a thing!)

Anyway . . . now your belly button doesn't do anything except look good in a bikini and collect a whole lot of funky stuff. Because the "innie" part has lots of little folds, it's a perfect place for dirt and dead skin cells to play hide-and-seek. Microscopic fibers from your clothes also like this game and play whenever they can. So, the next time you're bored out of your mind, stick a finger into those folds and fish out some smelly, dirty hunks of dead skin, laced with a little leftover underwear cotton.

SOME TOE JAM WITH YOUR TOAST?

So what is that stuff tucked between your toes? Well, it's a stew of sorts. Your skin is constantly shedding its dead cells. (See DANDRUFF on page 35 for more on that.) Your feet, which practically have little faucets with hot and cold running sweat pouring out, moisten the cells. (See BODY ODOR, page 21, and FOUL FEET, page 63, for more gross details). And since your socks are made of cotton or wool,

the fabrics break down into tiny little fibers that get added to the mix.

Have you ever rolled clay into little balls between your fingers? Well, that's exactly what your toes do with the dead skin cells, the sweat, and the sock fibers! Add a little dirt, picked up while you were padding around without shoes, and there you have it—toe jam! Delicious!

BODY ODOR

Did someone just run over a skunk, or is that you? Quick! Stick your face in your armpit and take a whiff. Still standing? Must've been a skunk. At least this time.

GET A WHIFF OF THIS

Why do our armpits—and various other body parts—get putrid when we don't bathe? What's the problem? Here's how it works.

Say you've been in-line skating or playing soccer and it's hot. The sweat is pouring off your head and dripping down your back. Lucky you! If you weren't sweating, you'd be a dead duck. When you get too warm—whether it's because it's 100 degrees in the shade, you've just run 20 blocks, or you've got a fever—your body has to find some way to cool down.

Ever watch your mom boil water? The water molecules, which are all close together at first, break loose from each other and start to float off into the air in the form of steam.

Sweating for Dollars

Can you imagine paying money to sweat? There are grown-ups who will actually fork over big bucks to sit in a little room that has been heated to temperatures of close to 190 degrees. In steambaths and saunas, folks get to sit wrapped in a sweat-soaked towel and drip like a broken faucet for 10 or 20 minutes at a time. They think all that sweating helps to remove impurities from the body. All it really helps to do is sweat away water—water that will be replaced with the first couple of drinks they have! They might just as well flush a few dollars down the toilet. There's simply no accounting for grown-ups' tastes.

The water evaporates, making the kitchen air moister and warmer. Sweating works the same way. As water on the surface of your skin evaporates, it sends heat off into the air. On an average day, you'll sweat away four cups of liquid.

Sweat is made in little sweat shops deep in the bottom layer of your skin, called the sweat glands. There are two kinds of these glands—ECCRINE (*eck-ren*) and APOCRINE (*app-ah-kren*). The eccrine glands send out an inside-out shower that cools your skin down when you get overheated. There are eccrine glands all over your body, especially on your forehead, neck, and back. Eccrine sweat doesn't smell bad, but then, all sweat is not created equal. . . .

meets up with all the bacteria hanging out on the skin's surface, things start to heat up. Bacteria love that oil and salt mix (think french fries without the potatoes) and end up inviting all their friends to a party at the "Underarm Mall." And where there's bacteria, as you surely know by now, there's smelliness.

TIME FOR A QUICK PIT STOP

So what do you do if you suspect you have problem pits?

First off, stop that bacteria in its tracks. Take a bath or shower every day and soap up with an antibacterial soap. Give your favorite T-shirt a wash between wearings, too.

One easy and quick way to snuff out smelly pits is to splash rubbing alcohol under your arms.

Health-food stores sell pit sticks made from green tea, which is a natural antibacterial. And if all else fails, bring out the big guns . . . "no-stink" sticks like deodorant.

The apocrine glands are the skunky guys. These are the glands in your armpits, around your nipples, and in your underpants—places where there are a lot of hair follicles. The apocrine glands don't actually start to work until you hit the teenage years. Then, boy, do they start to make up for lost time! These glands get cooking at the worst possible times—just when you're about to take an important math test, or to ask that really cute kid out to a movie. When you're embarrassed or nervous, chances are good that your palms will get moist, your armpits will dampen, and beads of water might dot your forehead. And if you're not careful, you will *reek!*

The actual sweat—the water, salt, and urea (yup, the same stuff that helps make pee-pee)—has almost no smell. But the apocrine glands make sweat with a little oil mixed in. When this oily sweat

THE PUTRID PAST

Have you ever run the water, filled up the tub, sat on the bathroom floor reading a magazine, and then mussed up the towels to make it *look* like you bathed? If so, you would have loved living in the 1400s! Remember Queen Isabella? The lady who launched Christopher Columbus on his voyage to the New World? She took only two baths in her entire life! Truth is, for about 400 years, taking a bath was considered disgusting, unhealthy, and downright bad for you.

You can just imagine what it smelled like back then! People throwing pails of pee into the street. No one washing their pits after a rough sporting event. You needed an iron nose to survive in those days. In fact, perfume was invented to cover up the odor!

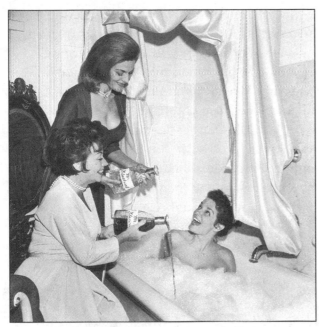

Do you think these ladies pouring expensive perfume into their friend's bath are trying to tell her something?

Deodorants kill the bacteria that live under your armpits where it's warm and wet and oh so lovely. No bacteria? No smell!

Antiperspirant goes one step farther and actually shuts down sweat production. Aluminum salts build an invisible wall that keeps the sweat from reaching the surface (and the bacteria that wait there). But since it's made from strong chemicals, antiperspirant should be used only if nothing else is working.

Sweat Stats

Now you know almost everything there is to know about those damp spots. But you're not a perspiration pro just yet. Read on!

❋ Ever wonder why the hottest places on earth serve the spiciest foods? That salsa or curry might burn your tongue, but it'll also cool down your body by revving up your sweat glands.

❋ If you watch a lot of medical shows on TV, you might occasionally hear the paramedics who are rushing a patient into the emergency room yelling that the poor guy on the gurney is DIAPHORETIC (*die*-uh-fa-*rett*-ick). That's a fancy way of saying that he's sweating all over. People having heart attacks sometimes have this symptom.

❋ Is a "cold sweat" different from an hour-of-soccer-in-June sweat? Sure it is. People with illnesses sometimes break out in cold sweats, such as when the blood sugar levels of a person with diabetes get out of whack.

❋ What do you think is the sweatiest part of your body? Nope. Not your armpits. It's your palms! The soles of your feet run a close second.

BURPING

Okay, I'm confused.

When a baby burps everybody makes a big deal about it. Moms even walk around patting baby's back, actually encouraging Little Junior to do the deed. But now that we're all a little older, let one loose at the table and you're sent to your room faster than you can say "excuse me." What happened? Did I miss something? At what point did it suddenly become a crime? And while we're on the subject, just what is a burp?

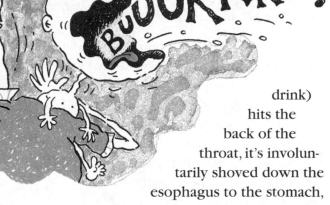

SQUELCH THAT BELCH!

How is a great burp born? It all begins with an innocent act . . . a bite of burger or a long sip of something cool and frosty. As you eat and drink and talk and laugh, something else besides that food or drink slides down your ESOPHAGUS *(eh-saf-ah-gus)*, that nifty tube that leads from your throat—also called the PHARYNX *(far-inks)*—to your stomach. At the end of the line, a set of strong muscles, called SPHINCTER *(sfink-ter)* muscles, controls what gets into the stomach and what doesn't (sort of like a bouncer at a hot nightclub).

That burger and super-size soda are now down the hatch and have made their way past the guards at the stomach door and into the big party—your stomach. Unfortunately, something else has snuck in, too. Air. Before you

know what's happened, you are suffering from an attack of ERUCTATION *(err-uck-tay-shun)*, or—as we normal people call it—burping.

What's one thing that has no place in your digestive system? Air! If you burp a lot, it might be because you have AEROPHAGIA *(air-o-fay-gee-a)*. (That just means you're an air-swallower.) Now that you know all this impressive medical lingo, let's find out what happens when you let a big one rip!

Swallowing, like breathing, happens automatically. When food (or drink) hits the back of the throat, it's involuntarily shoved down the esophagus to the stomach, along with whatever air is tagging along. While that's happening, the EPIGLOTTIS *(ep-ah-glot-is)*, which is a small triangular piece of cartilage that forms a little lid over your windpipe, snaps down so food can't get into your lungs. (After all, food in your lungs is a definite biological no-no!) When too much air gets into the stomach this way, the stomach blows up like a balloon. (That's when your jeans get too tight and you have to undo the button.)

That air has to go somewhere, so some of it gets squeezed out, making a reverse trip back up the esophagus. As this happens, the epiglottis gets partially "unsnapped" by the force of the air pushing up. That noise you make when you burp is your epiglottis flapping away!

Belch Busters!

WARNING! The more you burp, the more you're going to burp. That's because every time you burp, you swallow more air. At some point, you will burp at the wrong time, like when you are a grown-up asking for a pay raise, and it will cost you big! So you'd better stop now, while you still can (and you *can* if you concentrate)!

❋ Don't talk with your mouth full. It will soon be full of more than words and food. It will be full of air, too.

❋ Say "so long" to straws. They trap air, and air is the enemy. (Chewing gum is another air magnet.)

❋ Slow down! Don't try to beat the world record for most food eaten in a minute. Take your time.

❋ Take it easy on the carbonated drinks. They can be double trouble. Not only do they make you burp, the sugar in them can make you a fabulous farter, too!

You'll be happy to know that not everyone is offended by the roaring rip of a burp. In some cultures, especially among the Bedouin tribes of the Middle East, burping after a meal is considered a sign of politeness, an audible way of "applauding" the cook's skills. Maybe that's why camels burp a lot, too.

By the way, some of the air gets squeezed *down,* too. Any air that makes it to your IN-TESTINES *(in-tes-tinz)* will end up as part of that other great talent: farting. (See FARTS on page 54 for all the fragrant details.)

C

Pacific, and parts of South America could be dangerous to your health. And in centuries even more distant, cannibalism existed almost everywhere.

Why would one person want to eat another person? It's *got* to be more than just hunger!

Religious beliefs often played a big part in a person's decision to chew on Cousin Charlie. In central India, the Binderwurs ate their sick and aged in the belief that this act would make the goddess Kali happy. In Mexico, thousands of human victims were sacrificed and then cooked up by the Aztecs. A favorite dish there was called *TLACATLAOLLI* (don't even try to pronounce it!)—corn and man stew!

In many cultures—especially those that survived

CANNIBALS

What's the grossest thing you've ever eaten? Was it liver and kidney stew? A bag of moldy, soggy potato chips? Pizza loaded with anchovies and smelly olives? Well . . . it's time to thank your lucky stars you're not a cannibal!

HUMAN ON RYE, AND HOLD THE MAYO

In many places around the world, on every continent, in times just recently past, humans ate other humans. Up until about a hundred years ago, a trip to central or western Africa, Australia, New Zealand, the islands of the

"Don't tell me we're having boiled explorer for dinner AGAIN!"

by hunting—eating the dead was a sign of respect. For instance, in some tribes, the tribespeople believed that after a great warrior died, a bite off the old fellow would bring some of his fearless spirit to them. Many tribes ate only the heart, or sometimes the liver or kidneys, but not the rest of the body. Still others cooked up the whole person. To be eaten after death was a sign of the utmost respect in these cultures—an honor to be given only to the very finest of folk.

Among certain tribes in the Amazon, every funeral featured some dead-guy soup. Here's how that worked. Let's say it's time to bid a fond farewell to old Uncle Mel, dead at 102. (He led a long, full life, so don't be sad.) Wrap him up in his hammock and cook him up in a big clay pot. Take the remains out to the river and wash the charred bits off until you get down to the bones. Grind them into a fine powder and add them to a bowl of corn soup. If you are the lucky next-of-kin, you get to sip a hot bowl of Uncle Mel Chowder!

Maybe you've seen cartoons or old adventure movies where a couple of explorers in Africa are captured by a tribe armed with big shields and even bigger spears. The explorers are taken to the village and tossed into a big black pot—a pot big enough to hold two full-sized adults. This, of course, is total hogwash!

A Nasty Note

The word "cannibal" comes from the Spanish word for "Carib"—referring to an ancient tribe of West Indian people-eaters. In fact, Christopher Columbus would have been eaten if he had landed just a couple of islands over from where he did. The island he landed on was settled by the peaceful Arawaks. The man-eating Caribs were just across the water! Lucky break!

There *was* cannibalism in Africa, but a different kind. Here people ate other people not to honor gods and not out of respect for the person who had just died. Rather, they ate people to get rid of their enemies. In parts of the Congo, enemies captured in battle were held prisoner, fattened up, and then dined upon. These cannibals believed that their enemy's spirit would be completely destroyed if the body was eaten, too. After all, if the body was eaten up and gone, there would be no place for a ghost or spirit to hang around in, now would there?

A MATTER OF SURVIVAL

Every once in a while, people have had to resort to eating other people if there was no other way to survive. One of the most famous incidents of survival cannibalism occurred in 1846. An ill-fated group of pioneers, led by a fellow named George Donner, left Illinois, bound for California. Unfortunately, while crossing what is now known as the Donner Pass in the mountains of Nevada, they got trapped in a fierce snowstorm and could go no farther that winter. Of the 87 people who started out on the trip, 40 ended up as food for the others. The survivors who escaped in the spring were haunted by the experience for the rest of their lives.

Back in 1609, early American settlers at Jamestown, Virginia, found themselves in a similar sorry mess. The Jamestown settlers were unused to farming and had come to the New

*Mmm . . .
tastes like chicken.*

World with little food. They chose a piece of land to settle on that was swampy and mosquito infested. A terrible drought led to a water shortage. Within a few months, many had died. Food was so scarce that they were forced to eat rats and shoe leather. When the shoe leather and rats were gone, to many it seemed there was only one other option: to eat the other recently dead colonists. One unlucky settler was caught eating his dead wife and was quickly executed as an example to the other colonists to think twice about becoming cannibals.

In 1972, a plane crash high in the Andes Mountains in South America saw the survivors—Uruguay's rugby team—faced with a horrible decision. At first, the survivors expected a rescue party to come along and find them. But later, when it became clear that no one could get to them because of record snowfalls, they found themselves with no choice but to eat the people who had not survived the crash. They spent 70 days on that mountain, with only the battered remains of their airplane for shelter. They were incredibly brave and strong. They were determined not to die. And they did what they had to do to survive.

What would you have done in these situations? Do you think you would be able to eat another person if your life depended on it? A hard choice!

COCKROACHES

If this has happened to you then you know just how creepy it is. You go away for the weekend to visit your great-aunt (you know—the one who smells of mothballs and pinches your cheeks every 10 seconds). When you come home, you walk into the kitchen, turn on the light, and it's like the whole floor is moving. There are about one million *things* swarming all over the place.

The swarming things see you. They say something like, "Hey! Who turned on the lights? Uh-oh, big sucker about to step on us!" And before you can move your feet, they're gone, back into the woodwork. Party's over!

"WHAT'CHA GOT? I'LL EAT ANYTHING!"

Hard. Soft. Sweet. Sour. Alive. Dead. Doesn't really matter to a roach. They'll eat the sweat out of your sneakers, the grease on the stove. They'll eat the glue on your postage stamps and the wiring in your TV set. They will eat the fingernails of sleeping sailors aboard a ship. They even eat left-over bits of their own bodies!

They will eat paper, soap, and paint. Oh, and food, too. They *love* food!

And, if there's nothing around to eat at all? Hey, that's okay too! Roaches can go for incredibly long periods of time without eating anything. They can also survive on just about anything. And that is the secret of their success. When times get really tough and there's nothing to snack on, they'll turn on each other and dine on their friends. Just rip open the stomach and chow down! (See? There are all kinds of cannibals in this world.)

When it comes to disgusting houseguests, nothing can top a roach. That's because where there's one, there are zillions. Crawling through the cupboards. Swarming through the floorboards. In your toothpaste and your shoes. Chillin' in the fridge, and leaving cockroach ca-ca wherever they wander.

The good news is that of the 4,000 known species in the world, only 25 species get in the way of humans. The bad news is, those 25 species that live in our homes leave almost-invisible piles of roach poop all over the place.

And *that* is a real health hazard. Sixty percent of the over 11 million people who suffer from asthma will end up more than just grossed out by roaches. They will end up wheezing and gasping for air.

Clearly, roaches have *got* to go! Unfortunately, that's almost impossible.

KING COCKROACH

Dinosaurs roared for about 130 million years before they disappeared. We humans have only been hanging around on earth for about 2 million years. But cockroaches are 350 million years old and still going strong. These guys make that bunny that sells batteries look like a dead duck.

The biggest roach of all, the Madagascar Hissing Cockroach, sure is a handful.

At one point in this planet's life, roaches ruled. They were kings of the world during the Age of Coal, roaming happily in the steamy swamps. Let's face it: To hang out that long, you need to be tough. And these creepers are!

Roaches are completely amazing. Chew on this. In space, an astronaut will pass out at 12 Gs (that's 12 times the force of normal gravity—a crushing amount of pressure). At 18 Gs that poor astronaut's internal organs will be squished. But roaches? No problem! They can make it to 126 Gs without even breaking a sweat! They can also be frozen, then thawed, and walk away as if nothing had happened. Not to mention their ability to survive lots of the poisons humans use in a vain attempt to get rid of them.

Cockroaches are crazy for cleanliness. They spend hours washing themselves, licking their feet and sucking on their own antennae—two very important body parts if you are a roach. They use their antennae to poke around and sniff out food. And as for their feet? Read on! Imagine deciding what to have for dinner by sticking your toot-sies in your food. Well, that's what roaches do. If they like what they've stepped in—if it tickles their toe-tastebuds—then it's time to dine. Of course, just about everything tastes good to a roach!

But roaches do more than just eat and bathe. They know how to have a good time. When they're not busy eating or cleaning themselves up, they're out looking for ro-mance. One little cockroach finds a mate, has babies, those babies have babies, and those ba-bies have babies. At the end of a year, there could be about 10 million new cockroaches as a result of one romantic evening. (But don't worry. That would happen only if *all* the ba-bies survive and reproduce. They won't.) And for a real baby factory, no one can beat the German cockroach. One mom can produce about 500,000 tykes a year! That's a lot of birthday cake!

Gross but Good

Belive it or not, roaches are perfect for ex-perimenting with. Doctors use them to study heart disease. Cancer docs use them be-cause roaches grow tumors kind of like the ones that humans get. Even the nerve cells of the roach brain have a lot in common with ours, and, thanks to those cocky little fellows, many neat discoveries have been made that help to explain how our brains work.

Scientists at the University of Tokyo plucked the wings off of a bunch of roaches, in-serted little electrodes in their antennae, and stuck on tiny backpacks full of electric circuits and batteries. They discovered that they could then steer the bugs like a car. Hang a left. Turn right. Stop. Go. The point? They hope to use roaches in rescue work, such as in collapsed buildings, by mounting tiny cameras on their backs. Next thing you know, they'll be getting tiny Congressional Medals of Honor!

GOOD RIDDANCE TO ROACHES

So how *do* you get rid of the little creeps? You can't stomp on all of them. There are way too many. But short of filling your house with clouds of poisonous gas, here are some envi-ronmentally friendly ways to say "bye-bye" to those bugs.

✳ The Environmental Protection Agency is looking into allowing folks to use "roach motels" that are filled with parasitic worms, harmless to humans but death to a roach. They invade the roach's body and release a toxic bacteria that kills it. Then, after all the roaches are eaten, the worms die because roaches are the only thing they'll eat!

A boy and his cockroach. "Cocky" will live for about 7 years and grow to be over 4 inches long. No, he won't fetch or roll over.

✳ Some people swear that sprinkling boric acid powder along cracks in the floorboards and around electrical outlets will snuff the roaches out. The roaches lick up the fine, poisonous powder when they clean themselves.

✳ Centipedes love to eat roaches, especially the babies. So you could stock up on centipedes and replace one bug with another.

✳ Geckos also adore roaches. When those lizard lips meet cockroach carcasses, it's like a fiesta!

✳ The winner of Australia's 1991 Inventor of the Year award came up with a cockroach zapper, a lot like those bug zappers in everyone's backyards. The roaches creep in to stuff themselves with the roach bait, and end up fried!

The Roach Hall of Fame

✳ Biggest? The Hissing Roach, from Madagascar, is as big as a mouse. Try flattening that one with your shoe!

✳ Neatest trick? Roaches can flatten themselves to almost the thinness of a piece of paper and slide into tiny cracks in the wall. Their oily coating makes them extra slithery.

✳ Best pet? Australian giant burrowing cockroaches are the size of an adult finger. One fellow in Sydney sells them as pets for $50 a pair. He says you can go away on vacation and never worry about feeding them. Yeah, but can they fetch your slippers and roll over and play dead?

✳ Family ties? Roaches belong to the same family as grasshoppers and crickets (Orthoptera), but aren't nearly as cute.

CROCODILIANS

There are things lurking in the murky waters that you should know about. Don't believe me? Just ask Captain Hook! They glide through still waters, silent and deadly, and in the blink of an eye, they'll drag a good-sized mammal into the water, drown it, and rip it apart with their razor-sharp teeth. Trust me. There's nothing scarier than finding yourself nose to snout with a creature that has 100 sharp teeth packed in its jaws!

FROM KING-OF-THE-WORLD TO STUCK-IN-THE-SWAMP

For over 100 million years, dinosaurs called the shots. Those "terrible lizards" (that's what their name means) swaggered around, squishing everyone and everything underfoot. But they didn't last, and we're not exactly sure why. One of the best theories is that a giant meteorite slammed into the earth, sending up clouds of dust that blotted out the sun. The impact instantly killed many plants and animals, and it made a mess of the environment. With food scarce, only the small creatures survived. All those big dino-brutes with huge appetites starved and died. But a few of their scrappier relatives are still dragging their very long tails around. They're the CROCODILIANS (*crock-o-dill-yuns*)—crocodiles, alligators, caimans, and gavials.

Back in the days of the dinosaur, crocodiles were twice the size they are now—up to 40 feet long—about the size of a bus. They were so fierce, they even *ate* dinosaurs!

The Better to Eat You With!

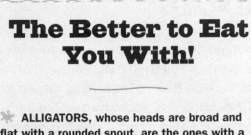

❋ **ALLIGATORS**, whose heads are broad and flat with a rounded snout, are the ones with a bad overbite. Their upper teeth completely hide the lower ones.

❋ **CAIMANS**, which live mostly in South America, are about half the size of alligators, but they manage to pack over 70 teeth into their slender mouths.

❋ **CROCODILES** have one notch on each side of their narrow heads . . . the better to show their really pointy fourth tooth with.

❋ **GAVIALS**, which live in India, have the most teeth—over 100 pearly whites tucked into an extremely long, pointy snout.

Today there are 22 different species of crocodilians, and they all spend a good chunk of their time near water. Some can grow to over 20 feet long. Talk about something you do not want to trip over in the dark!

Stay away from the caiman's mouthful of super-sharp chompers.

TABLE MANNERS

With all those sharp teeth, you'd think crocodilians would be master chewers. But they aren't. They use those teeth to clamp onto whatever chunk of meat they've decided to eat. An alligator, for example, will take an animal that it's snagged and shake its head violently or spin around in circles until it tears off a piece small enough to swallow without chewing.

If you can't tell the difference between an alligator and a crocodile by looking at their snouts and teeth, flip that big old gator over and examine its belly. Alligators have smooth stomachs; crocodiles have a bony plate covering their tums.

Why is knowing the difference important? Because crocodiles are the only ones that have a hankering for a bite of human flesh from time to time. Alligators don't care for the taste of us as much. If it makes you feel any better, even big crocodiles prefer to eat a dab of deer or a hunk of hog over you. Pointy-snouted crocodiles prefer fish. Most crocodilians do their hunting at night. During the day they bask in the sun, mouths wide open.

Bottom line? Stay out of still, swampy waters—especially at night. And if you run into a 20-foot-long creature with teeth like swords—run, and run fast!

And lest you get the totally wrong idea about crocodilians, remember this. They may like to tear hunks of flesh from other animals, but they are kind and loving parents to their young. And while your mom may cart you around in a minivan, mommy crocodiles transport their babies in their open mouths. Don't forget to buckle up for safety!

Down but Not Out

Many crocs and gators have had the bad luck to find themselves on a special list. No, it's not the after-school detention list. It's the endangered species list. As a cartoon alligator said, "Skin me alive and call me luggage!" Well, that's the problem in a nutshell. Their skins, made of all those bony plates, make strong-as-steel shoes, belts, and bags. Hunters had almost wiped crocs and gators off the face of the earth before the governments of the world stepped in (in the early 1970s) and put a bounty on the hunters' heads instead. Now many crocodilians are no longer considered endangered, but there are still laws in place to make sure they have a fighting chance to survive.

DANDRUFF

Don't you just love it when it snows? You get to make snowmen, pretend you're an Olympic snowboarder, or throw snowballs at strangers (and then duck so they can't see you). But what if that snow were made of clumps of oily dead skin? What if it were a blizzard of yellow-gray? What if it were all over your shoulders?

HAIR YE. HAIR YE. HAIR ALL ABOUT IT!

Dandruff's pretty yucky stuff. But before you can get to the bottom of why your scalp sometimes sheds, it helps to know about that blond or brown or red stuff sprouting from your skull. You spend a zillion hours a day combing it, and another zillion deciding if you should part it on the right or the left. It never does what you want it to do and it sticks up and out no matter how much you brush it. All this effort and energy spent worrying about a part of your body that is dead. Yup, that's right. Dead.

The stuff we call hair is actually an outgrowth of your skin, growing from a thing called a FOLLICLE *(fol-i-cull)*. There are 5 million of those suckers on your body—about 100,000 just on your head. The follicle is alive, capable of making new cells. But hair, alas, cannot make itself new. It can only get shoved up and pushed out of its cozy little home.

The only places where hair does not grow on your skin are the palms of your hands, the soles of your feet, and your lips. You may not see all the hairs on the rest of your body, but trust me, they're there—too fine to see. This very fine hair is called VELLUS *(vee-lus)*, and even a completely bald man's head is covered with it.

35

Hair-Raising Facts

❋ Human hair grows about 6 inches a year.

❋ At any given moment, 15 percent of your hair follicles are on vacation. That's because every few years, your hair roots get worn out and take a really long rest. For six months a lazy little resting follicle will do a whole lot of nothing.

❋ Do blonds really have more fun? That's hard to say, but they definitely have more hair than brunettes or redheads. No one quite knows why.

❋ When your hair is wet, it can stretch to 1½ times its length.

❋ A strand of your hair is stronger than the same size strand of steel.

❋ Every day, between 50 and 100 hairs break off, so don't panic when you check your hairbrush and find it full of hair. It doesn't mean you're going to end up like Uncle Bill—bald as a billiard ball!

❋ When human hair gets to be about 3 feet long it will generally stop growing. (However, there are exceptions, as you'll see in the next hair-raising fact.)

❋ In 1989, a woman in India made her claim to fame with hair that was 21 feet long, supposedly the longest in the world. That's three times longer than Michael Jordan is tall!

❋ People have been unhappy about the color of their hair for a long time. Hair dye has been around for 3,000 years. Ancient Romans even used pigeon poop to achieve that bleached blond look.

❋ Why do we have more hair on our heads than anywhere else? It provides some cushioning in case we get a blow to the head and it's a kind of permanent hat to keep us warm and protect us from the sun!

So what are those nasty flakes that dare to decorate dark shirts and cause us such embarrassment?

You might think that dandruff is caused by a scalp that's too dry. Wrong. There are actually two culprits here. The first is a head that's shedding too many skin cells. The second is the oil produced by the sebaceous oil glands on your head. The oil acts like glue, causing the shedding skin cells to stick together.

To some degree, everyone has dandruff—otherwise known as scalp flakes. Snakes shed their skin and so do you, just not all at once. Our bodies are constantly making new skin cells, the old stuff flaking away and the new skin rising to the surface. You just don't notice the shedding because there's nothing to trap

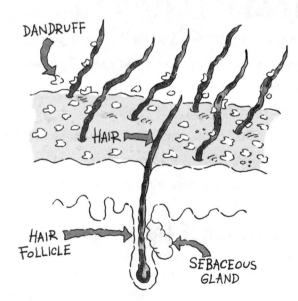

the flakes of skin. Every day, billions of skin cells float off into the air. In fact, most of the dust in your house is flaked-off skin. (Quick—

get out the feather duster!) But on your head it's a different story. Your hair is like a jail, holding the skin cells prisoner. It's harder for the shedding flakes to find their way to freedom. Add a few drops of oil produced in the sebaceous glands and suddenly you've got flakes the size of . . . well, cornflakes! Now there's an appetizing breakfast thought!

No two snowflakes are alike, and it's the same with dandruff. Flakes can range from small and white to big, yellow, and greasy, depending on what's causing the dandruff. The same things that cause skin rashes can cause dandruff—things like dermatitis and psoriasis.

Itchy scalp? Snowy shoulders? That's dandruff.

(See SKIN ERUPTIONS, page 144, for more on those gross things.) And dandruff isn't limited to just your scalp. Eyebrows can shed, too.

BEAT THE BLIZZARD

What can be done about this dreadful dermatological disaster? Well, first of all, be grateful for those snowy flakes. If your scalp didn't constantly shed dead skin, it would keep growing thicker and thicker until you would need a wagon to cart your head around in!

Then, keep it clean. Shampooing regularly is the easiest way to fight the flaking. Remember, oil is the bad guy here. If washing with your normal shampoo doesn't stem that "snowfall," try a special dandruff shampoo. A natural product you can use is green tea shampoo, available at health-food stores. It's excellent for fighting dandruff. Just don't confuse it with regular tea. It's still shampoo.

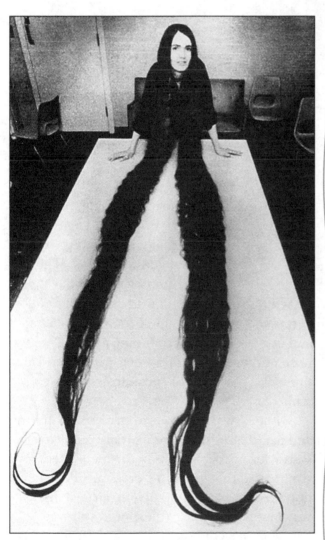
Diane Witt has some of the longest hair in the world. It hangs down an amazing 10 feet.

DIARRHEA
Well, it's the color of poop, and it sure smells like poop, but how come it comes out like pee? If you want to know more about what causes those ghastly trots, check out POOP on page 121.

E

doesn't do a whole lot except give you a place from which to hang your earrings, catch the sound vibes all around us, and, incidentally, give wax a place to hang out. Earwax is like mucus for your AURICLES *(awe-ri-kulls),* which is the fancy word for those flesh-funnels on the sides of your head! (See SNOT on page 160 for more on mucus.)

EARWAX

Great. Just what you need when you're trying to be cool. A hole in your body that leaks yellow-brown clumps of chunky stuff. And while scraping, sniffing, and studying those chunks can be an amusing way to pass the time, that's not what earwax is made for. Here's the scoop on why it's there.

WAX WORKS

If you're gonna get a grip on earwax, which is called CERUMEN *(sah-room-in)* by medical folk, it helps to understand its purpose.

The outside of your ear—the part that sticks out and has all those weird folds—

That opening in the center of your ear is actually the doorway to the external auditory canal. (The word "auditory" means having to do with hearing.) Think of it as a thrill ride for germs and dirt, made up of lots of tiny hairs and over 4,000 wax-producing glands. The purpose of the wax is to trap dirt, insects, and anything else that tries to sneak inside your ears while you're not looking.

But earwax does more than ward off dirt and insects. The wax and hair also act like a warm, fuzzy coat—heating the air as it enters your ear, so that when it's cold outside you don't have a blast of 20-degree air making its way into your brain. (You should still wear a hat when it's cold outside to keep from freezing your *auricles!*)

Cotton Swabs and Other Deadly Weapons

Remember what your mom told you about never putting anything in your ear except for your elbow? Well, this is one time she's right! If anyone comes at you with a cotton swab . . . run! The same goes for napkin corners and sharp, pointy objects. Basic rule of ear . . . leave that wax alone. It's there for a reason. Of course, you can swipe at the stuff that thinks it's a piece of jewelry dangling from your earlobes with a warm washcloth, but otherwise, remember what your mother said and *stay out!*

Mother Nature's Recipe for Earwax: Stir up secretions from the sweat and oil glands, especially the fatty acids and enzymes that beat up on bacteria and proteins. Mix in some flakes of dead skin to give it that attractive golden color. Mush it all together and you've got a fingertipful of gross, goopy earwax!

Not all earwax is created equal. Oddly enough, some people have wet, greasy earwax, and others have a drier wax, kind of rice-like. Caucasian and Black people usually have the wet, greasy variety, Asian people the dry, ricey kind. No one knows why.

WAXY BUILDUP?

Most of the time, your ears are self-cleaning. Imagine a really slow-moving layer of wax crawling like a lazy caterpillar from deep inside the ear canal to the opening, where it dries up, flakes, and then falls out. If you wear earphones a lot, or live in a big city where there's tons of dirt and grime to keep out of your ears, you might make more earwax than the average kid.

Sometimes when the wax accumulates, it gets plugged up and stops moving. Sounds have a hard time getting in, so you can't hear your parents when they yell at you to clean up your room. And while this may seem good at first, you eventually miss out on hearing all the juicy stuff, too (like the fact that the principal wears a hairpiece).

If your ears get clogged to the point where you can't hear well, call your doctor. She will pulverize that waxy blob with special drops that dissolve fat. Then she'll either flush it out with warm water from a syringe or scoop it out with a special little spoon called a curette. Gross!

WHILE I HAVE YOUR EAR . . .

Your ears have two jobs to do. First, they let you listen to that cool new band at super-sonic sound levels. But equally important, ears keep you from falling down by helping you to keep your balance.

Everyone has three parts to their ears—the outer, middle, and inner—and each part has a job to do. The outer ear is pretty simple: a sound-wave catcher and a tube, with that little wax factory and all those tiny hairs to help trap invaders. It's inside the ear where most of the work is done.

The inner end of the auditory canal leads to a cellophane-thin screen called the eardrum, the gateway to the insides of your ear. The vibrations of the eardrum deliver sound to the middle ear, where it's passed along to the inner ear to be converted into signals the brain can understand. The EUSTACHIAN (*you-stay-she-un*) TUBE also waits on the other side of the eardrum, sliding down to your nose and throat. It's the part that gets blocked when you're on an airplane. That happens whenever the air pressure on one side of your eardrum is different than it is on the other side (at high altitudes on a plane, for example, or when you have a cold). When your ears "pop," you know the pressure has equalized.

The middle ear officially begins just past the eardrum. Middle ears are the parts that get infected and send you screaming through the house in the middle of the night. The bad guy here is the Eustachian tube. In kids, the tube is short and wide and the lower end gets blocked easily. Germs sneak in

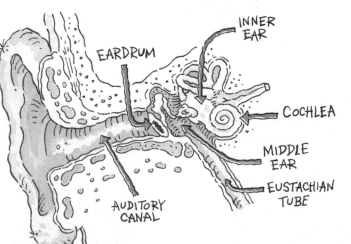

EARDRUM

INNER EAR

COCHLEA

MIDDLE EAR

EUSTACHIAN TUBE

AUDITORY CANAL

A Nasty Note

If you think your ears have it bad, try being a dog. They often end up with ear mites, tiny bugs that burrow into those big flappers and make themselves at home. (See MITES, page 102, to learn about the kinds that like to crawl around on you.)

But dogs' aren't the only ears that get invaded. Bugs, especially cockroaches, like to slither into human ears. Emergency room doctors often are asked to pull bugs from people's ears. How? They pour a lot of oil into the ear and drown the bug before trying to grab it with tweezers. That way it won't fight on the way out!

through the nose and throat, decide they like it in that cozy tunnel, and hang out there! Before you know it, you're swallowing bubble-gum-flavored antibiotic "bug-juice" four times a day.

The inner ear, even though it's only the size of a small marble, does the really important part—the hearing-and-standing-up-without-falling-down part. It has many tiny little parts. One of the most important is the COCHLEA (*co-klee-uh*) which looks like a snail shell. The cochlea contains thousands of tiny hairs that vibrate in response to the sound waves they receive. These vibrations are turned into signals that get sent to the brain.

But enough of the anatomy lesson. Let's get back to the really gross facts about your ears.

HAIRY EARS

Your great-uncle Elmo probably has more hair growing from his outer ears than he does from his head. As you get older, if you are a "he" (here's something swell to look forward to, guys), your ears may begin to sprout a forest of fur. You will be able to tell the person that cuts your hair, "Just a little off the top . . . and 6 inches out of the ears!"

For a total gross-out, old Uncle Elmo will also have little clumps of hair stuck in his left-over earwax! That extra hair comes from male hormones, the same critters responsible for men's furry chests.

While outer-ear hair is gross, inner-ear hairs are another story. When sound waves cause your eardrum to vibrate, these vibrations get passed into your inner ear by tiny bones. The inner ear is lined with hairs that are rooted in nerves. (This is in the cochlea. Remember that?) When the hairs vibrate, the vibrations rev up the nerves, which in turn send messages to the brain. Bald inner ears can't relay these messages, and a person who has hairless inners will not be able to hear a thing! (Really loud sounds cause

Spin Cycle

Try this. Trust me. It will help you understand the way the inner ear controls balance. Put this book down and spin yourself in a circle for 20 seconds. Now try to stand up straight. Can't do it, can you? Know why? It's because there's fluid in your ears, traveling in the semicircular canals. And right now it's sloshing all over the place. Your brain gets totally confused, flakes out, and you fall down!

these hairs to deteriorate, in a way causing your inner ears to "go bald.")

THE NEWS ON NOISE

While we're on the subject: Listening to your favorite band with the volume turned up to "stun" may seem cool. But unless you want to walk around with a hearing aid for the rest of your life . . . *don't do it!*

Sound is measured in something called DECIBELS (*des-i-bulls*). Anything above 90 decibels can damage your ears if you listen to it long enough. So read on for a guide to gauging decibels.

SAFE RANGE

Watch ticking: about 20 decibels
Background noises during a walk in the country: 40 to 50 decibels
Normal conversation: 60 to 70 decibels
Heavy traffic: about 80 decibels

RISKY

Motorcycle: 85 to 90 decibels
Rock concert: about 100 decibels

DOWNRIGHT DANGEROUS

Jackhammer: about 120 decibels
Jet airliner at takeoff: about 150 decibels
Your gym teacher telling you to do 50 push-ups: about 70 billion decibels (Just kidding.)
WARNING: If you have to shout to make yourself heard, the noise around you is too LOUD. (Huh? What was that? I couldn't hear you!)

Now, wiggle your ears to show you understand all this!

EDIBLE BUGS

If you had been invited to a recent dinner party at the New York Entomological Society you would have feasted on the following: Sizzling cricket and veggie tempura. Warm wax worm fritters. Roasted Australian grubs. Mouthwatering mealworm pizza. And for dessert? Chocolate cricket pie. (Just can't get enough of that cricket pie!)

I'll bet you're sitting there, right now, thinking, EEEOOOOUUU! The idea of eating bugs is about as appetizing to most of us as the idea of drinking motor oil. But, believe it or not, in much of the world, tasty bug dishes are considered a real treat!

BAKED? BROILED? BOILED?

Once you know the facts—that bugs are packed with vitamins and minerals, loaded with protein, and are considered quite tasty—you might change your mind and begin loading your lunchbox with "Termites on Toast." For thousands of years, man has feasted on bugs, burping in delight after dining. Think about it. If we can eat spareribs,

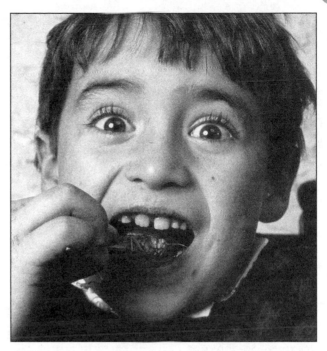

Crunchy, delicious, and nutritious, too!

which come from pigs that eat garbage, why not nibble on an insect that eats only grains and veggies?

What kind of bugs make the tastiest treats? Earthworms and larval insects, such as caterpillars, are the best loved. Canned caterpillars grace the supermarket shelves in Mexico. In the Orient, silkworms are served up in soup, scrambled, or simply fried. Tarantula egg omelets are popular in the rain forests of Brazil, as are the tarantulas themselves (Wrap it in a big leaf, cook over a slow fire, and eat up!) Live grubs, plucked fresh from fallen trees, are cause for a party in parts of New Guinea.

Grasshoppers, as food, are universally appreciated. In Japan and China, they're fried and served with a side of rice. In fact, they are an excellent source of protein, a big "yes" for good health. Cook 'em up like this: Pull off the wings, small legs, and the bottom portion of the hind legs. Off with their heads, too! Put them in a frying pan with a little oil and brown lightly. Add a dash of salt for some extra zest.

Rumor has it grasshoppers taste a bit like beef. And it's certainly much easier to pull off a

Got a Sweet Tooth?

Before you turn your delicate little nose up at sitting down to a bucketful of fried ant-bellies (as they happily do in movie theaters in Colombia), chew on this. Ever had honey-glazed doughnuts? Honey in hot tea? Well, what do you think that stuff is? Food drizzled with bee spit-up, plain and simple!

When bees drink flower nectar it's converted to honey in special sacs in their throats. Back at the bee hive, they hurl up that honey, then store it in the honeycombs. Bet those fried ants aren't looking so bad now, are they? By the way, not only can you eat honey, you can eat the whole bee! Bee suppliers will provide hints on de-stinging them before cooking.

BARF BAG

grasshopper's head than a cow's! The biggest problem with grasshopper dishes is the amount you need. One recipe for "Oaxaca-hoppers" (Oaxaca is a place in Mexico—don't even try to pronounce it!) called for "1,000 grasshoppers, the younger the better!" So, what're you waiting for? Better start gathering those grasshoppers!

No matter where you travel, from India (where red-ant seasoning is a specialty) to Central America (where no wedding is complete without honey ants) to China (where they eat sun-dried maggots), billions agree. Those tiny little critters are simply yummy! In fact, on just about every continent except North America and Europe, insect-eating is a way of life. And even Americans are beginning to get on the bug-wagon. Fluker's Cricket Farm in Baton Rouge, Louisiana, and the Grub Company in Hamilton, Ohio, both produce edible insects for discriminating (and daring) American palates.

RUSTLE UP SOME GRUB

Ever wonder where this expression, spoken at every cowboy cookout, came from? Maybe it came from the fact that pioneers crossing the frontier lived on locust stew. The Navaho Indians had a nifty recipe for grilled grasshopper. And the Paiutes ate shore-fly pupae, which they scooped up by the ton from lake edges. (They dried them in the sun, mixed the bugs with acorns, berries, and seeds, and fried them in their own grease.) As for grubs—those short, fat, worm-like insect larvae—many swear they're better than peanuts.

MEALWORM DELIGHT

What will it be tonight? If you're tired of chicken, how about asking Mom to whip up mealworms for your next meal? Interested? Read on.

Eating Bugs Saved His Life!

When an American Air Force pilot named Scott O'Grady was shot down over Bosnia in 1995, he survived for six days by eating ants. He was guided by the *Air Force Survival Manual*, which tells which bugs are the tastiest and most nutritious!

Mealworms are the larval stage of a kind of beetle that loves to devour grains. They are yellowish-gold in color and tasty as can be. As amazing as it sounds, there are actually mealworm "ranchers" right here in the United States who do nothing but raise and sell them. Think of them as "hamburger" for folks who like to eat bugs.

All bugs taste better if they are cooked while they are still alive (or fresh-frozen), just like lobsters, so get your mealworms fresh from a dependable dealer. Your mealworms will come packed in bran, which, as you all know, is a Mom-approved food. They need to eat while they're waiting to be cooked or they will eat each other. (That's what the bran's for.) After all, you don't want your dinner to dine on itself now, do you? They are sometimes shipped rolled up in newspaper, which you probably won't want to eat. But mealworms aren't as fussy as humans, and they just adore eating the news. Leave a small piece of apple or pear out for the worms to eat. The fruit will push whatever newsprint they have nibbled on out of their intestines.

Now it's time to get cooking. Rinse the little fellows in cool water in a colander (you know, that pot with all the holes that your mom uses to drain pasta). A gentle pass with a blow-dryer will blow away any yucky particles still clinging to them.

When they've been bathed and blow-dried, pour them out onto wax paper. They can't get too far on smooth surfaces (never learned to ice-skate, I guess). Remove any dead worms, which are darker in color.

You might want to pop them into the refrigerator at this point. Cool bugs are a whole lot less jumpy than warm ones. (After all, you don't want your little mealworms jumping out of the frying pan before they're done!)

When your mealworms are nicely chilled out, they are ready to be rinsed once again, then patted dry with

Ounce for ounce, mealworms are an excellent source of protein. But would you really want to eat enough of them to equal the amount of protein in a slab of steak? (That's a lot of worms.)

paper towels, just like you do with a piece of fish or some raw shrimp. Have your mom or dad stir-fry them in a little oil or roll them in bread crumbs and sizzle them in a skillet until crisp on the outside and tender on the inside. Now, enjoy! They're finger-licking good!

By the way, you can substitute earthworms for mealworms. The French call them *Ver de Terre,* which sounds very fancy. (That's the French for you.) In fact, an international cooking contest was held to find the best earthworm recipe. They received hundreds of entries—for salads, stews, appetizers, soups, and desserts. But the winner was Applesauce Surprise Cake. I bet you can guess what the surprise part was.

EELS

Pretend you're a fish down near the ocean floor. Pretend that you're really, really sick. In fact, you're almost dead. But instead of being offered a nice bowl of hot chicken soup and permission to watch TV all day, you feel something wriggling up your butt—something green and very, very slimy. Oh no! It's started to snack on your innards! By the time it's finished, you will be a wrung-out, tossed-about bag of bones. You have just been dined upon by a slime eel (more on him later).

EELS EVERYWHERE!

Eels may look like snakes, and move like them too, but they aren't snakes. They're fish. There are about 600 different species of eel, grouped into about 20 families. Wherever there's water, there are eels—from Iceland in the north to New Zealand in the south. Some eels prefer fresh water. Some like the salty seas. But even freshwater eels will head for salt water when it's time to have babies.

The next time your mom whines about all the things she does for you, tell her about AMERICAN EEL and EUROPEAN EEL mommies. Here's what they do just to have babies. Even if they live in a stream in Ohio, even if they do their slinky swimming up in Sweden, when they are ready to lay their eggs, these eels swim to the Sargasso Sea, between Bermuda and Puerto Rico. To

This moray eel may be all smiles for the camera, but keep your distance. Once he sinks his teeth into you he won't let you go. Well, not until his head is chopped off, that is.

get there, they sometimes have to slither across land. Eels have a thick layer of mucus all over their bodies that not only helps them glide through the water with ease but also allows them to wriggle onto (and sometimes across) land without drying out. It can take them as much as a year to get where they're going! Once they arrive, they dive down 1,000 feet beneath the surface, lay their eggs, and die. Talk about making sacrifices for your kids!

When the eggs hatch, the larvae will start to head home. The American eels will reach their coastlines in about a year. The Europeans take about three years to reach their home-town lakes. At first, they are transparent and are called glass eels. As they change from sea creatures to freshwater fish they are called elvers, which is considered a yummy food item in Europe. (See SICKENING SEAFOOD, page 140, for other disgusting meals that come from the sea.)

What do eels eat? Depending on their size, everything from tiny little shrimps to other eels. Ever been told not to play with your food while you're eating? Well, since eel mommies aren't around to teach their babies basic table manners, little eels don't know any better. Let's say an eel has snagged a squid. With squid in mouth, he will spin that poor squid round and round, like an Olympic ice-skater doing a scratch spin. You can't even see his little eel face, he's going so fast! The only difference is that the skater will spin 5 times in one second, while eels are spinning an amazing 6 to 14 times a second! To understand this all better, next time your mom cooks chicken, get a drumstick, still attached to the thigh. Spin it around and around until it all falls apart. (And don't tell her I told you to do it, please!) That's kind of what eels do. They grasp it. Jerk it. Pull it and twist. Then spin themselves silly. Then they eat.

An Eel? Not Quite!

Lampreys look like eels and lurk just about everywhere except the waters off southern Africa. But they have no jaws. Instead, adult lampreys have a round, suckerlike mouth with rows of horny teeth and a tongue like a file. A hungry lamprey attaches itself to a fish, digs into its flesh, and proceeds to suck all the bodily fluids—and the life—out of it.

Young lampreys don't have sucker mouths. They live burrowed into the muddy bottoms of streams and seas for over four years, and feed by producing oozing strands of mucus that trap whatever food happens to come by.

R-EEL-Y GROSS EELS

CONGER EELS These are the brutes of the eel family. They can grow to 9 feet long and weigh as much as 150 pounds. They live in the Atlantic and the Mediterranean. But apart from the fact that you might be scared to death if you swim into one, they are blind as can be and are actually quite harmless.

ELECTRIC EELS These eels live in the Amazon where the waters are very murky and it's just about impossible to see anything underwater. By giving off an electrical charge they create a force field around themselves. If the field is disrupted by another creature or a rock, they can tell and, in this way, they're able to navigate in the murky waters. They also use their electrical powers to stun their prey. They can deliver a 500-volt

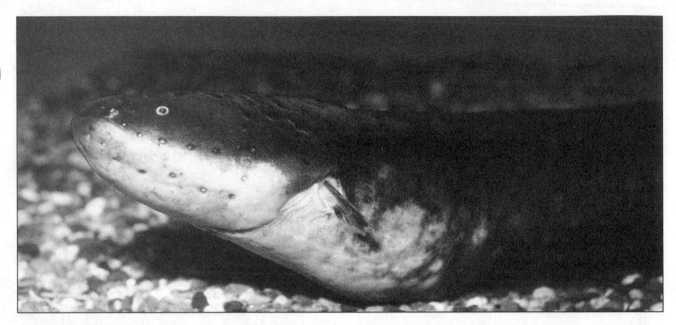

This fresh water electric eel can deliver a furious jolt of power (about 500 volts in case you're interested). Large mammals that survive the jolt often fall into the water and drown because they're so dazed by it.

shock—strong enough to knock over a horse standing in shallow water. Repeated discharges can kill a full-sized adult!

MORAY EELS The most dangerous of the eels is the MORAY EEL, which lives in tropical waters, hiding in the rocks and reefs. Unlike most fish, which can only go in one direction, morays can swim both forward and backward. Most grow to be about 5 feet long, but some as long as 10 feet have been spotted. They have very sharp teeth and very hearty appetites.

When a moray bites, it won't let go. Pulling on it will just tear off more of your flesh. You will have to cut off its head and break its jaws after it's dead to get it off of you! Fortunately, morays are really quite shy unless you mess with them. By the way, their flesh is poisonous, so fight the urge to snack on them the next time you're hungry.

SLIME EELS A name that says it all! Just about the most disgusting creature under the sea is the SLIME EEL. These are so wretched that even scientists, who are usually very polite

when they name things, call them "hagfish" or "slimehags." What makes them so gross? Well, first of all, they are completely covered in mucus, which oozes from about 90 slime pores that line them from top to bottom. This slime is their not-so-secret weapon. When approached, they throw out coils of disgusting slime-streamers. The water becomes thick and gunky, and it feels like you are swimming through a vat of gelatin. To add to their yuckiness, their mouths are surrounded by four pairs of probing tentacles. And inside that mouth is a single tooth on the roof and a tongue covered with two rows of strong, pointy teeth—perfect for chewing their way through their victims.

No other sea critter wants to eat them. Think about it. If you've ever had a really bad cold and tried to swallow some of that mucus stuck at the back of your throat, you know what it feels like when you finally do manage to swallow. That's a bit like trying to eat a slime eel. (Turn to SNOT, page 160, to read more disgusting details about mucus.)

Slime eels dine by slithering into dead or dying creatures lying on the sea floor. Some-

A Nasty Note

If you have a run-in with a slime eel and try to rinse the slime off your body with water, you may be in for a surprise. Instead of thinning out, it increases in volume when mixed with water. Best way to remove it? Peel it off!

times they slide in through the mouths of their victims. Other times, a glide through an eye socket or the butt will do the trick. Once inside they gobble up everything but the bones and skin. Fishermen hate them, because they can slink into their nets and suck their trapped catch dry. One large fish was found with over 100 hagfish gobbling away at its innards!

But all that protective mucus comes with a price. Even slime eels can suffocate in their own snot if they produce too much. To remedy this, they coil themselves into tight loops, then form a simple overhand knot, through which they draw their bodies. A big sneeze *(gesundheit!)*, a quick backflush of the gills . . . and the slime comes bubbling out like a mucus volcano. The extra mucus is wrung out!

You can call it a slime eel or a Pacific hagfish. Or you can simply call it totally gross.

EYE GUNK

You can wink 'em. Blink 'em. And for extra fun you can even cross 'em. No doubt about it—eyes are totally cool. But those adorable baby blues (or browns or greens) have a yucky side, too. They can turn as pink as Barbie's Dream House and ooze a slimy river of pus. If you have allergies you sometimes need a crowbar to pry them open in the morning. And every once in a while they sprout weird blobs on their lids. Eye caramba!

ROSES ARE RED, EYEBALLS ARE PINK

When your eyeball starts to feel like you have sandpaper in it . . . when your eye feels hotter than the pavement in the middle of July . . . when a yellow, sticky slime is oozing from under your eyelids . . . when your eyeballs turn the color of strawberry ice cream . . . it's time to see a doctor. You have an eye infection!

Old Eye's Tales

✳ "Reading in dim light will make you go blind." Wrong! If that were true, our ancestors (who didn't have electric lights) would have each walked around with a seeing-eye dog! Dim light might make your eyes tire easily, but that's about it.

✳ "Using computers can ruin your eyesight." Wrong again! The worst thing that will happen is that your eyes will need a rest. Also, it sometimes helps to lower the light in the room when you're pulverizing your favorite space aliens on screen.

✳ "Sitting too close to the TV will damage your eyes." Hogwash! Kids can focus on things up close better than grown-ups can. As you get older, your need for a soft spot to place your butt will be more important to you than your need to be up close, so sitting 2 feet from the TV will probably end naturally.

✳ "Your eyes can freeze in the crossed position." Honestly! What do they take us for?

CONJUNCTIVITIS *(con-junk-ti-vie-tis)* is its official name, but you might know it as PINK-EYE. It happens when the CONJUNCTIVA *(con-junk-tiv-ah)*, the membrane that lines the eyelid and covers the eyeball, becomes swollen, and sometimes there's a yucky discharge, too. The bad guys here? Bacteria, viruses, and even eye makeup can cause this irritation. Pinkeye is not usually serious, but if you do get it, know that it *can* spread quickly to other people's eyes. Now, it's not as if you rub eyeballs with your buddies, but you probably *do* rub your own eyes with your hands. Then you lend your friend a pencil that has bacteria on it. He rubs his eyes and . . . ta da! Pinkeye. Because it's so contagious, some doctors will make you stay home from school if you have pinkeye. But then, you probably wouldn't want to be seen in public with puffy, pus-crusted eyes anyway. Be thankful.

STYES (it rhymes with "eyes") are another pain-in-the-eye. Each eyelash has a little gland at its root that secretes an oily goo called SEBUM *(sea-bum)*. This goo is what keeps the skin of your eyelids soft so that they can blink. But that sticky sebum is also a bacteria trap. Sometimes, certain kinds of bacteria creep into a gland and set up camp, and before you know it, the gland swells up. You now have a HORDEOLUM *(hor-dee-oh-lum)*, the medical word for a sty—the swollen, red, painful lump tucked in between your lashes. And like a small volcano, those lumps sometimes "come to a head" with an eruption of yellow pus. In some ways, a sty is a bit like having a pimple on your eyelid. Luckily, medicated ointments and hot compresses will send those bacteria to their graves!

When the whites of your eyes look like they've been dipped in a bowl of ketchup, your eyes are BLOODSHOT. That doesn't mean your eyes are bleeding. You can't see them, but your eyeballs are covered with tiny blood vessels that nourish your eyes every minute of every day. When those little vessels are unhappy, they get engorged, which means they swell up. Soon, they're big enough to see. Allergies, rubbing your eyes, and really dry air can all bring on the big blood vessels. The cure? Keep blinking your eyes as much as you can. Your own tears will calm those vessels down. And speaking of tears. . .

Bloodshot eyes are a real pain, especially when they're caused by conjunctivitis, a condition that can make eyes crusty, swollen, and oh-so-itchy.

HEY, CRYBABY!

What is that salty stuff that drips from your eyes when you jab your elbow against a piece of furniture, or see a really stupid movie where some cute little baby animal's mommy almost dies? I guess I don't really need to tell you they're tears. But they're a lot more than just saltwater. In fact, they have a lot of the same ingredients as your pee! They're a neat mixture of 98 percent water, bits of glucose, protein, ammonia, uric acid, citric acid, ascorbic acid (vitamin C), potassium, sodium, calcium, and a *lot* more stuff!

Why do we cry? When we're upset our brains produce certain chemicals and our bod-

ies produce stress hormones. Scientists have found traces of these chemicals and hormones in tears. The crying helps us flush out the chemicals produced by our strong emotions. So next time you feel blue, bring on the tears!

By the way, you cry all the time. Every time you blink, a thin "eyewash" of tears slides over your eyes, washing away bits of dust and dirt. So each blink is like a little shower for your eyes. Those tears are packed with bacteria-killing enzymes, which usually protect your eyes from infection. Tears are made in the LACRIMAL (<u>lack</u>-ri-mal) GLANDS, which are located behind your upper eyelids, in case you feel like impressing someone with how brilliant you are!

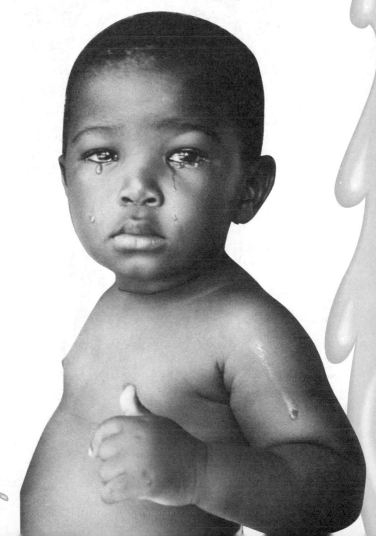

Ever wonder why your nose "cries," too? Tears drain through the corner of your eyes into a special passageway that leads into your nose. Before you know it, you're a damp, oozing mess.

MR. SANDMAN, MEET MR. MUCUS

It's morning. Your alarm has been ringing for 10 minutes and it's time to rise and shine. But your eyes have hunks of yellow crust hanging from the corners. Sure, it's fun to pick it and flick it, but what on earth is it?

Surprise! You've got mucus in your eyes (the same kind that's in your nose and your guts). Where did it come from? Well, tears actually have three layers: an oily layer to keep the tears from evaporating, lacrimal fluid to wash away dust and dirt, and a mucus layer to help the tears stick to the eye. At night when you're asleep, the fluids keep on flowing but you stop blinking. Even though your eyelids are shut, the seal is not completely tight and some of that mucus escapes and dries out. Before you know it, Mr. Sandman has left you enough "sand" to keep a herd of camels happy!

HOW EYES WORK, MADE EASY

Eyes are *really* complicated things. And to understand why they mess up every now and then, it helps to know a bit about what's going on in there.

Your eyeball really is shaped like a ball. But you can't slam-dunk this ball. In truth, it's as fragile as one of Grandma's precious little china figurines. It has to be protected. Your eyeball sits in a hollow in your skull called the ORBITAL CAVITY. That hollow is lined with a protective layer of gushy fat. (Bet you didn't know you had fat eyes!) Eyebrows, eyelids, and eyelashes help guard your eyeballs from injury. And a squishy jelly called the VITREOUS HUMOR (*vit-ree-us* *hue-mer*) helps the eyes to keep their shape.

The SCLERA is the tough white covering on your eyeball. And, as you already know, the CONJUNCTIVA is a clear membrane on the front of the eye and inside of the eyelids. It covers everything but the CORNEA *(cor-nee-uh)*, which is the clear covering that lets in light and keeps out the bugs!

The IRIS is the part that's colored—blue, green, brown, or any combination of those lovely shades. You can remember that, because there's a flower called an iris, and flowers come in pretty colors, too. The iris expands or contracts to control the amount of light that passes through the PUPIL, which is that black

hole in the middle of the iris. The pupil closes up in bright sunlight to keep too much light from flooding in, and it opens up in the dark to let more light in.

The iris is surrounded by a liquid called the AQUEOUS HUMOR. The CILIARY BODY and MUSCLE control the shape of the LENS. The lens in your eye is kind of like a movie projector. It lies just behind the pupil and it projects light onto your very own "viewing screen"—your RETINA.

The retina is made up of millions of tiny little CONES and RODS that "capture" the light. The cones let you detect detail and color, and the rods help you see outlines and shapes (but not color). Rods are the ones that help you see in the dark. (Cones, which help you see color, work best in bright light.)

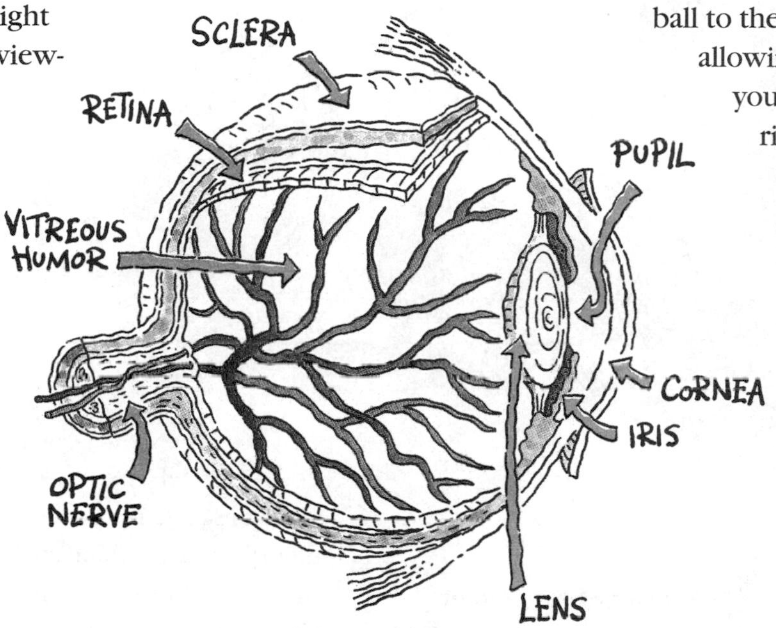

The rods and cones send electrical messages along the OPTIC NERVE, the superhighway that leads to the brain. The brain translates those messages into images, or, in other words, your sight.

EYE MUSCLES connect the eyeball to the orbital cavity, allowing you to move your eyes from left to right and up and down. Just think: without those neat muscles, you wouldn't be able to roll your eyes when your mom tells you to clean your room.

SCLERA

RETINA

VITREOUS HUMOR

OPTIC NERVE

LENS

PUPIL

CORNEA

IRIS

FARTS

You're sitting at your cousin's dance recital. The room is so quiet you can hear a pin drop. Then, without warning, it happens. That unmistakable noise . . . that unforgettable smell . . . you have just farted. But before you move to Antarctica, where no one knows you yet, keep reading.

DID SOMEONE IN THE ROOM "CUT THE CHEESE"?

There are a ton of clever things to call a fart. But whatever you call it, that gassy feeling has an official name—FLATULENCE (*flat-chew-lints*). And flatulence ends in farting. Everybody, from the Queen of England to the President of the United States of America,

does it. (Feel any better yet?) In fact, the average person crop-dusts a room about 14 times a day. If you could catch all the gas your body makes in 24 hours (and you'd have to be a little odd to want to), it would fill half a quart.

Farts comes from two sources. Some farts are simply swallowed air that never got burped out. The rest happen when the bacteria that live in the intestines break down undigested

WARNING: Farting in public will not impress your friends. And, if you happen to be near an open flame when you let her rip, you might just blow up a few buildings. (Just kidding about that last one.)

food. The by-product of that breakdown? An interesting leftover gas with an aroma that sometimes smells like rotten eggs. Most of the gas you make is absorbed through the spongelike walls of the intestines. But sometimes, one of the gas bubbles sneaks out when no one is looking. Let's find out why.

BEANS, BEANS, GOOD FOR YOUR HEART

The foods you eat can add to the stinkiness of the air around you. Beans, the butt (sorry) of a thousand jokes, are a troublemaker because they contain a funky sugar called RAFFINOSE that the body simply can't use. So when you eat beans, there are usually a lot of bean leftovers for the body to get rid of. Brussels sprouts, broccoli, cabbage, and whole grains also have a lot of this kind of sugar, and eating too much of them can turn you into a little Texaco Station.

FRUCTOSE is another sugar that can make you a real stinker. Many sweetened fruit drinks, and

10 Foods That Can Make You "Airborne"

1. **Beans**

2. **Bran**

3. **Broccoli**

4. **Brussels sprouts**

5. **Cabbage**

6. **Carbonated beverages** (double trouble—air and fructose in some of the sweetened ones)

7. **Cauliflower**

8. **Dairy products** (for those who can't break down lactose)

9. **Onions**

10. **White bread** (carbohydrates are real troublemakers!)

especially sodas, have this ingredient added to them. Start reading those labels or be prepared to pass air!

Ever heard of SORBITOL? That's a sugar that hangs out in pears, peaches, prunes, and apples. It's also sometimes used in gum to make it sweet. And yes, it can make you let loose a stink-bomb from time to time.

FIBER, which is found in things like bran, adds to the

general stinkiness of a fart. Because the acid in the stomach can't break down tough fibers, that job falls to the bacteria in the large intestine. And, by now you surely know that where there is bacteria, there's smelliness.

So, is there anything you can do to keep from becoming airborne every time you eat a bean? Well, believe it or not, being in good physical shape can help. If the muscles that support the intestines are strong, the intestines will work better. (Hit that floor, right now, and give me 50 sit-ups!) Exercise also helps to move things smoothly along

cause problems for some people because their bodies can't break down LACTOSE, a natural sugar found in dairy products. (Now you know why they call it cutting the cheese!) For others, dairy products are no problem at all.

ANATOMY OF A FART

What exactly is in a fart? There are five neat ingredients. Oxygen, nitrogen, hydrogen, carbon dioxide, and methane. But sometimes a chemical reaction will also produce hydrogen sulfide, a particularly nasty combination of two chemicals and the same stuff that

through your digestive system. So if you're feeling a little explosive, try going for a walk. (That'll also give you the chance to relieve yourself of some of those nasty stink bombs outdoors, without knocking everyone in the room over.)

It's not just the foods you eat that determine your fragrance factor, but also the speed at which you eat them. Gobbling down a bowl of baked beans at the speed of light is a recipe for disaster. But here's the tricky part. Each person's body reacts differently to the foods we eat. Some people can practically blast off after eating broccoli, while others have no reaction at all. Milk, ice cream, and cheese can

THE PUTRID PAST

Gosh, the things some people will do for a buck! And the things others will pay to see! In France about a hundred years ago, one of the most popular entertainers was a fellow who went by the name "Le Petomane" (which means "the Fartiste" *en Français*). He would blow large quantities of air through his butt, and even play tunes with that particular part of his anatomy. And you thought air guitar was cool!

makes that rotten-egg smell.

Ever wonder what makes some farts noisy, and some silent (but oh-so-deadly)? After food leaves your stomach, it heads for your intestines, where wave-like motions called PERISTALSIS (*per-eh-stall-sis*) squeeze the food and gas along. Certain foods that are hard to digest make for "rougher seas." The waves come along too fast and the gas surfing along doesn't have time to get absorbed into the lining of the intestine. (On the other hand, a slow, gentle ride allows the gas to be absorbed.) But when things get rough, well, that "surfer" is going to get slapped around a lot. Pretty soon, the gas finds itself being propelled through your butt at supersonic speeds. That can lead to a noisy exit!

Remember that you are not the only person on earth who has ever laid an egg. But please try to help cut down on air pollution. If you feel a toot coming on, be kind and head for the bathroom where you can explode to your heart's content.

FECES

The word "feces" is a big favorite among doctors and those weird guys on nature shows. But what is it? Well, feces is the fancy word for plain old poop, and if you want to know more about that, see POOP on page 121.

FLEAS

It would be great if only dogs and cats got them. Unfortunately, humans do, too. For thousands of years, man and his best friends (not to mention many other animals) have been battling a tiny, little pain-in-the-fur—the FLEA, one of the yuckiest, most irritating insects around.

A FLEETING LOOK AT THE FLEA

There are lots of different kinds of fleas— about 1,600 to be exact—and just about each one specializes in tormenting a different animal. Dog fleas don't like the taste of people. People fleas think cats taste yucky. Rabbit fleas wouldn't be caught dead eating anything but bunny blood. And before people started bathing every day, fleas were just an ordinary part of life for humans—everyone had them. Let's start to scratch the surface of this nasty creature.

Ever find yourself face-to-face with a flea? Here's what they look like. They're about 1/8 of an inch long, wingless, flat-bodied and covered with bristles and rows of broad spines called combs. Their flat bodies are perfect for sliding through animal fur and the bristles prevent them from slipping back. Tiny barbs on their feet hook them on tight, and their hard, pointy heads are perfect for burrowing.

The Joint Is Jumping
(and Other Flea Facts)

❋ Fleas are the kangaroo of the insect world. They can jump 50 to 100 times their body length. Let's say you are 5 feet tall. If you were as agile as a flea, you could jump on top of a 25-story building! You could jump more than a quarter of a mile! You would most certainly be an Olympic gold medalist!

❋ Fleas are not only strong, they're fast! That awesome leaping flea's acceleration is 50 times greater than that of the space shuttle after liftoff.

❋ A flea can jump 30,000 times without stopping. Can you?

❋ Boy fleas have . . . ahem . . . how to put this politely . . . not one, but two weenies.

Fleas suck . . . literally. They are actually mutant flies that took to dining on dead mammals in prehistoric days. Over the next million-or-so years, the taste of freshly drawn blood became the equivalent of a burger and fries to these disgusting little creatures. Over time, the flea evolved into the creature we know today.

Mee-ouch! Fleas love burrowing into furry spots like this cat's ear because all that fur provides a safe place to settle down to a meal.

IT'S A FLEA'S LIFE

Flea eggs are the size of a pinhead. When fleas hatch, they are called larvae, and those larvae are starving. But no strained carrots for them—baby fleas love to eat their parents' poop. But if there's nothing else to eat, the larvae will simply eat each other! Within a few days, the larva will make a cocoon just like a caterpillar does, becoming a pupa. If it's warm and toasty out, it won't hang out in its cocoon tent for more than a few weeks, although a cold-weather pupa might stay all cuddled up for as long as a year. Finally, out pops a grown-up flea, hungry as heck and in the mood for food!

How does a flea find a snack? Some are drawn by warmth, some by the carbon dioxide of exhaled breath, some by the breeze caused by a moving animal or person. Before you can say "stop scratching," they are sucking up blood. And your poor pets—or even worse, you—are an itchy mess.

FLEEING THE FLEA

Throughout history, people have tried one desperate remedy after another in an attempt to make their fleas flee.

Feeling a little itchy? Try greasing your clothes with hog lard. If that doesn't work, spread mounds of cow-poop all over your floor and allow it to harden. What? You're still scratching? Grab some splinters from a tree recently struck by lightning and hang them from your neck. These are all flea remedies from the olden days. Only prob-

THE PUTRID PAST

During the Dark Ages, people thought that the more you suffered, the greater your chances of making it to heaven. So when some people got fleas, they did nothing to get rid of them. St. Aloysius, who cared for the sick during the Great Plague, was so kind to fleas that it was written of him: "Though his cassock [a type of robe] was swarming with all sorts of vermin, he'd not take the life of a flea!" Unfortunately, fleas took his life! He died of the plague, which was spread by our foe, the flea.

In the 1800s, flea circuses were the thing to do. During the 1830s, Signor Bertolotto's Fleas featured fleas at sea, a flea harem, and fleas ballroom dancing to a 12-piece flea orchestra complete with tiny instruments. They would actually dress the fleas in tiny little costumes and wire or glue them to one another. The fleas would hop like mad to escape, making it look like they were dancing! Believe it or not, the tradition still lives on—a woman in Manhattan has a flea circus today!

The largest flea collection in the world is housed in the famous British Museum in London. Is it just me or is this totally crazy? This is not just an "only in England" kind of thing, either. There are flea collections in the Smithsonian in Washington, D.C., and the Canadian National Museum in Ottawa.

lem is, none of them worked.

In ancient Egypt, there were professional flea-catchers. But the poor flea-catcher didn't head out looking for his prey with a little net and a magnifying glass. No, sirree! Instead, someone would pour milk all over him and let him stand alone in the room with the pests. As soon as he was completely covered with fleas, he'd walk out and the room would be left flea-free.

In Europe, women wore flea sticks—tubes with sticky stuff such as tree sap inside. They wore them around their

necks, or they fastened them to strips of animal fur, knowing that fleas love animal pelts. The fleas were supposed to nest in the fur instead of on the fur-wearer's skin. These must-have fashion items were the furry forerunners of feathered boas and fur stoles.

Here's an early Roman method for getting rid of fleas that had nestled into someone's ears. Get a wooden plank. With the middle supported and the ends free (kind of like a see-saw), tie the flea-bitten person to the plank so that his ears are extending past the edge of the wood. Hit the other end (near the feet) with a heavy mallet, causing the ear to shake hard enough to make the fleas drop out. Seem extreme? It might not if you had fleas in your ears!

The prize for the silliest flea-killer goes to Queen Christina of Sweden, who amused herself by executing fleas with a miniature crossbow (just 4 inches long) and tiny little arrows. She also had a "flea cannon." Don't believe me? It's on display in a Stockholm museum. Check it out!

Today's solution? Cleanliness (vacuum often) and anti-flea spray for your house, and a flea bath and powder for your pets.

FLIES

Talk about the good life. A female fly spends 40 percent of her time doing absolutely nothing—just hanging out daydreaming. Another 30 percent of her time is spent upchucking all over the despicable things she's about to eat, followed by a nice chunk of time sucking up the puked-up mess. Oh . . . and just for a little added fun, flies pee every few minutes. And to think that a fly has just done all that on your picnic lunch!

CHAMPION UPCHUCKERS, PRIZEWINNING PEE-ERS

No doubt about it. Barfing and peeing are the big events in a fly's life. Here's why.

You have teeth and a tongue in your mouth, but flies don't. Instead, they have little sponges. Flies eat by blotting up their food.

Facts on the Fly

Here are 10 things you've always wanted to know about flies.

1. A fly responds to light 10 times faster than we do, alerting it to the dangers of that rolled-up newspaper you are about to swat it with. And they are fast devils, too. Their wings beat about 180 times a second. Try flapping your arms that fast!

2. Scientists know of more than 120,000 different kinds of fly, but some think there may be upwards of one million different types of fly out there, most of which are still unidentified.

3. Flies fly in the face of the laws of gravity. They can scale walls and walk upside down on ceilings, thanks to special glands on their feet that produce a sticky, glue-like substance.

4. A fly has bristly hair all over its body. Perfect for germs to hide in.

5. The tongue of a fly has a gooey, spongy surface.

6. Mommy flies lay 75 to 150 eggs at a time—and hatch 600 to 1,000 babies in a lifetime. One average-size trash can can serve as a "nursery" for 30,000 flies a week. (See MAGGOTS on page 96 for more info on these fly babies.)

7. Scientists call the group that the flies belong to DIPTERA. Diptera means "two-winged" from *di*, which means "two" in Greek, and *pteron*, which means "wing" in Greek.

8. Flies have no lungs. They suck air through a hole in their midsection. And they have almost colorless blood because they have no hemoglobin (which is what gives our blood its ruby-red color when it mixes with oxygen).

9. There are flies everywhere human beings live, from the coldest corners of Alaska to the warmest tropical beaches. There are even flies in the deserts that survive by eating other bugs.

10. MOSQUITOES are in the same insect group (Diptera) as flies. (And because they are soooo gross, they get their very own entry on page 103.)

Now, if you've ever tried to blot up a hamburger, you know it's impossible. You can only blot a liquid, so flies have to turn everything they eat into honest-to-goodness bug juice. To do that, they spend a monumental amount of time vomiting.

When a fly throws up, it's not because it has ridden a gravity-defying roller coaster one too many times. The chemicals in its puke help turn that hunk of apple pie it's just snagged at your picnic into a liquid. This is the fly's way of mixing enzymes and digestive juices with its food *before* the food gets into its body.

Most of us have a sweet tooth, and flies are no different. They love sugary things. Ever dip your finger in a bowl of sugar and lick the sugar off? If you were a fly, you could dip your feet in that bowl and taste the sweetness without even licking. But then, you would have very hairy tootsies—1,500 little taste hairs festoon those fly footsies. Flies are ten *thousand* times more sensitive to food tastes than we are! But they don't just love sweets. A fly might have a craving for a big, steamy pile of fresh cow manure one minute and for a taste or two of your peanut-butter-and-jelly sandwich the next. You never know where a fly's mouth (or feet) may have been!

Flies also pee every few minutes, and that frequent peeing comes with a price—dehydration (a fancy way of saying "drying to a crisp"). Flies must drink a lot to avoid drying up, so they are very thirsty creatures. Fortunately, animal poop is loaded with water. That's why flies love pasture-patties. It's the fly's equivalent of an ice-cold water fountain after a hot ball game!

CALL IN THE SWAT TEAM

Flies may seem kind of basic, but they are actually very highly evolved, complicated insects that are well adapted to survive under even the most terrible conditions. They live everywhere on the planet except underwater and in the frozen parts of Antarctica and the Arctic.

Surely you have swatted at a housefly, a horsefly, or a blowfly? But there are some even yuckier kinds. FLESH FLIES eat only decaying meat—nothing fresh for them, please. FILTER FLIES feed on the slime that collects inside your bathroom and kitchen drains. STABLE FLIES (or HORSEFLIES) are bloodsuckers, always willing to swoop down on a barnyard animal (or even *you*) for several bloody gulps. EYE GNATS love to graze on the moisture in your eyeballs. And for pure yuckiness, nothing tops the FACE FLY, which likes to hang out and eat mucus from a cow's nostrils and eyes.

And although they may be small, flies are one of the deadliest critters out there. When

THE PUTRID PAST

Losing your hair? The ancient Romans had a surefire remedy. First, they'd mash up a couple hundred houseflies, making them into a paste. Then, they'd rub the fly-paste on their bald spots, and wait for the hair to start growing like crazy. After all, flies are just about the hairiest bugs out there, right? Well, guess what? It didn't work, and a bald Roman stayed a bald Roman.

flies come from the nearest poop pile into your backyard, they don't stop to wipe their feet! Millions of bacteria come along for the ride and many will stay behind on your picnic lunch.

Flies carry more than 100 different disease-causing bacteria—including those that cause nasty illnesses like diarrhea, food poisoning, cholera, and typhoid. (See BACTERIA, page 6, for the horrible details about germs.) In certain parts of the world where the sanitation isn't very good, flies are more than just annoying. They're killers.

So what to do? Cleanliness is next to fly-less-ness. Pack up your garbage, clean up after your pets, and wipe the fruit punch off the floor when you spill it.

Oh . . . and just in case all else fails, keep that flyswatter handy at all times!

FLY AWAY? NOT QUITE!

As if spreading illness and filth weren't bad enough, certain flies can get into farmers' crops and really ruin them. In the 1940s, scientists began spraying crops with a powerful pest killer called DDT. They confidently boasted that with DDT around, fruit flies (and other annoying bugs) would soon go the way of the dinosaurs. Unfortunately, the fruit flies quickly adapted to the foul spray, but birds that shared the same air space didn't. You could say birds began "dropping like flies." The DDT also seeped into the soil and the water and was absorbed by fish and humans. In 1972, the government banned its use. Oh, well . . . back to the drawing board.

A Nasty Note

In 1912, a "swat the fly" contest was held in Canada. The winner was a girl named Beatrice White, who killed 543,360 flies, which weighed in at a total of 212 pounds! She won a $50 prize for her efforts. (Amazing what a kid can do with no TV to distract her.) Together, the contest entrants swatted a grand total of 2.8 million flies! I wonder who got to add up the results?

FOUL FEET

Thank goodness gym class is over. It was all you could do to keep from taking the teacher's whistle cord and knotting it around her neck! Now you've got 60 seconds to change and get your sorry butt over to the other side of the building. Quick, out of those shoes. Hmmmm. What's that sour, revolting smell? It's . . . it's . . . Oh no! It's your feet!

STINKY PINKY TIME

There is actually a scientific name for feet that reek. It's called BROMHIDROSIS (*brom-hi-dro-sis*). Ain't science grand? Such a nice, official-sounding name for something so nasty.

Each of your tootsies is packed with about 20,000 sweat glands! In fact, each of your feet can produce a half a cup of sweat each day. (See BODY ODOR on page 21 for more on the nasty details of stinky sweat.)

Bacteria love the scenery down in the foot region. So, naturally they vacation there in droves. After all, that sweaty foot food is *so* tasty. Nice, sweaty socks just add to the fun, trapping heat and moisture. Since bacteria thrive in warm, moist climates, before you know what's happening those little fellas are having a foot fiesta! And we know what bacteria fiestas smell like. Fetid!

OH MY ACHING FEET!

There are more troubles brewing down in those toes of yours. Because your poor feet bear so much of your body weight—and because people insist on cramming their feet into shoes too small for Cinderella—feet are prone to lots of problems. One of them is BUNIONS, which form when your toes—and especially your big toe—get scrunched over a long period of time. The bones in the toe get deformed and stick out in a kind of hump on the side. It's ugly. Painful, too.

CORNS are another shoe-too-small problem. Do not confuse these with the on-the-cob variety. Foot corns are areas of the skin that have gotten thicker because of constant pressure on them. But everything underneath that thickened skin is a tad tender, so your poor feet become sore. Corns have a big brother called a CALLUS, which you usually get on the balls of your feet—the fleshy pad just below your toes.

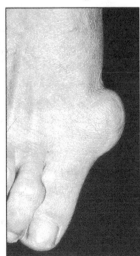

A big, bad bunion blooms at the base of this woman's toe. She's obviously been wearing shoes a size too small.

Calluses are sometimes painful, but often they're not. In fact, some folks in remote parts of the world where shoes are rare end up developing super-thick calluses over almost the whole sole of their foot, allowing them to walk barefoot on sharp stones without a single "ouch."

Bottom line? Don't cram your feet into too-tight shoes.

5 Ways to Have Fragrant Footsies

Do people run away screaming when you pull off your shoes? Besides taking a daily bath or shower, try these tricks to make your toesies smell like rosies.

1. Soak your toes in salt water. Mix about a half cup of kosher salt (the kind with extra big crystals) into a bowl filled with a quart of warm water. Don't rinse afterward. Just pat your feet dry.

2. Try a footbath of ice water and lemon juice. The combination of cold and citric acid (from the lemon juice) slows the sweat glands down a bit.

3. Try spraying an underarm deodorant on your feet. Same stinky problem—same solution.

4. Wash your sneakers from time to time— then dry them in the dryer to keep them sweet.

5. Have a "sock hop." Change your socks a couple of times a day.

FREAKY FISH

Forget those little fish that just swish along in the sea, looking pretty. Here's the haul on some flesh-ripping, bottom-feeding, truly terrifying, deep-sea do-badders.

SHARK ATTACK!

Let's face it. Bees kill more people every year than sharks do. So how come bees don't have a menacing theme song and a thrill ride at Universal Studios? Maybe it's because they don't weigh 4,000 pounds, aren't 21 feet long, and don't flash seven rows of teeth when they smile.

Ever fight with your brothers or sisters? No hemming and hawing. I'll bet you do! Well, get this. Shark siblings start picking on each other before they are even born! The bigger ones eat the little ones while they are growing in Momma Shark's womb. Only the strongest will live to make it out of Mommy. How's that for sibling rivalry?

There are close to 300 different species of sharks. Most of them are harmless to humans, despite their reputation, but here's the scoop on a few of the exceptions.

GREAT WHITE SHARKS are the most famous underwater predators, flesh-hungry and vicious . . . or so they say. Truth is, they usually reject human flesh after just one taste (although that single bite could be a big one). Weighing in at a hefty 5,000 pounds, great whites want far more fat in their diet than even the plumpest humans can provide. We are too stringy and have too many bones. They'll take a nice blubbery whale or a pudgy sea lion over a measly little human being any day.

But just in case, you better stay out of the

deep waters of the Atlantic, Pacific, or Indian Oceans if you want to avoid these sharks.

HAMMERHEADS and MAKOS are some other sharks with an evil reputation. Hammerheads are odd-looking creatures with heads shaped like . . . well . . . hammers, with an eye and a nostril at each end of the "hammer" (the better to see and smell you with, my dear). Makos are lightning-fast, able to swim at upwards of 55 miles an hour, and have an unusual fondness for head-butting boats.

Interestingly, the biggest sharks (up to 50 feet long), the whale shark and the basking shark, are among the least ferocious. They don't even eat fish, preferring tiny shrimp-like creatures.

In addition to being carnivores (another word for meat-eaters), sharks are the garbage disposals of the seas. When the bellies of dead sharks are cut open, it's not uncommon to find cans, bottles, propeller blades, and even anchors in their guts.

Is it true that a single drop of blood in the water will send a shark into a frenzy? No! They can smell it, but the scent usually doesn't make them wild and crazy. Instead, sharks often find their food by sensing electromagnetic impulses. They have special organs called the AMPULLAE OF LORENZINI (_am_-pew-lie of _lor_-en-_zee_-nee), small, gel-filled pits in the snout and other parts of the body, which can detect the electrical fields given off by all living things. They are so sensitive that they can pick up a heartbeat from a block away!

A ROUNDUP OF ROGUES

Let's see what else we can reel in.

Fishermen who pull up a PACIFIC GRENADIER (_gren-a-deer_) in their nets for the first time often get the surprise of their lives. As these deep-dwelling fish are dragged to the surface, the rapid change in pressure causes the gases in their bladders to expand too rapidly, making their stomachs pop out of their mouths and their eyes bulge wildly! No one wants to eat 'em after they've seen *that* corpse!

Getting an armful of porcupine quills isn't much fun. And there's a fish with the same trick up its gills. When a PORCUPINE FISH meets up with a hungry bully in a dark underwater alleyway, it gulps huge quantities of water. This makes its body swell up like a balloon covered with stiff, bristling spines. Unlike real porcupines, however, these fish don't release their quills, and they can't swim very well when they are all puffed up. But who wants to eat a mouthful of prickly porcupine anyway?

It's easy to see why you would never want to find yourself face-to-snout with a great white shark.

Man Bites Shark!

Looking for a little revenge? Think *Jaws* in reverse and have Mom or Dad cook up a shark for dinner one night soon. Try this dandy little recipe, direct from Iceland—a country not known for its cuisine. (After you read this, you'll understand why.)

Remove the inner organs from one shark. Bury the shark in the sand, or better still, toss it into an open barrel. Leave it there for three years. (Yes, you read that right. *Three years.* Did I say this was fast food?) The shark will ferment nicely, becoming like a soft, ripe cheese with the lovely aroma of ammonia. (If you're not sure what ammonia smells like, think day-old dirty diapers.) This tasty dish is called "*Hakarl*," and that's probably what you'll do after you eat it!

Or try "Shark Fin Soup." After you've sliced off the fin, brave soul that you are, salt it and leave it to dry in the sun. It's loaded with gelatin, which makes the soup a lot like eating liquid mucus. Mmm-yum! (See SICKENING SEAFOOD on page 140 for more tasty recipes from the deep.)

You'd better be careful when you go fishing off the coast of Southern California. You could end up with something truly nasty on your line. The kelp beds there are home to a fish called the SCULPIN *(skul-pin)*. Their fin tips have a cute little attachment—venom sacs loaded with a painful poison! If you catch a sculpin on the end of your fishing line and get stung, heat is the best remedy. Stick the affected part in hot water, as hot as you can stand it without burning your skin, and keep soaking it in that hot water for at least an hour.

You might not think STARFISH (sometimes called SEA STARS) are gross at all. After all, they come in pretty colors and all they do is hang around, bothering no one. And they're

This bat star has terrible manners. You should never let your stomach hang out of your mouth while eating.

kind of interesting because their bodies revolve around the number five. We have two legs, two eyes, two ears. They have five arms, five reproductive organs, and a five-part digestive system. But since this is a book about yucky things, here's a slimy sea star fact. When they eat, they push their stomachs out through their mouths, nearly turning themselves inside out!

When you step into the ocean, watch where you walk, especially on a calm day. You might find yourself stepping on something that will not be happy to see you—a STINGRAY. Stingrays live mostly on the ocean floor in tropical waters, but some like temperate seas and even cold water. Stingrays are flat and like to press themselves down into the sand. If stepped on, the stingray will deliver a nasty sting to the unsuspecting victim.

Ray roundup. On top, bull-nose rays go nosing around. Below, a southern stingray.

Each stingray has a long tail tipped by a stinger that would make a bee green with envy. It's covered with a sheath of cartilage that's like a twist-cap on a soda bottle. That cap breaks apart as the stinger enters a victim's skin and venom pours into the wound. The stinger has a serrated edge, like a kitchen knife, to add insult to injury. The sting should be treated in the same way as a sculpin sting (see page 66). But to avoid stepping on those flat-as-a-pancake rays in the first place, why not just shuffle into the water slowly the next time you go for a dip?

HEY! EIGHT ARMS!

If you happen to be like me, when you think of an OCTOPUS you think of long, rubbery tentacles covered with suckers, ready to squeeze the life out of you. Actually, octopuses are very shy

True or false? Giant octopus eats fishing boat! The movies would have us believe that one octopus could devour an entire ship. But the truth is shy octopuses flee from strangers (and big, strange boats).

and spend most of their days lying on the ocean floor. If you're a sea lion, seal, or otter, however (and if you are and you're reading this book, boy, am I impressed!), you probably think of an octopus as a big, gooey, rich piece of cake. Totally yummy!

So what does an octopus do when it sees a sea lion licking its lips? Easy. It inks him! Octopuses have a special organ called an ink sac. It sends out a cloud of dense brown-black ink, which not only blinds enemies (who can see through all that ink?), but messes up their sense of smell as well. And even if the sea lion gets a bite of one of those eight octopus arms, don't worry. It will grow back!

If, after reading all of the above, you are still foolish enough to mess with an octopus, you should know that some of them can mess with you right back. The Australian blue-ringed octopus gives off a poison which can paralyze and even kill you. *Octopus vulgaris,* the best-known of all, makes a poison called CEPHALOTOXIN (*seff-al-ah-tox-in*) in its salivary glands which kills many of its predators instantly.

Longing for more underwater trashiness? Turn to SICKENING SEAFOOD on page 140 and JELLYFISH on page 85.

FRIGHTENING FASHIONS

Jeans. T-shirt. Sneakers. There, you're dressed! Be grateful. In times past and places far away, things were very different and getting dressed could be pretty complicated, not to mention downright painful. Depending on where you lived, you might get to make the following fashion statements on a daily basis.

TEENSY WEENSY FOOTSY WOOTSIES

Some like them big . . . some like them *really* small. In China, for almost a thousand years, if you were a girl, the tinier your feet were, the more beautiful you were thought to be. So, young girls had their feet "bound," which meant their feet were wrapped tighter and tighter every day. Eventually, the bones in the toes broke and bent back and everything was forced and folded into an upside down V. The goal was for the girl to end up with a foot that measured about 3½ inches long. But, as we all know, you can't really stop your feet from growing to whatever size they want to be—nor should you!

Walking with bound feet was almost impossible, but that was okay because the girls whose feet were bound were usually wealthy and had servants and rich husbands to take care of them. In fact, that was how people knew you were rich! If you had to actually do things yourself, like cook and clean and take care of your family, you probably had big (or at least regular-sized) feet. With baby-sized feet, you got to sit around all day. (A good thing, since those little footsies wouldn't hold you up anyway!) This practice began in the tenth century and continued until 1911, when it was finally banned.

Go measure your own feet right now, and then imagine being the size of one of your parents. Bet your feet wouldn't hold you up. Bet you'd topple right over if you tried to do anything. Bet you're happy you didn't grow up in China 500 years ago!

Bound until bent and broken—that was often the fate of the feet of wealthy Chinese women.

MAKEOVER MADNESS

The next time you see your mom applying lipstick, tell her all about the makeup used in the 1700s in France and parts of the American colonies. Women wanted to have very white skin. To get that "look" they applied makeup made from white lead (yes, indeed . . . the very same lead that can poison you after repeated exposure) mixed with flour or cornstarch. To go with their chalk-white faces, they liked very red lips and gums. But there was no makeup counter at the corner drugstore back in those days, so they crushed a kind of insect called the COCHINEAL (*ca-cha-neel*) in their fingers and rubbed the crushed bug on their mouths. That stained them a bright red color. For good measure, a little dead insect on their cheeks added a spot of color to the greasy whiteness of their faces.

Many people had rotten teeth in those days and had to have them pulled. But no one wanted that gaunt and drawn toothless look, so women wore PLUMPERS—balls of cork that they jammed into the insides of their cheeks. Comfy!

What to wear with a chalk-white face? Big hair! In the 1700s in France, hair got completely out of hand. At the king's court, women piled their hair into poufs that were up to 3 feet high. Their hair was so big, they had to sleep sitting up. It took so long to get their hair fixed properly that they would keep their 'dos intact for months on end. Get the picture? Dirty, smelly, and a perfect place for rodents and bugs to hang out!

Women weren't the only ones on the big-hair bandwagon. Men wanted big 'dos, too. Any man who wanted to be considered upper crust went to the barber and had his

What do you think would be harder? Balancing a 3-foot-high tower of hair on your head or squeezing through a doorway wearing a dress 5 feet wide?

hair completely shaved off. Next, he paid a visit to the neighborhood wig maker. For a price, this fellow would make a set or two of fake hair, elaborately curled and styled. Really rich people could afford wigs made of human hair. But the less wealthy had to turn to horsehair or yak hair. Some poorer folk wore wigs made of thread! Wigs had to fit really tight so they wouldn't "flip" and they were unbelievably itchy, no doubt because they, too, made perfect bug hotels.

BUNS OF STEEL!

If you think your dress-up clothes are uncomfortable, pity the men of the middle ages. In the 12th century, because everyone was always fighting with everybody else, warriors started wearing clothing made of small linked iron rings called CHAIN MAIL (not to be confused with those stupid chain letters that come in the mail!).

By the 1400s they'd gone a step further. Men started wearing clothing made entirely of plates of iron. Knights sent to battle rode off wearing 50 pounds of metal. It was perfect for

Like mother, like daughter. Female members of the Karen tribe in Thailand still wear traditional brass neck rings.

deflecting arrows and lances, but boy did it chafe!

And while we're on the subject of metal fashions, let's dart around the globe to Thailand where the threat of tigers leaping at one's neck led to a strange fashion craze. To protect those vulnerable necks, folks started to wear wide metal bands at their throats. It soon became a sign of beauty for women to wear a foot-high stack of metal around the neck. Girls were fitted with a heavy iron or brass neck band on their fifth birthday, and every few months another band was added until the neck was a foot long. By the time the women were grown-ups they were carting around 30 pounds of metal!

But there are a couple of problems with this particular fashion statement. The neck doesn't actually grow longer. Instead the shoulders are pushed down until the muscles that hold the head up can't function properly. Women who, for whatever reason, had to have their rings removed discovered they couldn't hold their heads up anymore! As a matter of fact, removing those neck rings became a common punishment!

And while we're still on the subject of metal . . . there's nothing like a too-tight pair of undies to ruin your day. But if you think that's uncomfortable, shed a tear or two for women in America and Europe in the mid-to-late 1800s. Some of them wore undergarments made of iron! They wanted to have tiny little waists and be shaped like hourglasses. So corsets stiffened with whalebones or metal were laced around their midsections as tight as could be. Unfortunately, they were so tight that women's ribs were actually breaking. And forget about breathing. Lungs just couldn't inflate properly. So many women fainted from lack of oxygen that special sofas called "fainting couches" were invented. And we think spike heels are bad!

A woman needed a strong helper to get dressed back in the days when whalebone corsets were in style.

FUNGI

Ever had this happen? You decide to clean under your bed because it's beginning to smell weird down there. You happen to find a half-eaten peanut-butter-and-jelly sandwich—a midnight snack that got tossed off the bed as you tossed and turned. Only the bread isn't white anymore, and blue-green bread has never been a big favorite of yours.

FUN GUYS

Meet the FUNGI (*fun-guy*) family! They come in all the colors of the rainbow—blue, green, pink, orange, white—and in all sizes. They adore bread, fruits, and veggies (eating habits only a mother can love). If only they didn't show their affection for food in such a revolting fashion! Just about any food left in the fridge (or under your bed) will eventually become host to a mold party. (And mold is a fungi—but you knew that already, right?)

Fungi are not plants, they're not animals, and they're not even really fun. They are a life form all their own. They can be very tiny or bigger than the biggest whale in the ocean. The air you are breathing contains millions of tiny fungi "seeds" called SPORES. There are more than 100,000 different types of fungi. Some can save lives. Others can kill you in seconds. Knowing which ones are which can be a handy bit of information to have.

Unlike a plant, a fungus can't make its own food by using the sun's energy. Instead, a network of millions of tiny threads absorbs nutrients from other things both alive and dead. Mushrooms and toadstools (that's what people call the poisonous ones) are the best-known fungi. But there's a lot more to these creatures than meets the eye.

If you love mushrooms you might be tempted to nibble on this lovely colony of fungi growing in the woods of New York state. Resist the temptation! Some mushrooms are deadly and only a trained expert can tell which ones are safe to eat.

The biggest living thing on earth is neither an elephant nor a whale, but a fungus growing in Washington state. This living, still-growing mound of mold spreads over two and a half square *miles*—over 1,500 acres. It has been alive for hundreds of years, and it's still going strong.

Some fungi have even changed the course of history! In the mid-1800s, in Ireland, an evil fungus crept into the potato crops and destroyed them. Potatoes were such an important part of the Irish diet that people soon had little to eat. Many starved and died during what is now known as the Irish Potato Famine. Things were so bad that thousands of people left Ireland and moved to North America.

Gross but Good

Yeasts, the smallest fungi, dine on sugars. Yeast cells reproduce quickly, dividing into two, then four, then eight yeast cells . . . until they have created quite a crowd. And in this quick division, there is something that can be used to make neat things for people. Without yeast, there would be no wine, no beer, and no fluffy bread.

Here's how it works with bread. As the yeast eats the simple sugars in the dough, it leaves behind alcohol and releases carbon dioxide gas. The gas is what makes the bread rise.

And in 1928, a scientist named Alexander Fleming was growing some bacteria (you know—those little critters that make us smell so bad and get us sick from time to time) in a little dish. When mold started growing on the side of the dish, Fleming was *mad!* He was about to toss the experiment when he noticed that the bacteria closest to the mold had died. Being a scientist, he figured something was up, and he started asking himself some questions. It took almost 15 years before the stuff he discovered could be used to help people, but his discovery—PENICILLIN—went on to save millions of lives.

Don't Be a Spore Loser!

Certain toadstools can do a real number on a person. Many of them produce nasty poisons. Several varieties will make you sick, and some, like the pretty, red-topped FLY AGARIC, can make you *very* sick. Others, like the appropriately named DEATH CAP, can put you permanently underground. *Never* eat any mushrooms you find growing in the wild. The evil ones look a whole lot like the good guys.

EATERS OF THE DEAD AND LUNCHERS ON THE LIVING

Fungi basically fall into these two categories: Those that eat dead things and those that eat living ones.

SAPROBES (*sap-robes*) are the fungi that eat dead stuff—plants, trees, insects, and animals. Many mushrooms fall into this category, and you can find them happily sprouting from the trunks of rotting trees.

The fungi that move in on living things fall into two types. PARASITIC (*par-ah-sit-ic*) FUNGI don't really care for the taste of man, but from time to time they'll come along for the ride. They cause athlete's foot and ringworm, and a mouth rash called thrush. (See PARASITES on page 115 for the toe-curling facts on those gross problems.) PREDATORY (*pred-ah-tor-ee*) FUNGI are meaner. They go after really tiny worms and single-cell creatures, then trap them and eat 'em alive.

A FEW FUNGI FACTS!

❋ Think of a mushroom as a big iceberg with only the tip sticking out. The other 90 percent is buried underground. The part that you see is called the FRUITING BODY. Its job is to send out spores. Down in the dirt you'll find the HYPHAE (*hi-fee*), the tiny threads that soak up the nutrients.

✳ Picture a large orange glob of mucus-like material, slowly slinking across hunks of rotting wood. Lovely, eh? If you've ever seen anything like this, you've seen a SLIME MOLD. You can usually find them on damp, decaying, dead trees and logs. They

This oozing plasmodial slime mold will travel outward about 9 inches a day. Watch out behind you. . .

slowly "crawl" over the surface, eating the bacteria that live on the wood. Ugh!

✳ LICHENS (*like-inz*) are two creatures in one, part green plant and part fungus. Neither part can live without the other. They sprout up everywhere, from the driest desert to the deepest seas. You can see them growing on the surfaces of rocks or on the trunks of trees.

✳ The STINKHORN FUNGUS, true to its name, reeks! The whole tip is covered with a foul-smelling spore-filled slime that flies and beetles just can't resist. It smells like rotting flesh.

Don't let that delicate white veil fool you. This stinkhorn fungus lives up to its name.

GROSS GRUB

Sharpen those knives, grab a stack of napkins, and forget that boring tuna fish sandwich. Why eat grilled cheese when you can dine on sheep feet, frog's legs, and other assorted yummies?

It's amazing what some people will eat. You might be freaked out by the thought of chomping on "Braised Fungus" (a Chinese dish), but, of course, it works both ways. In some parts of the world, people would be grossed out at the thought of eating a bacon cheeseburger! Of course, no matter where you travel, it pretty much comes down to one thing. It all tastes like chicken!

WARNING: Reading about some of this stuff is sure to twist your tummy!

FROM AARDVARK TO ZEBRA

Imagine unpacking your lunch box and finding bear paw on a bun or some nice, steaming giraffe stew. How about having your mom offer to cook you up a few plump rats or a juicy bite of bat? You've seen them on nature shows. Now see them as you never have before . . . on a plate, with ketchup on the side! Cat, dog, elephant, frog, giraffe, monkey—from Aardvark to Zebra, just about every animal is eaten in some part of the world.

In Dutch, AARDVARK means "earth pig." You might know that these goofy-looking animals love to eat ants and termites, and they have a nose only a mother could love. But I bet you didn't know that they themselves are a big dinner favorite with African hunters. (In case you're wondering, yes, true to their Dutch name, they do taste like pork.)

Closer to home, Texans sometimes have a hankerin' for ARMADILLO (baked in its shell, of course, and stuffed to the gills with potatoes, carrots, apples, and a little salt). And

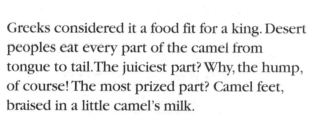

don't forget alligator, another snappy-tasting main course!

Broiled, boiled, or barbecued, BAT is another food favorite around the world, especially in China, where bats are a symbol of long life. In Samoa, they bake them in clay ovens, then fry them up with onions. (Order *"pe'a"* in a Samoan restaurant and bat's what you'll get.) Australians and

Talk about fresh "fruit"! These fruit bats are sold live in the markets of Indonesia.

Africans like a bat snack, too. And with hundreds of different types to choose from, you'll never get bored. Hunters catch them by sneaking into bat caves and getting them with fishing nets. (Just in case you were thinking of trying this yourself . . . never cook up a bat caught during daylight hours. It may very well have rabies!)

CAMEL is another everyday favorite: the ancient

Greeks considered it a food fit for a king. Desert peoples eat every part of the camel from tongue to tail. The juiciest part? Why, the hump, of course! The most prized part? Camel feet, braised in a little camel's milk.

CATS and DOGS have been dinner items for centuries. Throughout Southeast Asia, the Pacific Islands, and parts of Africa, eating dog meat is believed to prevent disease. There are even special breeds raised for meat just like cattle is, such as the black-tongued Chow in China.

THE PUTRID PAST

BACK in ancient Rome, suckling puppy was served at festivals honoring the gods. And when the Aztecs ruled Mexico, the Mexican Hairless dog was a major food staple. Little fattened pups were sold by the hundreds in the markets near Mexico City.

American wildcats like COUGARS and LYNX were part of the Native American cooking tradition. HOUSE CATS taste something like rabbit. One standard dish in Ghana is stewed cat, which is made with tomatoes and hot red peppers and is spooned over rice. A great Chinese delicacy is *"Lung Fung Foo,"* which translates as the poetic name "Dragon, Phoenix, and Tiger Soup." It's not made of any of those things, however, but from fillets of snake, pork, old cat, and chicken. No wonder they decided to be poetic!

HUNGRY ENOUGH TO EAT A HORSE?

You could do that, of course. (They do in France.) But try ELEPHANT if you're really starving. At 13,000 pounds, one elephant can feed a family for a long, long time. When African elephant herds become overpopulated, the government has to step in and thin them out. The meat is dried and sold in local markets. (The elephant's trunk is considered to be the best part.) If that's not gross enough for you, you might like to know that the Akoa, a tribe of pygmies, like their elephant served with a side of live maggots! (For more on MAGGOTS, see page 96.)

Feeling FOX-y? Come to Switzerland and

Forget steak. These Vietnamese merchants are selling roast dog, a delicacy that's more expensive than chicken, pork, or beef.

have some *"Fuchspfeffer,"* or in plain English, "Pepper Fox," popular with hunters.

Got a hankering for something really different? In Africa, GIRAFFE bone marrow is one of the greatest delicacies around. The bones are baked first, then the marrow is sucked out.

Or how about munching on a MONKEY? Apes, baboons, chimps, lemurs, and gorillas are all eaten in parts of Africa, Asia, and South America. In fact, monkey meat almost caused a war. When the Zaire soccer team visited Egypt, they brought their own monkeys to cook for dinner. But in Muslim countries, monkeys are considered sacred, so the Egyptian cooks, who were Muslim, refused to touch the animals. Angry words flew back and forth and diplomats had to be trotted out to smooth things over.

The practice of eating monkeys carries other great risks, though. At least two of the most deadly viruses of recent years—EBOLA and HIV (the virus that causes AIDS)—have been linked to monkeys. (See VIRUSES on page 184 to learn the scary details on these killers.)

Back to That Bear Paw

Hundreds of years ago, BEAR was one of the most widely appreciated animal meats in North America, loved by both Native Americans and European settlers. If they needed fat to fry in, they used bear fat! Want to know the original recipe for "Boston Baked Beans"? Beans, bear, and maple syrup! And the first mince pies were stuffed with minced bear meat!

Bear is also big in other countries. In Russia, grizzly bears are smoked, just like pork hams. In Japan, the Ainu tribes drink bear blood for strength. And in China, *"shon tsan"*—bear paw—is considered a great treat. Here's the recipe: Wash a bear paw, then pack it in clay and bake it in an oven. Let it cool and crack the clay off. (The fur will come off with the clay.) Simmer the paw in frequently changed water until that "bear" smell starts to go away. When it's very soft, add some sherry and shredded ham and chicken to the liquid and stir. They swear it's un-*bear*-ably good!

ANYONE FOR A NICE PLUMP RODENT?

Oh-la-la! France is known for its fine cooking, but in parts of France, RAT is considered a fine bit of dining—especially if the rat has drunk a little too much wine. Rats plucked from the wine cellars are cooked *à la bordelaise*—with a little olive oil, red wine, and shallots, grilled over a fire of chopped-up old wine barrels! (To find out how truly disgusting this is, turn to RATS on page 128.)

In some parts of Africa and China, rats are as popular as hot dogs are here. (And if you can stand to find out what goes into hot dogs, see MISERABLE MEATS on page 99.) West Africans love the giant rat the best, and in Ghana over 50 percent of locally produced meat comes from rats! Up in the Arctic, "Mice in Cream" is a real hit. (One of the ingredients is ethyl alcohol, the kind of alcohol that makes people drunk, which might help to explain why people like this dish.) The mice are marinated for several hours in a vat of alcohol, fried in salt pork fat, then simmered in another cup of alcohol with eight cloves of garlic. Cream is added and it's ready to serve. Sound tasty yet?

While we're busy licking our chops at the thought of eating a rat for dinner, how about some other rodents? SQUIRREL, for example, was a staple of the early American settlers. And everyone knows about Groundhog Day, but did you know GROUNDHOGS were practically the peanut butter and jelly of many Native American tribes a few hundred years ago?

WHICH CAME FIRST?
THE CHICKEN OR THE EGG?

Let's start with eggs—100-year-old ones, to be exact. In China, this dish, called *"Pi-tan,"* is con-

THE PUTRID PAST

Today, orangutans are found only in the lowland jungles of Borneo and north Sumatra. But once, when they were more far-flung, their lips were considered a delicacy in Vietnam.

sidered to be real party fare. Of course, the eggs aren't really 100 years old, just four or five. (But believe me, that's old enough.)

Want the recipe? Soak some raw chicken, duck, or other birds' eggs in a mixture of salt (lots of salt!), gardening lime, lye, and tea leaves for three months. Then dig a hole in the ground and mix up a bed of clay, more lime, ashes, and a little more salt, and bury those eggs.

Three or four years later, when you're really, really hungry, dig them up and peel them. The yolks will be green and cheesy. The whites will be yellow and gummy. The smell will knock your socks off (shove your schnozz into a hunk of blue cheese to get the idea). Dip the eggs in vinegar, and don't forget to wipe your mouth when you're done!

While we're talking about eggs and China, don't forget to try "Bird's Nest Soup." Swiftlets build their nests out of their hardened saliva. That dried-up wad of solid bird spit is the main ingredient of this favorite Chinese soup. Soak the nest overnight, then spread the softened nest on a plate. Carefully try to pick out all the feathers and twigs, toss it into a pot with chicken broth, onions, sherry, and some egg whites. And, voilà! Soup's on!

H

HALITOSIS (BAD BREATH)

Before you go to bed at night, chances are some pesky grown-up nags you to brush your teeth. Finally, to quiet them down, you actually do it. You do an OK job because the last time you went to the dentist you had a cavity—and *that* was no picnic!

So now it's morning and you've just woken up. You've hardly opened your mouth when your dog crawls into the other room with one paw over his nose. Even your mom doesn't want to kiss you, so you know your breath must be *really* stinky. The official grown-up word for stinky mouth is HALITOSIS (*hal-uh-toe-sis*) and you've got it.

So what happened? It's not like you got up in the middle of the night and ate a box of onions.

OH, NO! MORNING MOUTH!

Rivers are wet. Oceans are wet. The sneakers you left out in the rain last night are wet. And so's the inside of your mouth. But while you were under the covers last night, dreaming of

A Nasty Note

Sometimes the problem isn't your mouth, but what you put in it. Sweet Aunt Agnes loves onions and garlic. But kissing her is enough to make you gag. Why? When certain foods are digested, the unused leftovers are carried through the bloodstream and then exhaled through the lungs. Each time she breathes out, Aunt Agnes is blowing broken-down garlic on you!

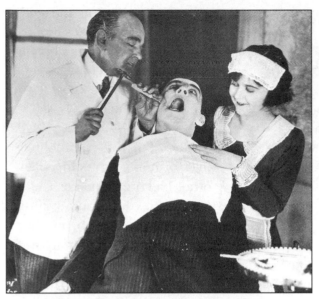

Thank goodness your dentist doesn't use a hammer and chisel to clean a patient's teeth!

becoming a great rock star, your body slowed down its production of SALIVA *(su-lie-va),* better known in real life as SPIT. (See SPIT-TING on page 167, to learn how to successfully lob this icky stuff.)

Spit is neat stuff—99 percent water, with a splash of mucus thrown in. But it also has all sorts of cool chemicals in it that help kill bacteria, constantly washing those bad guys away. It's sort of like a shower for your teeth. Saliva is made in three special glands—the SALIVARY GLANDS—tucked beneath your jaw and up near your ears. These little factories churn out about a quart and a half of spit every day. But at night the glands chill out, and spit production slows down.

That's when the bacteria come out to play. With no spit to wash them away, they can party to their heart's content. Your mouth is not exactly the cleanest place to be under the best of circumstances. In fact, it's the most unsanitary part of your body, teeming with about 10 *billion* bacteria. All night long, while you and your salivary glands sleep, the bacteria build up, their numbers multiplying with every passing hour. What you are smelling, when you get a whiff of someone's stinky mouth, is the "B.O." of 10 billion bacteria. Fortunately, that good-morning tooth-brushing usually reduces the bacteria bash to no-stink proportions.

CHEW ON THIS

So, how come people have bad breath even during the day? What else causes it?

PLAQUE One bad guy in the breath wars is PLAQUE *(plak)*, a sticky, see-through film made of mucus and food particles. It's a magnet for bacteria and it clings to your teeth like glue. Not only does it hang out on your teeth, it attaches itself to your gums and tongue, too. Now you've got an almost invisible, swarming team of bacteria stuck in your mouth. (Feel like brushing yet? I know I do.)

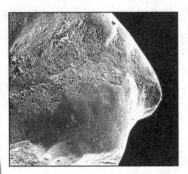

This photograph (taken with a powerful electron microscope) shows the sticky plaque that we can't see with just our eyes.

TARTAR Tartar *(tar-tur)* is a definite tooth bad guy. It's a stony substance made up of hardened plaque and minerals. It settles like concrete on your teeth and has to be scraped off every six months or so by a dentist armed with a fistful of sharp, metal weapons. Left on your teeth, tartar can create pockets between your teeth and gums that become a home for plaque and bacteria. This can eventually lead to gum disease. And diseased gums are smelly gums.

GINGIVITIS When bacteria in plaque dive down below the gum line, you get GINGIVITIS *(jin-je-vie-tis)*, which is as disgusting as it sounds! Your gums swell up, turn red, and bleed. Bacteria trapped within the plaque get ornery and give off toxins that irritate the gum tissue. Eventually, those toxins will eat away at the gums, making

THE PUTRID PAST

Did you know that as recently as the early 1900s doctors were suggesting cigarettes as good medicine for sore throats and bad breath? Yikes!

them pull away from the teeth they are supposed to support. Now there's yet another hiding place for bacteria to hang out in. And before you know it, your teeth are falling out!

CAVITIES These painful holes that form in your teeth are another bad-breath-maker. The bacteria in your mouth can't eat the enamel of your teeth, but they sure can eat sugar! When you eat yummy stuff like cookies, cake, or chips—or even fruits and bread—the bacteria chow down, too. Their "poop" makes an acid that eats through the enamel of your teeth, creating even more places for bacteria to hang out. Before you know what's happened, the hungry bacteria have mistaken the insides of your teeth (called the DENTIN) for a bag of nachos and have nibbled their way down to the roots. "Drill, please."

FIGHT THAT FOUL FATE!

Don't want to have breath that smells like week-old gym socks? What can you do? When food hides out in your mouth, it starts to rot. And we all know what rotting garbage smells like. Unfortunately, your mouth is no different than a garbage can.

There's really no way around it. You've got to do what your mom and your dentist keep telling you. Use that toothbrush at least twice a day. A

Oral hygiene is important even for sea mammals. This 16-year-old killer whale is getting a little help with his brushing.

dirty mouth is a stinky one, plain and simple. Dental floss, that stringy stuff that gets out the food and plaque trapped in between your teeth, will finish up the job. With these two marvelous tools at your disposal, you can keep your breath fresh and clean—and maybe spend the money you'll save at the dentist's for something a lot more fun. An electric guitar or fillings? What's it going to be?

TESTING 1, 2, 3

You can sniff your trash can but you can't put your nose in your mouth. So how can you tell if your breath stinks? Try the floss test! Slide a piece of dental floss between a couple of teeth, then quickly hold it up to your nose. If you're still standing, your breath has passed the test. If you fail the test, floss some more. (Remember to brush your teeth again after flossing to make sure the gross pieces of food you cleared out don't stay in your mouth.)

More Mouth Magic

Besides frequent brushing and flossing, try these tricks to sweeten your breath before you sneak a kiss in the corner with that cute kid from homeroom.

❋ **Brush your tongue.** Hello! The bacteria in your mouth don't just hang out on your teeth. There's other furniture in that room! So make sure it's all clean.

❋ **Take a swig of water after you eat.** Water washes the bacteria down into your stomach where the acid pulverizes them! Get in the habit of cruising by the water fountain whenever you can.

❋ **Eat foods that rabbits love.** Celery, carrots, and other healthy snacks actually help fight plaque.

❋ **Peck at parsley.** When you go out to eat in a restaurant and see that sprig of green stuff on your plate, don't think of it as just decorative. The scent of this herb will help hide the scent of the onion rings you just downed, but you have to chew on it, of course. Breath mints are okay, with one important warning. Some have sorbitol—the stuff that makes you fart!

Would your school dress code allow you to wear a belt made of living desert locusts?

ICKY INSECTS

Some insects are so totally nasty that they deserve their own entries in this encyclopedia. But others—buzzing, biting, and just plain bad—deserve honorable mention. So here are some foul flying, crawling, or burrowing critters. You can spray them, step on them, swat them, and squish them, but they just won't go away!

80 MILLION LOCUSTS CAN'T BE WRONG

LOCUSTS are one of the few bugs to be mentioned by name in the Bible. And they are definitely bad news. Whenever you see the word "locust," you *know* something big is about to happen. A swarm of them was one of the 10 plagues used to convince the Egyptians to let Moses and his people go.

Locusts are a type of grasshopper—a very hungry type. They have to eat their own weight in food every day. Think of it. If you weighed 80 pounds, you would need to eat 80 pounds of food a day! This makes them a real menace. They travel great distances in huge swarms—40 to 80 million of them at a time. And there's nothing scarier than watching 80 million bugs headed right at you, especially if you're a farmer whose crops they're after!

People have tried to control locusts with huge nets, flamethrowers, and even lasers. Nothing has worked. And wherever they go, they leave almost no crops behind.

PRAY THEY GO AWAY

The PRAYING MANTIS is a big bug . . . so big that they call them mule killers in the South. That might be stretching the truth a bit (they're really only 3 to 5 inches long), but they can devour small lizards and birds. Praying? Sounds more like preying to me! Actually, they got their name because they hold their forelegs up in front of their heads as if in prayer.

Talk about dinner dates . . . After mating, this mantis female turned around and bit her date's head off. Maybe she wanted him off her back!

Mantis legs may look like green toothpicks, but they are made for more than just walking. They have sharp spines that grip a victim so it can't escape. Mantises make bug-kebobs by stabbing their food with a spike that they keep hidden when they're not attacking a victim. It works kind of like a switchblade, snapping out when there's something around that's good to eat. Food on a skewer! Yum!!

If a mantis can't find enough to eat, it becomes a cannibal! Babies eat other babies. Moms eat their own children. And the ladies always love to devour their husbands, usually after mating!

TERMITES

"Pssst . . . rotting wood over at 235 Elm Street. Pass it on." TERMITES love to eat wood, and if it's decaying it's even better! They have special microoganisms in their intestines that let them digest the toughest two-by-four. In Africa, the termites build high-rise condominiums. Their termite hills are

In Australia's Northern Territory kids don't play King of the Mountain, they play King of the Mound—the termite mound, that is!

as high as 30 feet (that's a three-story building, swarming with bugs).

But here's an even more alarming bit of news. Scientists at London's Natural History Museum in England have estimated that termites fart out between 20 and 80 million *tons* of methane every year! Think about it. All they eat is roughage! (Read FARTS on page 54 to find out more about gassy emissions.) And while they are fouling up the air, they are doing over a billion dollars' worth of damage a year to homes around the world!

WASP SPIT

Apart from that nasty sting of theirs—and we are talking very major boo-boo—here's a little wasp gross-osity. WASPS build their nests by first chewing pieces of wood into tiny bits, then spitting them out and mushing the material into walls for dozens of tiny little rooms. One egg is then laid in each tiny room. A wasp's baby food? Forget baby formula. They eat chewed-up, spit-out caterpillar. Thanks, Mom! And in case you were wondering. . .

The ICHNEUMON (*ick-new-mun*) FLY is really a wasp. This wasp is a parasite, which means it lives off of another creature at the other creature's expense. The ichneumon flies lay their eggs on other insects. When one of

This Malaysian beekeeper wears a "beard" and "shirt" made entirely of live bees.

those eggs hatches, the larva literally sucks the life out of its poor host! (To learn about some of the charming PARASITES that live off humans, turn to page 115.)

J

thing super-squishy and slimy—something that can leave you screaming in pain and swimming faster than an Olympic gold medalist!

Read on to discover how a couple of pairs of pantyhose can save your life if you meet up with one of these gross globs.

THE "NO-JELLY, NO-FISH" FISH

As usual, we have it all wrong. Those clear clumps floating in the sea are really not fish at all. They belong to a family called COELENTERATES (*si-lent-ah-rates*), which means "hollow gut." And they're not made of jelly either (so don't spread one on bread with your peanut butter). That blubbery mess of gelatin-like material is actually something called MESOGLEA (*mez-ah-gleeah*),

JELLYFISH

What can you expect from a creature who eats and poops from the same hole? Not much, you say? Well, think again. Jellyfish, formless blobs with no brain, no heart, and no lungs, can suck the life right out of you if you're not careful! For 650 million years they have been bobbing along just looking for a bite to eat. And sometimes they bump into things other than plankton (microscopic sea creatures that are the jellyfish's most-loved food).

Has this ever happened to you? You go out for a dip in the ocean on a hot summer day, just minding your own business, when all of a sudden you touch something truly yucky. Some-

A Nasty Note

No-brainers cannot recognize their enemies. They bump right into them. Loggerheads, leatherbacks, and other sea turtles love having jellyfish for dinner. Completely immune to the jelly's sting, they happily gobble up great globs of the stuff, tentacles, venom, and all.

One weird observation has been made, though. When sea turtles stuff themselves with Portuguese men-of-war, they give off a smell that attracts sharks. The sharks then rip the turtles limb from limb in a feeding frenzy. Kind of a nasty footnote on nature's feeding chain, don't you think!

a combination of minerals and simple cells floating in water, all held between two fragile layers of a kind of skin.

Jellyfish are 95 percent water. Basically a bundle of nerve cells that look for food and react to danger, they can be as tiny as a pencil point or as big as a pro-football player, with an 8-foot body trailing 100-foot-long tentacles. They come in a lovely range of colors from pastel pink or blue to bright orange-red or screaming yellow. Some even glow in the dark. And though some of them can be deadly, not all jellyfish sting, and most are actually very fragile creatures.

Make a fist with your hand. Now extend all your fingers. Now, make a fist again. And extend your fingers again. Keep doing this until you have propelled yourself across the Atlantic Ocean! Just kidding, but that's kind of how jellyfish move from here to there, by contracting and opening their bell-shaped bodies. (Hey. Did I say you could stop?) Using this jet-propulsion method, some jellies can swim the equivalent of a 33-mile swim by a human in one day.

BEWARE THE STING!

Jellyfish tentacles are the part you want to stay away from. One long tentacle can hide millions of stingers. Many jellies are armed with micro-

Swimming into a slew of sea nettles feels like swimming into a sea of razor blades.

Sting Fever

Ouch! Ouchouchouch! OUCH! You've just tangled with a mess of tentacles. Now what?

✳ First off, get out of the water immediately, before the sting interferes with your ability to swim. On the beach yet? Good! Next, do not wash the sting with water. Tiny bits of the tentacle with still-unreleased nematocysts will probably still be clinging to the area where you were stung. Pouring water on it will rupture the delicate membranes, causing them to swell, burst, and release even more poison.

✳ Instead, trickle some white vinegar on the wound. It will zap the protein-based toxins. Meat tenderizer (the kind you use on steak) mixed with that vinegar will take the pain away.

✳ For those of you who do not wish to carry an entire grocery store in your beach bag, some people swear that fresh pee will do the trick in a pinch! Is that gross enough for you?

scopic stinging cells called NEMATOCYSTS (*ne-mat-ah-sists*). When they touch anything, tiny triggers discharge hollow harpoons that inject venom into the unlucky victim. Amazingly, they never sting other jellyfish, which is incredible considering they have no brains to think with or eyes to see with!

Most jellyfish have stingers that are too small to penetrate human skin. But then there are the big guys, like the BOX JELLY, which is also called the SEA WASP. Australians try to avoid these critters. (They live in the waters surrounding Australia.) Swim into one, and your family might have to set off in search of a nice coffin for you! A sting can kill a person in about five minutes. A full-grown box jelly is the size of a basketball and can trail up to 60 tentacles, each 15 feet long. (That's the length of a

This Portuguese man-of-war's gas-filled float keeps it from sinking. The stinging tentacles below the surface of the water have paralyzed an unsuspecting fish that was probably looking for a hiding spot in what it thought was a floating clump of seaweed.

Another glob to avoid is the POR-TUGUESE MAN-OF-WAR, world famous for its enormously painful sting. For science-purists, it's not actually a true jellyfish, but rather a colony of hundreds of separate organisms, each with a special job to do, all working as a unit. Beneath its gas-filled float of bloat are long tentacles (up to 165 feet!) that paralyze whatever sea creature happens to get in the way. Then, wrapped up by a separate set of tentacles, the too-stunned-to-swim meal is digested.

Men-of-war occasionally bump into humans with painful, sometimes even deadly, consequences. Wracked with pain, and unable to swim, victims often drown!

SLIMY SIBLINGS

Here's the scoop on some other jelly bellies. LION'S MANE JELLYFISH are king-sized jellies! At 8 feet in diameter, their tentacles are longer than the length of a whale—up to 200 feet! They're killers, too. In fact, the murderer in one Sherlock Holmes mystery turned out to be a lion's mane.

MOON JELLIES are the ones we are most likely to see. They bob along all of America's coastline from north to south, east to west. They cause a painful, but harmless, sting and they can still zing you even after they're dead. So don't touch them, even if they are lying on the sand motionless.

SEA NETTLES can make you scream, too. A brush against their stinging tentacles will feel like you have just swum into a beehive!

Was that an oil slick? No, it's just the SEA THIMBLE JELLYFISH swimming in the calm Caribbean waters. They prefer to travel in large groups and so they bob along in mile-long packs, swishing darkly along the way.

So take care the next time you take a dip in the ocean. That innocent plastic bag floating around might not be garbage!

big old Cadillac for those of you who are measuring-impaired.)

Australian surfer-dudes have come up with the perfect protection against box jellies. If they are not wearing a wet suit, they pull on two pairs of pantyhose. One pair covers their legs. The other goes over their arms and shoulders, with the head sticking through a hole poked in the crotch. The jellyfish stinger's tiny nematocysts are not quite long enough to penetrate the pantyhose fibers.

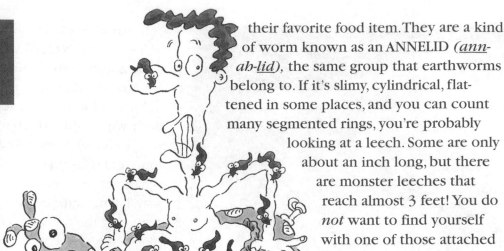

their favorite food item. They are a kind of worm known as an ANNELID (*ann-ah-lid*), the same group that earthworms belong to. If it's slimy, cylindrical, flattened in some places, and you can count many segmented rings, you're probably looking at a leech. Some are only about an inch long, but there are monster leeches that reach almost 3 feet! You do *not* want to find yourself with one of those attached to you!

The end of a leech comes to a point and is equipped with a special sucking disc which surrounds the leech's mouth. Depending on the type of leech we're talking about, it may hitch a ride on just about anything, from a lobster to a frog to a turtle to a juicy young kid. Then it draws the blood from its hapless host. Of course, not all leeches are vampires. Some like to suck on garbage or the flesh of dead animals, which is almost as disgusting.

Most leeches prefer waterfront property but LAND LEECHES are the ones you really want to avoid. They live in Asia and the islands of the Pacific and Indian Oceans, and they can be quite deadly. These leeches can literally suck the life out of you by draining a large volume of your blood. If you happen to find yourself hanging out in the rain forests of India or Ceylon and you see one, you might want to *get out fast!*

Gross as it is, a leech bite is almost painless. That's because the leech's slimy saliva has a natural painkiller in it. However, painless does not mean harmless. By the time you realize leeches are using your legs for a banquet, you might be too weak to walk. When leeches chow down, they secrete a substance called

LEECHES

If you should happen to find yourself in North Africa or parts of Asia, *do not* go skinny-dipping! In that part of the world there are super-gross LEECHES—wormy little creatures that lurk in the waters. They will swim up your butt or slither into the places you pee from, and start sucking your blood. They can even drop into your drinking water and attach themselves to the insides of your mouth or throat. And once they've settled in for a suck, they're mighty tough to get rid of! You will have become a leech-feast.

LEECHES REALLY SUCK!

Leeches are commonly called bloodsuckers, and with good reason. Blood is pretty much

HIRUDIN (*he-rude-in*) which is a powerful ANTI-COAGULANT (*an-tee-co-ag-u-lent*). This keeps the blood from clotting, so that it flows like a swift, red river. If several leeches attach themselves to you all at once, they can suck out so much blood that your body can no longer function.

KILLERS OR CURERS?

Here's the interesting paradox. Certain kinds of leeches can kill a person. But others can help cure diseases and speed healing of wounds. It can really pay to know your leeches!

In the olden days, leeches were used to treat just about every illness. Doctors believed that too much blood was what made a person sick. So they attached leeches to go after the "bad blood" and leave the good stuff behind. A special type of leech was bred to do that job.

They called that leech HIRUDO MEDICINALIS (*he-rude-oh me-dis-sin-al-is*). Let's call him Harry for short. Although Harry and his leechy friends can be found all over Europe, they were first bred in England (so let's call him *Sir* Harry). Sir Harry has some very special tricks up his suckers. For instance, his mouth contains substances that can ease pain and fight bacteria. And guess what—he's still used by doctors today.

THE PUTRID PAST

Native Americans knew about the healing powers of leeches. But here's an interesting note. How did the brave medicine men obtain the slithery suckers they needed? They would hire women to stand in water infested with them and wait for some hungry little suckers to come around and attach themselves to their legs. And in Europe being a leech catcher was an actual job title!

Hirudin is one of the leeches' prized possessions, and it's quite powerful. Doctors have figured out how to extract this incredible substance from the leeches and use it to keep blood from clotting during surgery. It's especially useful in eye surgery and in the treatment of strokes caused by blood clots. (A clot is when a bunch of blood cells stick together and get too fat to pass through the veins and arteries, kind of like a big truck stuck in a tunnel. Hirudin comes along and blasts that clot apart!)

One of the most important ways leeches are used is in recovery from high-tech microsurgery, such as reattaching fingers that have been severed in an accident. After this type of surgery, too much blood sometimes accumulates at the site of the injury. So doctors bring in Sir Harry and friends because they know they'll suck up that extra blood in a snap!

Here's how it works. The leeches are placed on the wound and covered with a light gauze wrapping until they get cozy and comfortable. (The gauze keeps them attached to the right spot.) After a while, the gauze is removed and the leeches settle in and suck away. They will drink until they are so engorged that they simply can't manage another drop. Swollen with blood—and now almost 10 times bigger than when they began—they fall off.

Then, someone has to pick

Every seen a leech farmer? Meet Dr. Roy Sawyer, shown here holding a handful of his favorite critters.

89

Nifty Bits of Leechology

❋ In a single meal, some hearty little leeches can eat enough to last them nine months.

❋ A typical leech can consume 10 times his weight at mealtime. Let's say you weigh 95 pounds—that would be like you sitting down and eating 950 pounds of food for dinner.

❋ There are more than 300 different kinds of leeches. Some suck on garbage, some on fish, some prefer animals.

❋ Leeches are neither male nor female, but a kind of boy-girl combo. Any two leeches that spend a romantic evening together can end up with bunches of babies.

❋ Some leeches have mouths with three jaws and between 60 and 100 teeth. (Good thing they don't have to brush 'em at night.) And to go with their multiple jaws, they have between 4 and 10 pairs of eyes.

❋ Attention all snowboarders! There are leeches even in the Arctic and Antarctica.

❋ When a leech is eating, it can't feel anything. You can actually cut off its other end and it will continue to suck away!

❋ Leeches are available in three designer colors— black, brown, or slime-green.

❋ Freshwater leeches find humans quite tasty. Saltwater leeches prefer seafood.

❋ Applying lime, salt, or ice cubes is a good way to get those nasty leeches to go eat somewhere else!

If you can get them to lie still long enough, you can extract a drug called orgelase from these medicinal leeches.

them up off the floor, a job only slightly less gross than emptying bedpans! (Believe me, a worm full of blood is a pretty yucky thing to touch!) Fortunately, by now they've drunk themselves into a deep sleep and can't wriggle away.

Scientists and bioengineers are busy trying to duplicate all these slimy leech substances in the lab. The natural painkillers will be useful for treating arthritis (which makes your bones and joints stiff and painful), and the blood-thinners can help prevent heart attacks and glaucoma (a disease that causes blindness).

LICE

Lice love scalps. Rich scalps, poor scalps, young scalps, old scalps, clean, dirty . . . any scalp will do! Every year, 10 to 12 million unlucky people will be blessed with a visit from lice. In fact, creepy-crawly scalps are one of the most common kids' ailments around! But lice aren't just a "hair" thing. They can burrow into some pretty private places and leave you scratching yourself silly.

What exactly are lice? Well, for starters, they are PARASITES (*par-ah-sites*), critters that live off other creatures' bodies. (See PARASITES, page 115, for more on some of their charming fellow freeloaders.) In the case of a louse (think "mouse/mice" and "louse/lice"), *you* are that creature! Your blood and tissue are louse food, your body is a louse house! And if you get lice, you *will* feel lousy!

FEELING LOUSY?

Could be because you are. "Lousy" originally meant louse-filled! Three kinds of lice call humans "home." There are head lice, body lice, and "underpants lice," also called crabs.

Six legs. No wings. About the size of a sesame seed. Lice aren't much to look at, but they sure are something to scratch at.

Lice generally fall into two different categories—biters and suckers. Biters chew through the skin, then chow down on blood. They also eat dead skin. Biting lice's favorite hotels are birds. In fact, almost all birds have lice! Sucking lice prefer to stay at an animal or people hotel. Only five types of mammals don't get lice—anteaters, armadillos, bats, duck-billed platypus, and cetaceans (*si-tay-shuns*), better known as whales, dolphins, and porpoises.

Head lice are the real bummers for kids, so let's go straight to the top and see if we can begin to scratch the surface. They may be tiny, but boy, can they have you headed for trouble!

ITCHY! ITCHY! ITCHY!

Each one of a head louse's six legs is equipped with a strong claw—perfect for grabbing onto a hair strand for dear life. And like chameleons, lice can change their body color to match any hair color, which makes them almost impossible to find. Shine a bright light on them and they'll dive even deeper between the strands of hair.

These body lice are going for a hike through a forest of human hair.

The Only Good Lice Are Dead Lice

Head lice are really hard to get rid of. But they've got to go! What's the best way to make them history?

❋ **HIGH HEAT** (temperatures above 150°F for at least 10 minutes) is the best solution. But since you can't toss your head into a pot of boiling water, read on for the only surefire way to de-louse.

❋ **FORGET ORDINARY SHAMPOO.** Go for a shampoo with an ingredient called Permethrin. It's nontoxic to humans, and pretty effective in killing lice. Since the old-fashioned alternative is pouring kerosene over your scalp and wrapping it in a towel, or shaving all your hair off, it seems worth a try!

❋ **CALL OUT THE LICE PATROL.** After that Permethrin shampoo, you'll need a pair of tweezers, one very patient grown-up, a magnifying glass, a nit comb (which has very close-together, pointy teeth), and a very long movie to watch on TV. It can take hours to get all the nits out. When you're done, both you and the grown-up will have a new appreciation for the term "nit-picking."

❋ **WASH AROUND THE CLOCK!** Head lice can live for two days without a meal. So wash anything that might have come into contact with your head— sheets, towels, pillows, blankets, shirts, hats, *any-thing*—with soap and really hot water. Then toss them in the dryer and set it on high for a double-whammy of heat.

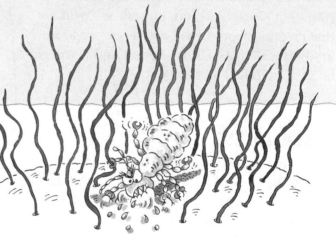

One rumor has it that dirty hair attracts lice. Wrong! Head lice are dainty critters who actually dislike dirt. Remember how your mom was always insisting you learn to share? Well, here's one instance in which sharing is a very bad idea. Sharing hats, combs, and brushes is what helps the lice hop from head to head. Here's how they do their damage.

Lice come equipped with two built-in "straws." When they find a spot of scalp they like, they grab onto the skin with their teeth, then thrust their sharp little mouthparts, those "straws," into the scalp. One straw injects saliva full of a chemical that keeps your blood from clotting. The other taps into the blood vessels, which it slices open and sucks from. Yuck!

Chow time for lice comes about every three to six hours, one hearty 45-second-long suck at a time. And when lady lice are not eating, they're busy laying eggs! A mommy louse is good for 200 to 300 eggs in her 30-day life span. But lice don't lay their eggs in nests, like birds. They prefer hair. Which brings us to. . . .

Lice eggs are known as NITS, but don't worry, you won't find these eggs scrambled up for breakfast. Nits are very small and shaped like tears, which is exactly what your mom's eyes will be shedding if you happen to get them! The nits are attached to your hair with a glue-like substance that is stronger than Super-

LIZARDS

Imagine leaving your butt behind when you get stressed out. If you were a **LIZARD** you might! Many lizards, when handled roughly, throw off their tails to distract their enemies. The broken portion of the tail keeps the attacker busy by wriggling around for a couple of minutes while the lizard slinks away. But in case you're feeling sorry for the poor little things, don't. In a few weeks, a new tail will grow from the stump.

Like their relatives the crocodilians, lizards look a lot like small dinosaurs. Some are actually very cute. But naturally, we're going to focus on the creepy, ugly ones. There are over 3,000 different species of lizards—from tiny (under an inch) to almost 12 feet long! There are iguanas and geckos, fat-bodied agamids and skinny skinks (these look like mutant snakes with legs). Some have sturdy limbs with sharp claws, and others look exactly like snakes. In fact, lizards are very closely related to snakes. They both belong to the family called SQUAMATES (*skwa-mates*). And with that bit of dandy scientific information

man. No amount of brushing or regular shampooing will break their super bond.

In 10 days the eggs will hatch, and the babies (which are called nymphs and are about the size of the period at the end of this sentence) will dive down in search of what every baby louse is looking for. You guessed it—blood!

Unlike head lice, BODY LICE are dirt-lovers. They creep into the seams of filthy clothing, then feed on the skin. Butts and tummies are their favorite hangouts. But laundering those foul jeans and giving a swipe with a hot iron will kill those lice and save a lot of itching.

The underwear variety of lice are sometimes called CRABS. But do *not* confuse them with the seafood. These creepers love hanging out in the parts of your body that you may think of as off-limits. The itching they cause is totally intense. Happily, kids rarely get them.

Think there's no such thing as a dragon? This Komodo dragon begs to differ with you. (I wouldn't argue with him if I were you!)

out of the way, let's get down to the disgusting details.

For starters, some lizards, geckos, for example, have no eyelids. When dirt and dust get in their eyes, they lick their eyeballs. Let's see you try and do that! And while most lizards are completely harmless to humans, for sheer scariness, a couple definitely stand out from the pack.

DANGER! MONSTERS AHEAD!

What can you expect from a creature whose name actually includes the word "monster" in it? A pretty ornery varmint! GILA *(bee-la)* MONSTERS are only about 2 feet long, but they can hurt you like the biggest *T. Rex*. These lizards pack a load of venom that can really make you sick. If you are in America's Southwest or in Mexico, be on the lookout for bead-

like skin and yellow or coral-colored markings. Look, but don't touch! Once a Gila monster sinks his teeth into you he will not let go. You will have to drown the critter to get it to open its mouth.

A Gila cousin, the MEXICAN BEADED LIZARD is just as persnickety and venomous. So be aware . . . and beware!

Who says there's no such thing as a dragon? Tell that to the folks of Indonesia (in Southeast Asia), home of the KOMODO DRAGON. Tipping the scales at 300 pounds, this 10-foot-long monster is the biggest in the lizard family. Give him a nice hunk of meat, like a small deer or a bush pig, and watch his beady eyes light up! They've been known to devour a human on occasion, too! A Komodo dragon's mouth harbors four rare and deadly bacteria. If the shock of being bitten by one doesn't kill you, the infection that will develop at the bite site surely will!

These lizards have claws like razor blades

These happy Komodo dragons are enjoying a feast of one of their favorite foods–fresh goat (very fresh, if you know what I mean).

This gaudy Gila monster is sucking on a mouse.

are the closest living relative to those dinos of the past, and they were able to survive extinction because of their small size—only about 2 feet long and weighing about 2 pounds—and their remote island location.

Tuataras have a third eye covered by a scaly flap on the top of their heads! They don't actually see with it but use it as a light sensor. These creatures are s-l-o-w! Female tuataras produce eggs only once every four years, and the eggs themselves take over a year to hatch. But on the flip side, tuataras can live for up to 100 years, so I guess there's really no need to rush.

and can rip the bowels from an animal in seconds—their jagged teeth are little "Jack-the-Rippers." And if a Komodo mom forgets to go to the grocery store, a younger brother or sister always makes an acceptable snack. In fact, just about any member of the dragon family makes a good meal.

Are there any real dinosaurs still walking the earth? Think not? Come to New Zealand and you'll see a creature called a TUATARA *(too-ah-tar-ah)*. These odd creatures

M

MAGGOTS

Take one dead, decaying rodent, stick it in a pool of polluted water, and sprinkle it with a pinch of raw sewage. Sound appetizing? Well, if you were a MAGGOT you'd be drooling by now! When it comes to eating the most disgusting things on earth, nothing comes even close to these slithery, slimy, scuzzy little creatures. But underneath that revolting pile of squirming worminess lies a truly amazing critter!

A delightfully disgusting sight—blowfly larvae eating some awfully gross meat.

Maggots are one of nature's garbage disposals. They break down the earth's leftovers into ever smaller parts until they can be reabsorbed into the soil. And as unsavory as some of their food choices may be, maggots are essential to our world because they help to redistribute vital elements.

OH BABY!

Everyone loves fuzzy little caterpillars, waddling along on their fat little feet. They build sweet little cocoons and when they grow up they become colorful butterflies. Now, a maggot is to a fly what a cute little caterpillar is to a butterfly—just a sweet, innocent, little baby. Only difference is, these sweet little infants eat animal poop, rotting flesh, garbage, and sewage, and have a face that only a mother could love!

Your typical maggot is an active little varmint, constantly wriggling around. A maggot is oval-shaped and is tapered to a point. That pointy part is the maggot's very small

Gross but Good

In the middle of disgusting, writhing piles of garbage and decaying flesh lies a medical miracle. Believe it or not, maggots make a great cure for infected wounds! During the 1500s, doctors noticed that injured soldiers whose wounds had gotten infested with maggots actually healed faster than those whose wounds had not. By the early part of this century, maggot therapy was common in many hospitals in America and Europe. But with the discovery of antibiotics, maggots lost their status as medical do-gooders.

Now all that is changing again. Dr. Ronald Sherman, a California doctor, has turned back to maggots to help him treat patients. Some bacterial infections are resistant to antibiotics, but not to maggots! One of Dr. Sherman's patients had terrible infected bedsores that would not heal, and the patient's body was literally beginning to rot. Dr. Sherman ordered 8,000 blowfly eggs and placed them on the infected tissue. The eggs hatched, the maggots ate, turned into flies, and flew away! Within four weeks, the man's wounds were healed.

Dr. Sherman now has a blowfly maggot farm. He collects the fly eggs and bathes them in a special solution that will produce maggots that are germ-free. When the eggs hatch, they are placed on the patient's wound, which is then sealed with a mixture of glue and gauze. A little window is left so that the maggots can breathe and can also be observed.

Maggots are now used in many major hospitals, and are especially good for treating bone infections. Bones don't have a strong blood supply, so antibiotics, which travel through the bloodstream, can't get to where they are needed. But maggots can, and do.

head. A maggot has no jaws or teeth so it can't chew its food. Instead, it secretes a kind of juice called FERMENT that dissolves solid food into a liquid that the maggot can then suck up. The other end of its body is broad and has two tiny black spots. You might think these are eyes, but maggots don't put their sunglasses there. That's how they breathe!

MAGGOT MILESTONES

If you were a fly, you'd know that the best place to lay eggs is on stinky stuff, such as garbage or rotting animal carcasses. That's where most newborn maggots are hatched. Since a mommy fly can easily lay 100 eggs at a time, you never get a single maggot, or even just twins. You get a horde—whole mounds of slithering maggots making the thing they are eating seem like it's alive and moving!

When they are born, maggots are slender, white, and very tiny. In the first 24 hours they

Housefly maggots, freshly hatched and ready to squirm.

UH-OH! MAGGOTS IN MY MEAT LOAF!

Trust me. There is nothing more disgusting than stumbling across a maggot-infested mound. So how do you get rid of them, once you've got them? Here are some helpful hints.

1. Get smart. Maggots in your trash can? Wrap your garbage, first in a plastic bag, then in yesterday's newspaper. And, no, it's not so the maggots can read the sports page. The printing ink is a turnoff.

2. Get floral. Some folks swear that geraniums will repel them. These pretty flowers smell like a skunk to a baby fly.

3. Get spicy. Maggots don't care for cloves, bay leaves, or citrus peels. If you find a heap of maggots, sprinkle cloves over them!

4. Get salty. Drown 'em in saltwater or just pour plain old salt all over them.

AND ONE LAST MAGGOT NOTE

As animals graze in pastures littered with cow or sheep poop, home to whole bunches of maggots, they will snort up a few of those little fellows. Before you can say "Tissue anyone?" the maggots have moved into the sheep's warm and cozy nose and made themselves right at home. Vets call them NOSE BOTS. I'd call them a pain in the schnozz.

And sheep aren't the only lucky bot-ees. Horses get them, too, but they get theirs on their legs. Flies lay their eggs right on those shapely thighs. The horses get itchy and start to scratch, but since they don't have hands they use their teeth. Next thing you know, the fly eggs are in their mouths, down the hatch and into their stomachs. The eggs will grow in the horses' tummies until they hatch and produce a bellyful of maggots! Vets try to keep this from happening by giving horses medicine that will kill the little bugs before they can do any harm.

will MOLT, or shed their skin. Over the next four or five days they will grow to be about half an inch long, and their color will change to dirty white. (You know how kids hate to wash their hands and faces!)

After eight or nine days, maggots turn dark brown and become PUPAE *(pew-pee)*. Their brown covering is kind of like a little tent inside of which they hang out and go through a transformation. When they get too big for the tent, it's time to spread those new, crumpled wings and take off for the nearest cow pasture! They are now grown-up flies! (To read about the adults' dirty habits, turn to FLIES on page 60.)

OH GOODY!
COW PATTIES FOR DINNER!

There are over 90,000 different types of maggot, and each is unique. Some are vegetarians and eat only plants and fruits. Some spread pollen the way bees do. Some maggots are too lazy to eat flesh, so they live in polluted ponds and have actually developed built-in snorkels so they can breathe underwater.

The very things that we find most revolting are the ones maggots love the best. The stinkier the swamp, the more oozing the open sore, the more reeking the garbage dump, the smellier the latrine, the finer the dining is to a maggot. To which I can only say, *"Bon appétit!"* (That's French for "enjoy your meal.")

MISERABLE MEATS

"Brains and intestines for dinner again? Aw, shucks! And I was looking forward to stuffed eyeballs." Think I'm joking? Think again. All around the world people chow down on some pretty strange cuts of meat. Got to get that protein in your diet somehow. (So what if it comes from pig's feet or deer knees?) Taste in food all depends on what you're raised eating. Let's sharpen up our carving knives and talk about the different parts!

You've heard of sirloins, ribs, and chops, but that's only a small part of the animal-eats. Just about every limb and organ of most every animal appeals to someone somewhere in the world. Let's start nibbling at the top of the animal and work our way down—a dining experience that just might make you lose your lunch!

HEY! MEAT-HEAD!

First of all, watch out for sneaky food names! There is no cheese in HEADCHEESE, but there is plenty of head. The meat from an animal head (usually a cow's or a pig's)—the cheeks, forehead, and nose, minus the brain—is removed and wrapped tightly in cloth, then set in boiling water to simmer for hours. Head meat has a lot of muscle, cartilage, and ligament, and when it is boiled it turns into a kind of clear, gelatinous substance with hunks of meat floating in it. The finished product is chilled until it hardens, sliced, then stuffed between a couple of slices of bread and gobbled up. Quite popular in merry old England!

Of course, if you don't want to go to all that bother, you can always just grab a pig

and slice its cheeks off, then boil them, as they sometimes do in Ireland.

TONGUE is a favorite in Poland, Italy, China, and France. (Lots of people in the United States like it, too.) It's lean, boneless, and has more protein than steak, with half the fat. And a cow's tongue is a big sucker—it can weigh up to five pounds! Butchers sell the stick-out-your-tongue part along with a big hunk of salivary gland and taste buds attached at the back. Best way to cook it? Boil it!

How about a taste of the French delicacy *"Yeux de Veau Farcis"* (you won't need to pronounce this one!). In English that means "stuffed eye of calf." Sounds great, huh? Here's the recipe. Soak some calves' eyes in cold water for a couple of hours, then boil them for 60 seconds. Remove the corneas, lenses, and irises with a small knife. Fill with chopped mushrooms. Dip in beaten egg and bread crumbs and deep-fry in oil. Talk about see-food!

BRAINS are considered a great treat in many countries. Avoid *"Ris de Veau"* (<u>ree</u>-de-<u>voe</u>)—calves' brains—if you think you are already smart enough and don't need any extra help in the brain department! And beware of monkey-brain dinners in the Philippines. The main course comes to the table *live,* then has the top of its poor head sliced off. Spoons are

A Manly Meal

In a great many countries, calf, sheep, and boar TESTICLES are a real delicacy. Chefs call them mountain oysters, which just goes to show you that food inventors are a truly sneaky bunch! South American gauchos, who are like our cowboys, have a whole food festival built around testicles as the main dish. Order plane tickets to Argentina if you want to be a part of the festivities. Then decide if you want them deep-fried, sautéed, or poached.

Cervelle d'agneu sounds good, but beware. It's really lamb's brains.

provided for all the dinner guests. (How about a barf bag?)

Dipping down below the shoulders, you can dine on the parts of the animal which food-people call OFFAL (and some of it really does taste just *awful*). Those parts are the hearts, lungs, livers, glands, and kidneys of our barnyard buddies. Liver is popular here in the United States. It's rich in iron, protein, and vitamin A, which is why your mom may have tried to serve it to you. Gross as it may sound, it's not bad, especially when it's smothered in onions and crumbled bacon.

SWEETBREADS— NOT SWEET, NOT BREAD

If you saw SWEETBREADS on a menu you might think that this dish sounded quite tasty. Well, don't be fooled! Not only is it not bread, it's not even remotely sweet. It's really the thymus gland of a young cow—the gland that makes lymph tissue, which is a part of the immune system. (By now, you're probably thinking "bleecch!") In France it's considered a real treat, even by picky kids.

You might also want to try TRIPE, otherwise known as—yup, you guessed it—cow stomach. There are four different cuts of stomach, from the paunch to the honeycomb, and all true tripe-lovers have a favorite part.

Animal FEET are another treat enjoyed in many parts of the world, including this one. Cow-feet-meat dishes are called "brawn," probably because you need to have a strong stomach to eat them. Don't like the idea of cow feet? You can nibble on pig feet or sheep feet, instead.

What about all the leftover BLOOD when an animal is butchered? Well, in Europe it gets cooked up into something called blood pudding. Here's how to whip it up. Take a cup of milk, a bit of sugar, some rice, barley, and ginger. Whisk in two pints of blood (pig or cow blood will do quite nicely) and some bread crumbs. Bake for two hours, then drizzle some melted butter on top, sprinkle with powdered sugar, and enjoy!

In Africa, the Masai Mara make blood shakes instead of milk shakes. They drain the blood from the neck of a live animal with a big straw, then mix the fresh blood with milk, swish it around in a gourd, then chug-a-lug to their heart's content.

MAY WE SPEAK FRANKLY?

Just in case you're feeling nice and comfortable, thinking miserable meats are only found in faraway places, think again. If you've ever had a bit of breakfast sausage with your pancakes, you've had a taste of intestines, because the casing that holds all the other ground-up goodies in a neat little tube is made from them.

Speaking of intestine casings, there's nothing like a nice, warm HOT DOG at a ball game—until you discover what's tucked inside! Many hot dog makers fill those puppies with meat by-products—which is just a nice way of saying ground-up organ meat. After a butcher cuts every piece of meat from a carcass, the leftover hunks of bone, cartilage, and muscle are fed into machines that scrape off whatever tiny bits of flesh are still clinging to the carcass. Unfortunately, those scrapings also include a dusting of powdered bone. Fat

When in Scotland . . .

Maybe it's the gloom and the rain. Maybe it's all those men walking around in kilts with nothing underneath, all drafty and cold. But for some reason, the Scots have one particular dish that they love and seem to find comforting. It's called HAGGIS, and it is a must-have at any proper Scottish celebration.

For starters, you'll need a sheep's stomach. Stuff the stomach with a mixture of chopped-up sheep heart, liver, lungs, and kidneys. A little minced onion is always a nice touch. Add suet (_sue-it_)—the solid white fat found around the kidneys and loins of cows and sheep—and oatmeal, to make it extra thick and gloppy. Simmer the stuffed stomach for four hours, then bring out the bagpipes. And if you get gas? Do a "Highland fling"!

and water (up to 40 percent) is added to this lovely concoction. The whole mess is then smoked and loaded with nitrites, which can cause cancer. Now, did you want mustard on your hot dog, or are you having second thoughts about the whole thing?

The longest sausage in the world takes shape, measuring over half a mile long. How would you like that with your hotcakes?

MITES

Whoever heard of Mighty Mite? Nobody. But just because these creatures don't have a cartoon series about them doesn't mean they're not everywhere (including perhaps on _you_ right now) or that certain species can't do damage.

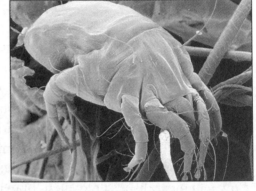

Dust dwellers uncovered— a dust mite as seen through a powerful electron microscope.

Mites are members of the ARACHNID family, and a kissing cousin of the tick. (See SCORPIONS, page 136, SPIDERS, page 163 and TICKS, page 173, for more on the mite's disgusting relatives.) They are also parasites. (See PARASITES, page 115, to read about other human-eaters.) And they are tiny—really tiny. The biggest mite in town is a mere quarter of an inch, and most can't be seen with the naked eye. In fact, many of us have mites (*Demodex folliculorum* for you Latin fans) inhabiting the hair follicles in our eyelids, eyebrows, ears, and noses. They cause no trouble, but magnified a few hundred times, they look pretty prehistoric.

MIGHTY MITES

DUST MITES are totally disgusting. They live on the flakes of your dead skin—those thousands of cells that fall off *you* and settle on your pillow, your sheets, your rugs—everywhere there's a speck of dust! Your bedroom is probably crawling with more dust mites than you would believe possible! And not only are their dining habits disgusting, the tiny particles of poop they leave behind cause major problems for people with allergies and asthma.

Then there are MANGE MITES. They say it's a dog-eat-dog world. But in this case it's a mite-eat-dog planet. These mites look like microscopic grains of rice, but they can mow a path through dog fur better than a ride-on mower in a grassy field. Before you know it, your poor pup is covered with hairless, scaly patches of raw, red skin.

One species of mite (the *ACARPIS WOODI* for you Latin fans) has wiped out entire honeybee colonies, with disastrous effect. No bees, no honey. No honey? Hungry bears. Hungry bears? Trouble in suburban trash cans. And so on and so forth.

Napoleon the Itchy

You've probably seen that famous painting of the short little French emperor with his hand tucked inside his coat. Ever wondered why the hidden hand? Rumor has it that his skin was crawling with SCABIES mites. Scabies burrow under human skin—feeding, laying eggs, and using people as their bathrooms as they go along. If you discover short, wavy red tracks between your fingers, on your wrists, in your armpits, your butt, or in those very private parts, you may have scabies. Each track has a little blister at one end. That's where the female has laid her eggs. Scratching them will only pop them open and lead to more mites feasting on you. Too bad Napoleon didn't know that.

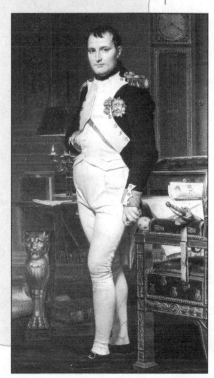

MOSQUITOES

Forget Freddy Krueger or those creepy fellows with the chainsaws. Want to come face-to-face with a real killer? In the past 200 million years, the mosquito has caused the deaths of more animals and people than any other single species or weapon, making it the most dangerous creature on earth!

It's a warm summer night. The mosquitoes have been driving you crazy. You have just smashed a pesky little buzzer that was sucking on your thigh. Now there is a revolting splotch of blood—your blood—where the bug used to be. This is completely disgusting! How can such a little critter drink so much blood? Here's the buzz on those skin-biting, itch-causing, disease-bringing varmints.

THE DEATH SQUAD

There are Hollywood movies about killer snakes, killer sharks, and killer spiders. Well, maybe they should make one about mosquitoes, because they are far more deadly.

Every year, a million people die because of mosquitoes, which belong to the same order as the fly—the Diptera. (Read FLIES on page 60 to learn more about the mosquito's nasty cousin.) Many more people get *really* sick.

In certain parts of the world, just one bite from one of these bloodsuckers can mean big trouble. Trouble such as the deadly diseaes malaria, encephalitis, yellow fever, or dengue fever (also known as breakbone fever—yikes!).

A Nasty Note!

Forget the bug sprays and the electronic bug zappers. Some people swear a necklace of stinky garlic is the best mosquito repellent. Maybe those Count Dracula movies were right! Garlic bread anyone?

KILLER LADIES

Mosquitoes are dainty-looking little creatures, no bigger than a quarter of an inch with a head no larger than the head of a pin. But they are also amazing, daredevil, fighter-bomber kinds of flyers. Some species of mosquitoes can dodge raindrops and arrive at their next meal totally dry. They can hover, loop-the-loop, and fly upside down, sideways, and backward. That makes them hard to swat.

If you smash a mosquito and it spurts blood, you've squooshed a female. They are the ones that feed on humans. Males drink only flower nectar and plant juice. (The ladies need blood to nourish their eggs, which can number between 100 and 500 at a time.) How does this killer lady choose her victims? Mosquitoes are supersensi-

tive to moisture, warmth, and the chemicals in your sweat. They choose the tastiest among us when it's chow time, which is why some people at a picnic get covered with bites, while others are left untouched.

One thing mosquitoes are drawn to is the carbon dioxide in your breath when you exhale. They also prefer moist skin to dry. And people with a lot of lactic acid in their bodies' chemistry will often be mosquito favorites.

By the way, if you think living where it is cold will keep you safe, think again. There are 3,400 different types of mosquitoes and they live everywhere, even close to the icy poles. In the Arctic tundra, when the spring snows melt, all the dormant mosquito eggs hatch at

the same time, emerging in swarms so dense they can block out the sun. They know they have only a short time to suck up all the available blood before it snows again. They are so vicious that the Eskimos that live there have to cover their faces with a thick layer of mud to survive the summer.

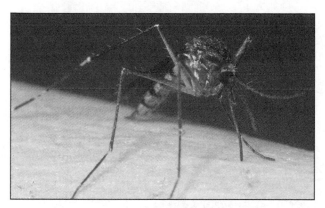

Mosquitoes have definite taste preferences. That's why you always get bitten and the rest of your family doesn't.

In the damp marshes of the rain forests, a single square foot of soil can house 10,000 mosquito eggs. The eggs have been known to hatch all at the same time. These baby mosquitoes hop onto the first available meal that happens by. And if there are enough of them they can suck that critter to death! When this happens, its called EXSANGUINATION *(ek-sang-wi-nay-shun)* and fortunately it happens only to small animals, not to humans!

TAKING A NOSEDIVE

A female mosquito dines by dive-bombing with her nose. (I'm sure you all know that annoying sound they make as they zero in for the kill.) Her nose has six sharp STYLETS

A she-mosquito needs to drink blood for its amino acids—the building blocks of protein. She needs lots of protein to make eggs. After a delicious dinner of your blood, she may lay hundreds of them!

(sti-letz), each as fine as a strand of your hair. Two are barbed—kind of like fishhooks—and are perfect for slicing into your skin. Two are like little saws—perfect for ripping and tearing. The fifth and largest stylet is a big "straw," which is lowered into the opening the mosquito has hacked into your skin. The sixth stylet injects saliva containing an anticoagulant that keeps your blood from clotting while Mrs. Mosquito has her "Bloody Mary" (or Larry). No clumpy blood for her!

Why does the bite itch? Because most of us are allergic to mosquito saliva. The reason everyone tells you not to scratch is that scratching just rubs the irritating saliva deeper into your skin. The big, red welt you see is your blood reacting to the presence of the mosquito spit.

A happy mosquito slurps up its human-blood meal.

When a mosquito bites a sick animal or person, she sucks up some of the disease with her bloody meal. She may then pass that disease on to the next person she bites. Mosquitoes can transmit a bunch of deadly fevers, especially malaria, which causes sky-high body temperatures and periods of intense sweating. (Malaria is actually a PARASITE. You can read about some others on page 115.) Almost 300 million people a year come down with it, many of them children. Pesticides to control the mosquito population only seem to work for a short while before the mosquitoes become resistant to them. Those hungry females just won't give up!

MUCKY MEDICINE

Feel like you're swallowing razor blades? Skin splotched with blotches the color of watermelon? Sounds like you need a doctor! Folks have been getting sick since . . . well . . . forever. Doctors have tried to make them better since forever, too. You may think it's disgusting when you have an earache and you have to swallow a couple of spoonfuls of that pink syrup that the pharmacist claims tastes like bubble gum. But boy, in the old days they had some pretty warped ideas of how to make people healthy. Read on. . . .

The ancient Peruvians were skilled brain surgeons, as this 1,000-year-old skull shows. (Well, actually, all it shows is that they could cut a nice round hole in a person's skull.) It must have been some headache to make the patient agree to this!

WHAT'S UP, DOC?

Ever wonder where the expression "I need this like I need a hole in the head" came from? Doctors have been sharpening their scalpels— well, actually, their sharp rocks—for ages. Even back in prehistoric times, almost 10,000 years ago, primitive surgeons were flashing their blades, anxious to perform an operation called TREPHINATION (*tre-fah-nay-shun*).

Let's say you had a really bad headache and made the mistake of telling a doctor. The good doctors figured that bad spirits were responsible for the problem. But how, oh how, could they get those evil critters out? Simple. Drill a hole in the person's head and see what happens. *Yikes!*

By 3000 B.C., this kind of brain surgery was pretty common. Sharpened rocks or shells were used to scrape a hole over the cranium. Then the doctor cut into the skull with flints or knives

106

and lifted out a small square of bone, which you got to turn into a necklace—*if* you survived the surgery!

MORE ANCIENT DOC-DOINGS

In southwest Asia, the great MESOPOTAMIAN (*mess-uh-puh-tay-mee-in*) civilization rose up in around 3500 B.C. One of the first civilizations to discover how to use metal, the Mesopotamians were also one of the first to develop a written language, and they left great stone tablets with all sorts of neat things written on them. One of these tablets, called the Code of Hammurabi, contained laws set down by a fellow named (surprise!) Hammurabi. A bunch of his laws had to do with doctors and medicine. In those days, if a surgeon performed an operation on a person and the patient died, the surgeon's fingers were cut off! Doctors probably weren't too eager to operate in those days!

In what is now India, ancient surgeons had an amazing array of surgical tools—20 different sharp instruments (saws, knives, needles, and scissors) and 101 blunt instruments (tubes, levers, hooks, forceps, and probes). And they needed them, because plastic surgery was invented in India. One reason for this is that it was popular to pierce a hole in someone's ear and then shove a humongous amulet into the hole. Unfortunately, all too often, the person's earlobe just fell apart and had to be surgically rebuilt.

By 2000 B.C., the Egyptians (you know, the mummy and pyramid guys?) were actually pretty smart when it came to medical matters. After all, scooping out people's guts during mummy-making gave them a pretty good idea of what went on under the skin. Archeologists even unearthed a step-by-step surgical book, including the operations that doctors should never try to perform. It came complete with chants and incantations to go along with the treatments.

Egyptian doctors thought that the butt was one of the body's most important parts, and they

Why isn't the man on the left screaming? A "physician" is cauterizing his patient's head in this illustration from a 15th century Turkish manuscript.

liked to administer medicine up through that particular opening. One of their most esteemed healers, a fellow named Iry, was even inscribed in hieroglyphics as the "keeper of the king's rectum" (you know, the end part of the bowel).

Back in those days, most doctors were part priest, part healer. Here are some of their typical cures. Burn yourself while cooking? Place a dead frog on the affected area that has been fermented in yeast and warmed in goat dung. Crocodile bite? Hold a slab of raw meat in place with bandages that have been soaked in honey. Splinter in your finger? Soak it in an ointment made from the skull of a shad (a fish) cooked in oil. Just feeling under the weather? Try a mixture of mashed mice and pureed poop. Alas, none of them actually work.

Ancient Chinese doctors have at some point turned just about everything into a get-well-fast cure. Ground-up minerals, bugs, plants, and my very favorite part—animal poop—were all combined to fight disease. Bull pee, dog poop—it all found its way into the Chinese drugstore! The Chinese had over 2,000 different substances in their medicine cabinets and made over 16,000 different medicines by combining those items!

HUMAN PINCUSHIONS

We don't take ox intestine pills anymore (aw, shucks!), but quite a few ancient Chinese practices have stood the test of time. Take ACUPUNCTURE (*ack-u-punk-ture*). It's been around for more than 5,000 years and is still being used today. The Chinese discovered it by accident. They noticed that soldiers who survived arrow wounds found that other chronic health problems—things like asthma and allergies—had gone away.

Acupuncture works like this. Dozens of very thin, very sharp metal needles are stuck into one or more of the 1,000 specific points on our bodies that are said to be energy pathways. The needles are then twisted to stimulate nerve endings. You know what's the weirdest thing about it? It tingles, but it doesn't hurt and it really works. American doctors didn't believe it at first. But now it's becoming a commonly turned-to medical practice, and many American doctors are learning how to pin the pin in the hurting body part.

Acupuncture can also work in reverse, deadening pain by blocking nerve impulses. It can be used to perform surgery without having to put the patient to sleep. And it can be used to control all kinds of chronic pain. Cool things, those needles!

FIRE ON THE BELLY

MOXIBUSTION (*mox-ee-bus-chun*), another ancient Chinese remedy that is still being used, is another real tummy churner. Got a backache? Stiff joints? In ancient times the healer would place a little mound of ground-up leaves on your skin at a pressure point. Now for the fun part. He or she would light a match and set fire to the pile of leaves. Yikes! It would raise a big, slimy blister which the healer then popped. Next, the burnt plant leaves were rubbed into the raw skin. Ouch! Probably invented before needles, moxibustion was a way to deliver drugs into the bloodstream. Nowadays, they still do moxibustion but they've eliminated the fire-and-popped-blister part.

MEDITERRANEAN MEDICINE

The ancient Greeks gave us great myths. And speaking of myths, the Greeks believed that the body was made up of four elements, which they called "humors." (No, not the "ha-ha-ha" kind of humor.) These humors were phlegm, blood, yellow bile (which we call barf), and black bile. (I think you can figure that last one out, but if you can't, does the number *two* mean anything to you?) The Greeks believed that too much of any one humor in your system made you sick. Too

Egyptian suadis, or witch doctors, sometimes used serpents to "cure" their patients.

much phlegm would give you a cold. Too much black bile? Diarrhea! And so on.

Healers figured out that the body could easily and naturally rid itself of three of those four humors—through drippy noses, tossed cookies, and the runs. So they hit upon the idea of "bloodletting" (draining the blood) to help rid the body of "excess" blood. Bet your own doc is looking pretty good to you now!

Despite the limitations of its medicine, ancient Greece gave us one of the greatest doctors of all time. His name was HIPPOCRATES *(hip-pock ra teez)* and his advice to other doctors was so sound that medical students today still swear his oath when they graduate from medical school. And what was that invaluable advice? "Above all, do no harm."

IN-THE-DARK DOCTORS

Looking for a medical person in Europe around the year 1000? To put it bluntly, there weren't any. After the Greek empire fell, around 150 B.C., the Roman empire rose up in its place. But the Romans had no interest in medicine and most of the doctors in Rome were Greeks. In time, the Roman empire crumbled as well, and with it, so did the medical profession. People had lost faith in medicine. After all, in those days, most of the time doctors couldn't really do much. There were no wonder drugs, no lasers, no anesthetics. So people began to put all their faith in faith-healing.

Soon there wasn't a doctor to be found.

Monks and nuns did the healing, and since they were monks and nuns, the only medicine they really believed in were miracles from above! The bottom line? Everything the Greeks had learned about the body over thousands of years was forgotten.

Here's a typical medieval European cure. Got a fever? Pray. Broken bone? Pray. Rash? How did you guess? Take a bath in the river and pray!

It was actually forbidden to study medicine in much of Europe and surgery was a no-no. People believed you got sick because you were bad. And since you were bad, well . . . too bad! About the only thing you could hope for was a miracle. Needless to say, a whole lot of people who got sick just didn't make it.

Things were so bad, they had to get better, and eventually they did. After the Black Death—a terrible plague that killed millions—swept through Europe, medical learning and the science of healing were embraced again.

Over the past 600 years, folks have figured out all sorts of neat tricks, from how to kill germs to how to replace an ailing human heart! And that's where we are today. Still using leeches (see page 88), still sticking pins in the backs of our knees and necks, but also capable of replacing old and crumbling body parts with new and better models.

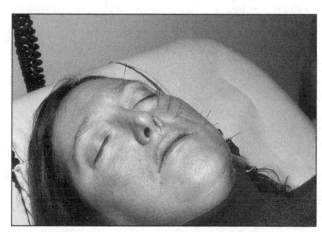

Acu-ouchy? Surprisingly, acupuncture is fairly painless.

"Ring Around the Rosy . . ."

Cute little nursery rhyme, huh? But did you know it was written about the plague, an epidemic of the disease known as "The Black Death" that wiped out a third of the population of Europe around the year 1350? The "ring" in the song refers to the telltale swelling that rose up under the armpits of an infected person. A "pocket full of posies" were flowers people carried to cover the smell of all the sickness. The part about "ashes, ashes" refers to the fact that the houses and possessions of victims were burned in an attempt to destroy all traces of the disease. And "all fall down"? Well, during the plague, people were doing just that—only permanently!

MY FACE HAS FALLEN AND IT CAN'T GET UP

If you think that only old-time medicine had a gross side, don't forget today's medical marvels of disgustingness—the FACE-LIFT and its buddy LIPOSUCTION (*lie-po-suck-shun*). Liposuction involves inserting a long metal wand into plump body parts—flabby hips, tubby thighs, paunchy tummies—anywhere fat lurks. The wand has an ultrasound device at the end that turns fat into a greasy liquid. The liquid is then sucked through the wand and collected in big jars.

Face-lifts are even worse. Wrinkly people actually pay big bucks for special doctors, called COSMETIC SURGEONS, to peel the droopy skin off their foreheads, drill a hole in their skulls, drive in a screw, and then literally hoist up the skin, anchoring it to the screw. For wrinkled cheek skin, the surgeon might just cut along the front of the ear, loosen the skin from the bone, pull the skin tight, cut off the leftovers, and then stitch the remaining flesh to the edge of each ear. Ouch! And you thought trephination was bad!

MUMMIES

What could possibly be more fun than spooning someone's brains out through his nose? Ask any MUMMY maker. There's more to mummies than simply wrapping a dead body in a lot of bandages. Their guts have to be stored in separate little jars. Then there's stuffing the scooped-out body with sand and tossing the leftover body bits to the cats. Sounds like a fab way to pass an afternoon, don't you think?

Back in ancient Egypt, at the same time they were busy building those pyramids (around 2000 B.C. for those of you desperate for a date), people believed that when you died, you crossed a river to your next life "on the other side." And you wouldn't want to show up there without your body. You never know, it might come in handy. But, as you know, bacteria love decay, and a dead body will start to do just that, especially in a place that's hot. (And trust me, Egypt is plenty hot!) So, pretty soon that dead body started to smell worse than your gym socks and dirty underwear put together. No one wanted to go on to the next life with a smelly, rotten body.

The mummy's curse, Hollywood style. Of course, a true Egyptian mummy's bandages wouldn't droop like this guy's do!

110

Movie audiences were scared silly by early mummy movies like The Mummy's Curse. *Hollywood mummy movies like this one were inspired by highly publicized tales of a curse on those who discovered King Tut's tomb in the 1920s.*

So something had to be done to keep that body looking and smelling good.

Folks had noticed that when they dried and treated the skinned hides of animals, these skins stayed soft, even after the animal was no longer alive. (Think leather jacket or fur coat.) But what to do with everything inside the skin—things like the lungs and the brains—all the wet, gooey stuff that keeps us ticking? They figured if you scooped out all those rotting hearts and lungs and livers, the body would stay preserved. (And they were right.)

HOUSE BEAUTIFUL, CIRCA 2000 B.C.

In Egypt, the "Beautiful House" was where you went if you needed a mummy made. That's what they called the place where the dead were embalmed *(em-bomd)*, which is a fancy word for what happens in the next few paragraphs. Of course, the beautiful house looked more like a butcher shop! In well-to-do families, not only did humans get mummified, cats and dogs and other family pets got the full-mummy treatment too!

The dead person's lungs, liver, stomach, and intestines were easy to get out.

They'd just make a good-sized slash on the left side of the dead person's abdomen, reach in, and pull! The important organs were each put in their own little pots, called CANOPIC JARS. Each jar came with a perky little statue of a god on the top to protect the part inside. Then, the insides of the body were rinsed with wine!

The brain was a little trickier. If you cracked open the skull it made kind of a mess, so they used a long wire with a little spoon on the end to get the gray stuff out. Up the nose it went, up higher and higher, until it reached the brain. Then, scoop by tiny scoop, it was spooned out through the nose. Egyptians didn't think the brain was an important part, so they fed the scooped-out brain bits to stray animals. The heart was the only organ left in the body. This is because the Egyptians believed that when the person reached the afterworld, their heart would be weighed on a balancing scale against a single feather. The dead souls "on the

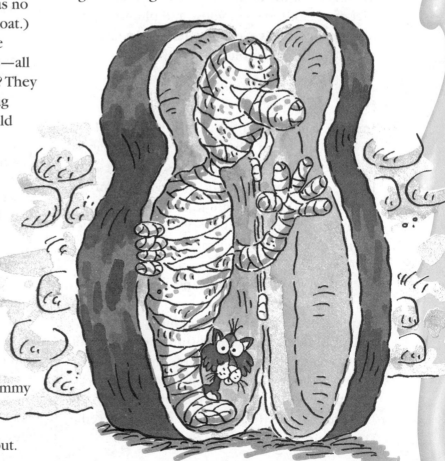

other side" would then see if the person was a good guy or a bad guy—a light heart meant a heart free of guilt. The Egyptians believed that if you passed this test, it was on to an eternity of fun and games in the afterlife!

The next step took 70 days to complete! The mummy makers would cover the body with natron and then let it sit for almost two and a half months! Natron is a salt, kind of like the stuff you sprinkle on your french fries, but with a slightly different chemical composition. (It got its name because it came from a lake called Wadi Natrun.) This nifty salt absorbed all the water from the body. Plus, it even had a mild antiseptic in it, which helped to kill any bacteria lurking on the corpse.

After being given its salt bath, the body was painted with a varnish-like substance from trees and plants called resin. Then, a mixture of oil, wax, and more natron was rubbed into the skin. The inside of the body was filled with sand, pieces of cloth, even sawdust, and plumped up like a pillow, to give it a nice fluffy shape. And then it was time for the best part!

IT'S A WRAP!

Imagine bundling up a package that took 15 days to wrap. That's how long it took to bandage a mummy. Some mummies had over 20 layers of bandages, and the average mummy had enough linen on him to cover a basketball court! Every finger and every toe was wrapped separately, and between each layer a coating of glue was applied.

Then it was into a coffin . . . and another . . . and another . . . and another. If you were an ordinary person, you might have just one inner and one outer coffin. But royalty got the "royal treatment"—multiple inner coffins of jewel-studded silver and gold, encased in a beautifully painted wooden coffin (or two). Finally, the whole thing was placed in a carved stone outer coffin called a SARCOPHAGUS

More on Mummies

✳ "Mummy" is the Arabic word for bitumen (bit-you-min), which is a fancy word for tar. Tar is a very dark, sticky substance, and the bodies of the mummies looked like they were coated with exactly that!

✳ You couldn't walk into a drugstore in Europe in the 1600s and *not* see jars of ground-up mummy. It was considered a wonder drug. A couple of spoonfuls a day of powdered dead guy was supposed to make you feel stronger. Tombs were plundered to supply the hot demand, and Egyptian families sold off old great-grandpa's corpse to the highest bidders.

✳ The Egyptians weren't the only ones who made mummies. In South America, in the Andes Mountains, the Incas mummified their king and then kept him propped up on his throne. Three perfectly preserved mummies were recently found high atop the Andes mountains.

✳ "Mummifying" can happen quite by accident. In very dry deserts, in freezing cold ice caves, and even in peat bogs, bodies can end up being preserved if the conditions are just right.

This Peruvian mummy was once a member of an ancient Incan tribe.

(sar-coff-a-gus). The bodies were well protected from the wind and sun and rain in one of those! Unfortunately, they were not safe from robbers, who took to stealing the jewels and gold from the coffins.

One can only wonder what happened to those thieves when their hearts were weighed before making the journey to the afterlife. Bet they didn't get to go!

N

NAKED MOLE-RATS

They look like water-soaked hot dogs with stubby legs and buck teeth. The only place they sprout hair is *inside* their mouths. And they've got a queen with a real attitude. Meet the NAKED MOLE-RAT. Naked? Hmmm. Now, it's not as if other rodents wear three-piece suits. What makes these guys "naked-er" than the rest?

IN THIS CORNER, THE UGLIEST RODENT OF ALL!

The naked mole-rat is the only known mammal that is almost completely hairless. When it's born, a mole-rat's skin is so transparent you can see its insides. They have no sweat glands, no fat layer, but scads of very wrinkled pink skin! Their tiny, beady eyes are so covered with folds of flesh that they can barely see, which is just as well, considering that they live underground in pitch-black burrows. The darkness comes in handy, since mole-rats are pretty gnarly looking. But hey, in the dark, everybody looks good!

Home for a naked mole-rat is Eastern Africa, especially Ethiopia, Kenya, and Somalia. Well, actually, *underneath* Eastern Africa. They live in underground colonies of between 20 and 300 pushing, shoving, squirming critters. But all naked mole-rats are not created equal. Although they are mammals, they act like insects in one very important way. Like bees and ants, mole-rats have a queen, workers, and soldiers.

THE QUEEN OF MEAN

A face only a mommy naked mole-rat could love.

Only her-royal-nakedness, the queen mole-rat, has babies. About every two and a half months she has a new litter of between 10 and 27 pups. But the queen needn't lift a regal finger after her children are born because all the other (childless) mole-rats help her care for her young. By the time the babies are about three months old, their days spent hanging around with the queen mum are over. It's time to get to work!

A colony of 300 mole-rats needs lots to eat. Tubers—plants such as potatoes—and roots provide most of their food. The mole-rats dig tunnels here, there, and everywhere, in the hope that they strike food. When they get lucky and hit a root or tuber the party begins. But naked mole-rats are careful party-goers. They gnaw a small hole in the tuber's rind, then carefully hollow it out from the center, neatly leaving most of the outer skin intact. Then, when they have filled their little tummies, they pack the dirt from their tunnel up against the partially eaten tuber and let the plant recover. That way, they can have their cake (well, their tuber, actually) and eat it, too!

Back to that mean queen. This lady is *soooo* nasty to all the other females. She shoves them around, stomps on them, nips at them, and yells and grunts at them continuously. They get so stressed out that it actually affects their reproductive organs. Until that queen dies and her reign of terror ends, no other female in the colony will be able to have a baby. But the real secret of her royal power lies in her pee. Little do the other mole-rats know that every trip to the potty is keeping them powerless.

WHERE MOLE-RATS GO WHEN THEY HAVE TO "GO"

Naked mole-rats actually have bathrooms in their burrows! Yup, they have special little chambers and they're the *only* place they do their peeing and pooping. When those rooms get filled to the rim, they close them up and scoop out a new restroom. But the queen's urine has a special hormone in it that makes the other mole-rats sterile (that means unable to have babies). As the worker mole-rats go to the "john" to have a tinkle, they are unknowingly rubbing their little wrinkled skins with the queen's powerful pee—pee that will keep them workers forever. Considering the queen can live for over 20 years, most mole-rats can look forward to a lot of years of dirt-kicking sacrifice.

In time, some of the brighter mole-rats figure out the system to some degree. As they get older and bigger, some of them are able to move up a notch from hard workers to lazy-good-for-nothing workers who loll around in the central nest chamber most of the day. Some mole-rats eat a lot and become heftier than the others, which makes them perfect soldier material. Soldiers hardly do anything except hang around in case a RUFUS-BEAKED SNAKE, a mole-rat's only real predator, comes slithering down one of the tunnels.

By the way, the naked mole-rat is neither a mole nor a rat; it's actually more closely related to the guinea pig.

So there you have it. The naked truth about the world's nakedest mammal!

A crew of naked mole-rat workers play "pass the dirt" as they excavate a new tunnel.

P

PARASITES The worms crawl in. The worms crawl out. They eat your guts and they spit you out. How true! There are several varieties of truly yucky microscopic worms that thrive on eating your insides out, and they're not the only disgusting creatures for whom people are the food of choice. Read on, if you think you can stand it.

WHAT'S FOR DINNER? YOU!

There are lots of critters that like to dine on our bodies. They are called PARASITES, and no, I am not talking about your friend who's always mooching money off you. Parasites live off the nutrients in your body, some sipping happily on the surface of your skin, others diving deep inside to really stuff themselves silly. And worms aren't the only ones!

Ticks, lice, fleas, chiggers, and scabies are just some of the bad guys who can make our lives miserable. (Some of those are soooooo disgusting they have their own entries. See TICKS, LICE, FLEAS, and MITES—with a side order of scabies—for all the news on what makes you itch.) Now for the disgusting details on some particularly nasty human-blood suckers. . .

SLITHERING SUCKERS

There are microscopic wrigglers that can creep into our bodies through tiny cuts in the feet (HOOKWORM). Once inside, they make their way to the intestines, where they latch on and start sucking blood, leaving their victims weak, to say the least. Certain ROUNDWORMS sneak in through meat that hasn't been refrig-

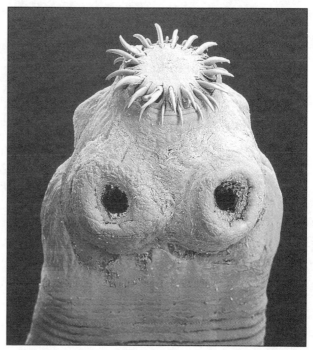

This gruesome monster is a tapeworm most commonly found in cats. The worm uses that circle of hooks to anchor itself to the inside of the cat's intestines.

A tapeworm is not something you want as a houseguest—because its bedroom is your intestines.

erated, and TAPEWORMS hide in pork, beef, or fish that was undercooked before it was eaten. Like the hookworm, the tapeworm's favorite spot is in your intestines, where it dives head-first into your intestinal wall. There it will eat and eat and eat until it grows to be 30 feet long! (That's as long as your classroom!) Every time you head to the can to do "number two," bits of the worm will break off and get pooped out. But until you get rid of that ravenous head, you will continue to be nothing but a walking, talking cafeteria for the tapeworm. By the way, the tapeworm eats by absorbing nutrients (that it steals from you) directly through its body.

Then there are PINWORMS, who hang out just inside your butt and slither out at night to lay their eggs—between your butt cheeks—in the dark. They will make you itchy beyond belief! How do they get there? When you dig in the dirt, the larvae sneak in under your fingernails. Maybe you fake washing your hands one night (you know, run the water, but don't actually get wet) and then you accidentally stick a finger in your mouth. All aboard, down the hatch, and here comes the itch! Is that gross, or what?

RINGWORM 'ROUND THE TOESIES

Your hair, toenails, and fingernails all have something in common. They attract some nasty stuff that checks right in and makes itself comfy. That stuff is called TINEA that finds your toenails, your scalp, your crotch, and the place between your toes just absolutely yummy!

When this particular kind of fungus moves onto your scalp or the skin on your body and sets up housekeeping, you have a dandy condition known as RINGWORM.

Of course, ringworm isn't actually a worm at all; it's a fungus. (Here we go again with the confusing terminology!) The disease got its name because of the ring-shaped marks the fungus leaves behind in its path of destruction. As it dines, it finishes with one spot and moves outward in a perfect circle in search of more chow. The outer part gets red and irritated. The inner part heals, leaving a red ring. (see FUNGI on page 71 for more on Tinea's creepy cousins.)

Tinea lives on the surface of the skin and feeds on the keratin—a protein that makes up part of the skin, nails, and hair. This unwanted guest/pest makes the skin go wild and fight back with everything from scaliness (think alligator skin) to fluid-filled blisters.

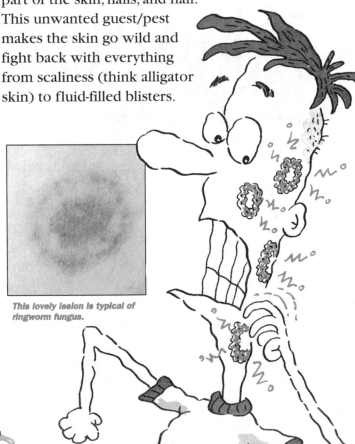

This lovely lesion is typical of ringworm fungus.

When a tinea fungus heads for your feet, look for trouble between your third, fourth, and fifth toes, sometimes spreading from between the toes to the soles of your feet. You will find scaly, peeling hunks of flesh and your nails might get thick and turn yellow. Unlucky you! You have a kind of ringworm called TINEA PEDIS, better known as "athlete's foot." (About half of you out there—the unlucky half—will end up with this itching nuisance at least once in your lives.) If the fungus moves upward and lands in your crotch, you will be the proud owner of a case of TINEA CRURIS *(crew-ris)*, better known as "jock itch." Warm weather and sweaty thighs make for good eating conditions for this pain-in-the-butt.

The tinea family has wonderfully diverse tastes. TINEA UNGUIUM *(un-gwee-um)* likes fingernails, while TINEA CAPITIS *(cap-it-us)* goes for the scalp.

How to fight these foul foes? They're all spread by direct contact. So don't even think about borrowing your friend's dirty socks, clothes, comb, or—heaven forbid—underwear! Athlete's foot can be picked up in locker-room showers, so many super-jocks wear rubber sandals while singing in the shower after a workout.

Should you be warped enough to actually wear someone else's dirty socks (even after this warning), special fungus killers available at your local pharmacy will come to your rescue.

And relax. If you borrow shoes at the neighborhood bowling alley, know that they have been sprayed with a fungicide— something that will kill that pesky nuisance. Same goes for the combs you see sitting in that bright blue soup at your neighborhood barbershop or beauty parlor. Those tinea don't stand a chance!

PEE

We've all been there. Long car ride. Lots of bouncing around in the backseat. Maybe that extra-large milk shake you drank 30 miles back wasn't such a hot idea. But the real question is, how does that thick pink shake turn so quickly into a clear yellow liquid? A liquid that's threatening to leak out from somewhere below your belly button before the next gas station comes into view?

BLOOD BATH

Whew! You made it to the bathroom! Not a second to spare! But even as you finish flushing, your body's busy making more PEE (us regular folks' word for URINE *[yur-in]*). And even though that pee might trickle out from somewhere down below your waistline, its trip be-

RESTROOMS 10 MILES

OH, YUCK!

Are You Kidney-ing Me?

✳ Your kidneys are only 4 inches long and weigh about five ounces (about the weight of a half-finished can of cola). And surprise! They really are shaped just like kidney beans. (Not to mention those cool 1950s swimming pools.)

✳ It's great to have two kidneys, and most of us do. But you can also manage just fine with only one, and many people do.

✳ The average person deposits about two pints into the potty between sunrise and bedtime. That's two pounds of the yellow stuff, by weight.

✳ About 44 gallons of blood gets washed by your kidneys every day. That's almost two bath-tubs full!

gins near the middle of your back, on either side of your spine, just below your lungs. That's where your KIDNEYS are.

Kidneys are the Most Valuable Players on the urinary tract team. (We'll get to the other players in a minute.) Like super-athletes who

A Nasty Note

Fresh pee is cleaner than spit, cleaner than your hands after you've just washed them, cleaner than that cheese sandwich you just ate. In fact, it's 95 percent water and 5 percent used-up cells, proteins the body didn't need, and salt. "Look Ma! No germs!" It's only when urine sits around and starts to collect bacteria, that it starts to turn funky . . . and begins to smell like dirty diapers. And, believe it or not, some people actually *drink* pee! People who follow Tantric Yoga swear by it! Mahatma Gandhi, who was a famous leader in India, was said to start every morning with a sip of the yellow stuff.

can play pro football and major league baseball at the same time, kidneys have two great talents. They are blood-scrubbing, fluid-balancing, wonder workers. Here's how they do their thing.

Next to your brain, your kidneys are the most complicated organs in your body. Every 60 seconds, a whole quart of blood gets pumped through these two little guys, and the stuff your body can't use gets filtered out. But you don't pee blood (unless there's something really, *really* wrong). So what does blood have to do with pee? Read on!

You know how Mom throws your dirty gym socks into the washing machine and half an hour later they're clean? Well that's the first job your kidneys do: they're washing machines for your blood. All day long, blood travels into your kidneys through your RENAL ARTERIES. (Arteries are tube-like passageways for blood.) These arteries keep splitting into smaller arteries, until they finally branch into tiny tubes called NEPHRONS (*nef-ronz*). The blood will pass through about a million nephrons, which have microscopic pores (a fancy word for a hole) that sort molecules by size and shape. A square block won't fit into a round hole, and big red cells won't fit through the tiny pores of the nephron. But some cells—the "garbage" cells (the ones the body can't use)—fall right through. And that's how those nephrons filter your blood. (Cool fact: If you laid the nephrons from both kidneys out, end-to-end, they would stretch for about 50 *miles!*)

Why does your blood need cleaning? It's not like it was playing in the mud! Well, let's say you've just eaten a bowl of kidney beans. (So why not? They seem appropriate here.) Your body will break down those beans into tiny pieces and take the parts it needs for energy. The rest is trash that your body needs to get rid of. Among the waste products is UREA *(you-ree-ah)*, broken-down, tired, old proteins. Another is CREATININE, *(cree-at-in-een)*, the stuff squished out when your muscles contract. These and other leftover bits, along with excess fluids (the water in that mega-sized shake you sucked up, for example), have to be washed

Even statues gotta go some-times! Peeing statuary can be found in gardens worldwide.

THE PUTRID PAST

✳ Back in the time of gladiators and chariots, Romans used to brush their teeth with pee, then swish a bit of it around as a gargle! They believed it made gums healthy!

✳ In Colonial America, clever housekeepers washed dingy windows with rags dipped in pee. Guess they thought that because it smelled like ammonia, it would work like ammonia, too!

✳ Anybody got a spare pig's bladder lying around? Oh, goodie! You can blow it up and play football the way the ancient Greeks did.

out of the blood and your body.

By the way, pee gets its yellow color from a special pigment called UROCHROME (but don't look for this color in your crayon box). If you've had a lot to drink it will be a pale yellow because the pigment is diluted in a lot of water, darker if you've been walking around feeling thirsty all day. In fact, if your pee is yellowish-brown, go and drink a glass of water . . . *now.* It means your body needs fluids.

WATER, WATER, EVERYWHERE

Your kidneys' other big job is to get rid of excess water. At the same time, the kidneys must make sure you have enough fluid in your body so that everything runs well.

Half of your body weight is water. So if you weigh around 100 pounds, 50 pounds of you is the wet stuff. It's in your blood, your cells . . . every inch of you; in fact, your body is kind of like a big sponge. The water in your body is salty

Gross but Good!

Not all that long ago, doctors would actually taste people's pee to test for DIABETES *(die-a-beet-eez)*, an illness that causes you to pass sugar in your pee, which makes it taste very sweet. Nowadays, they have little dipsticks that can "taste" it for them! When a doctor asks you to pee into a cup, diabetes is one of the things he or she will test for.

(probably because a zillion years ago life began in the ocean—but that's a whole other story). Now, if there's too much or too little water and salt in your body, your body will spazz out completely!

Imagine a glass of water on your front porch. Let's pretend that you have to keep it exactly half full or a big, ugly monster will gobble you up. Let's say it rains and the glass gets too full. You've got to pour some of it out—quick! Or let's say it gets really hot, and some of the water evaporates. You need to refill it—fast!

That's kind of like what the kidneys do.

Three stalls. One hundred women. Why is it that there's always a huge line at the ladies' room, but never at the men's room?

There's More Than One Way to Pee!

Here are a few fun ways to let your loved ones know that you gotta go—*now!* Stop the car, I've gotta:

✻ Take a leak

✻ Tinkle

✻ Go pee-pee

✻ Take a whiz

✻ Drain the lizard

✻ Visit the golden arches

✻ Powder my nose

✻ See a man about a dog

✻ Go to the john

✻ Shake the dew off the daffodil

✻ Hit the head

✻ Water a tree

✻ Play firefighter

✻ Make number one

✻ Go DMV (Drain the Main Vein)

✻ Urinate (used in polite company)

✻ Micturate (used in even politer company)

Or you could just say "Nature calls!" Then only *you* will know if it's number one or number two!

They make sure your body has just the right amount of fluid, and just the right amount of salt, to keep you working well.

THE WEE-WEE WAY OUT

The laundry's done. Your blood's been cleaned—pumped through those nifty nephrons. But the extra fluid from that six-pack of soda you drank at lunch has got to go, too. All that leftover URINE is now ready to leave the building. But how?

Attached at the end of each kidney is a long tube called a URETER (*yur-ah-ter*) that leads to a balloon-like organ called the bladder. This waterproof bag stretches easily to hold about a soda-can-and-a-half of liquid—about two cups. It's lined with muscles that contract to squish the urine out through a small tube called the URETHRA (*you-ree-thra*), the last stop before "splashdown." When the bladder is full, it presses on some sensitive nerve endings, and that's when you tell Mom she has to pull over to the side of the road. If the bag gets too full, well . . . you know what happens then. (Anybody got any dry underwear?)

PIMPLES

You went to bed looking pretty normal, but you woke up looking like Rudolph the Red-Nosed Reindeer! How did this happen to your poor little nose?! And wait, there's another crusty mountain on your forehead! You've got pimples, my friend. To learn more, read ACNE on page 1. (Just don't pop 'em!)

POOP

The average person eats about three pounds of food a day, 1,095 pounds a year. By the time you blow out the candles on your 70th birthday cake, you will have eaten 33 tons of food, or a pile about the size of six elephants. You will have pooped a pile about the size of a car!

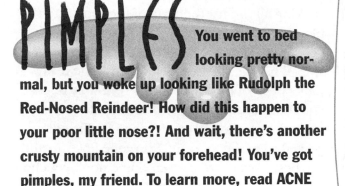

THE POOP ON POOP

You have just eaten a wonderful dinner. A thick, juicy cheeseburger, a tall glass of milk, a salad (okay, your parents made you eat that part), and a hunk of watermelon for dessert.

From the moment that food touches your tongue, your body starts breaking it down into smaller and smaller pieces so that it can get to the parts it needs—the proteins, carbohydrates, and fats that fuel your engines. Whatever's left over after that has got to get dumped.

You all know the difference between "going number one" and "going number two." (By the way, if both events happen at the same time is it called "going number three"?) But here are some other poopy numbers to know.

It takes about seven seconds for that bite of cheeseburger to make it from your ESOPHAGUS (eh-*saf*-ah-gus) down into your stomach. For the next four to five hours, strong acids in your stomach attack your dinner, turning it into a soupy liquid. Once this happens, a kind of gate, called a SPHINCTER (*sfink*-ter), opens up and the mushed-up food gets pushed into the SMALL INTESTINE (in-*tes*-tin).

Now, the small intestine isn't particularly small. In fact it's pretty big—over 20 feet long in a grown-up! But it's got to fit into a pretty small space in your abdomen, so it loops and coils like crazy. At the other end of the small intestine is—you guessed it—the large intestine, which is actually much shorter than the small one. (Go figure!) It's only 5 feet long, but it's three times wider than the small intestine.

The inside surface of the small intestine is lumpy and bumpy, covered with millions of things that look like tiny fingers sticking up all over the place, called VILLI (*vill*-eye). If you could somehow flatten those lumpy surfaces with a steamroller and stitch them all

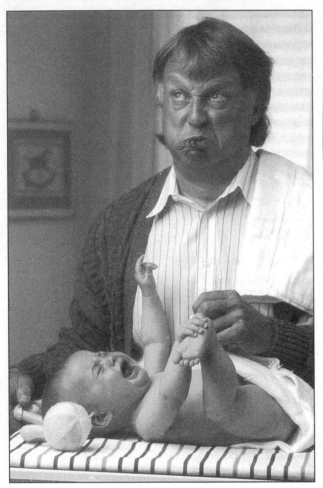

How long can Daddy hold his breath? Many fathers find out when they change their first poopy diapers.

together, they would be almost as big as a baseball diamond. (Seems awfully big for something with the word "small" in its name.) But that big surface area is a must. Here's why. . .

SMALL, BUT SUPER!

The small intestine is a hard worker. It has to take the soupy slime that's just been squished out of the stomach and sort it into carbohydrates, proteins, and fats, continuously breaking them down into smaller and simpler bits. The intestines move food by PERISTALSIS (*per-eh-stall-sis*), wave-like motions that squeeze the foods along. Like a snaky, slimy, spongy blotter, the intestine absorbs the nutri-

ents from each digested item as it squeezes it, sucking all the useful parts of the food into the bloodstream or the liver to be used to fuel your body.

What's left behind? Leftovers—the really junky parts of food, like tough vegetable fibers and the stuff that didn't get broken down enough to make the cut. It's kind of like being picked to play on a team. Everyone lines up and the best players are chosen. Some don't get chosen, so it's time for them to leave the game. And the only way out is through the LARGE INTESTINE, which is also called the COLON (*coe-lin*).

If there's any water left, it's the colon's job to absorb it. By the time the food has gotten to the end of the colon, all that's left is lumpy leftovers. The last 16 inches of the colon is called the RECTUM (*rek-tum*). The poop hangs out there until enough has accumulated to make a trip to the bathroom worthwhile.

The last stop on the trip to the toilet is the ANUS (*ay-nuss*), which has two really strong muscles. When those muscles are relaxed, look out below!

What's the exact recipe for that finished poop? Any water that wasn't absorbed, along with cellulose (you might know it as fiber), dead intestinal cells, and a whole lot of bacteria. In fact, a quarter of that pile floating in the potty is bacteria! *Yuck!* No wonder it stinks. Remember: bacteria = stinkiness. By the way, the official medical word for the finished product is FECES (*fee-sees*).

Suppose you have eaten only strawberry ice cream for three days straight. Why isn't your poop pink? Well, your body makes a liquid called BILE. It's produced in your liver and its job is to break down fats during digestion. And when its job is done, it has to get kicked out of your body, too. Bile has a yellowish-greenish-brownish color, and as it mixes with the other leftovers, it stains them poop color!

Take a Ride on the Poop Path!

The SMALL INTESTINE has three (count 'em, three) parts: The DUODENUM (*due-ah-dee-num*), which grabs "liver" juice from the bile duct to neutralize the acids in food coming from the stomach; the JEJUNUM (*ji-jew-num*), where much of the food absorption takes place; and the ILEUM (*il-ee-um*), where small meets large and the intestines merge.

The LARGE INTESTINE makes a sort of upside-down U. Its parts are: The CECUM (*see-cum*), which has a sphincter muscle to keep all that stuff from flowing back into the small intestine; and the ASCENDING, TRANSVERSE, DESCENDING, and SIGMOID COLONS, which have to reabsorb six liters of fluid a day! (That's three of those huge soda bottles worth!)

The RECTUM is the end of the road for poop.

The ANUS is the opening to the outside world.

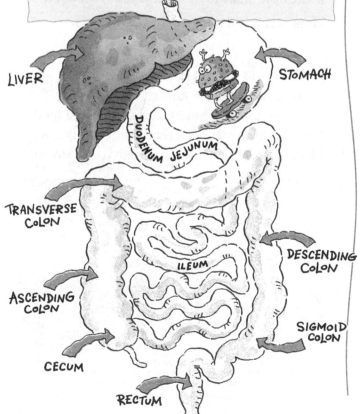

LIVER

STOMACH

DUODENUM JEJUNUM

TRANSVERSE COLON

ILEUM

DESCENDING COLON

ASCENDING COLON

SIGMOID COLON

CECUM

RECTUM

PARTY POOPERS

Poop problems turn up when the recipe for digestion gets thrown out of whack for some reason. Maybe some nasty bacteria snuck in; maybe you ate something that you're allergic to. Whatever. The end result? The Runs. The Trots. The Green-Apple Quick-Step. Use whatever name you like, it all boils down to one thing—DIARRHEA (*die-ah-ree-ah*)! In other words, poop that's *really* watery.

Diarrhea happens when the body rushes foods through the intestines to protect you from any bad stuff lurking in it. Occasionally, the stomach gets irritated and doesn't do a good job of breaking down the food in the first place, so your meal starts its cruise through the intestines in bad shape. That's what happens when you have a stomach virus. Other times, bacteria in poorly cooked or spoiled food can make you a frequent flyer to the bathroom.

Another reason for the runs? A trip to a faraway land where different, alien bacteria live! Along with a suitcase full of tacky souvenirs and dirty underwear, some people come home with "Traveler's Diarrhea," also called "Montezuma's Revenge," named after the bloodthirsty Aztec king who used to rip people's hearts out of their chests! Folks who have had it say the cramps you get feel just about that bad! (Incidentally, for those of you who are wondering, Montezuma was murdered by the Spanish Conquistadors, early explorers who came to the New World—the very first tourists, you might say. He trusted and helped them, but they later turned on him. So you can't really blame him for taking revenge!)

The opposite problem can occur, too. Sometimes when you don't drink enough water and you eat junky foods like chips and candy, the intestines work too slowly, take too long, and too much water gets removed. The contents of your intestines turn into a big

No, you don't need the whole roll to wipe.

PUKE

Who told you to read in the car, eat 12 hot dogs with "the works," or for that matter stuff yourself with cotton candy before getting on a roller-coaster? What's that you say? You mean you didn't know it'd make you puke? Learn more about why you spew—please (for the rest of us) turn to VOMIT on page 187.

brick, and trying to fit that big brick through that small hole is no treat. When your poop is stuck, with no way out, that's called CONSTI-PATION. Drinking a lot of water helps. So does brisk exercise and snacks of fruit and veggies. And if all else fails, you can always try prunes!

A ROSE BY ANY OTHER NAME

Why does poop smell bad? Well, the fragrance of poop depends a lot on the kinds of food you eat and the particular bacteria that thrive in your insides. Each person's poop has its own unique aromas. There are a lot of "good-guy" bacteria living in the intestines. They run a little vitamin factory, producing B vitamins and vitamin K. But they also munch on the dregs of the leftover food, producing smelly gases and two stinky chemicals, skatole and indole. (See FARTS on page 54 for more on stinky gases.)

Babies who drink only mother's milk have poops that don't smell bad at all. Guinea pigs, rabbits, and many other small mammals have droppings that smell sweet. In fact, rabbits' poop is so sweet-smelling that bunnies occasionally snack on it! And dogs adore deer droppings. Maybe they think they're chocolate kisses? (See BEETLES, FLIES, MAGGOTS, and VULTURES for all the poop on these poop-eaters.)

PUS

What did you expect from a word whose first two letters are P and U ? Something lovely? Hel-loooo! And whether it's splattered on the bathroom mirror after a quick pimple-popping or lurking beneath an oozing scab, don't let the fact that looking at it makes you want to hurl keep you from appreciating just how totally cool PUS really is.

WHY PUS IS A MUST!

Bacteria, as you now know, can cause all sorts of problems, from smelly farts to rotting teeth. You also know that bacteria can be real troublemakers when they get under your skin. But

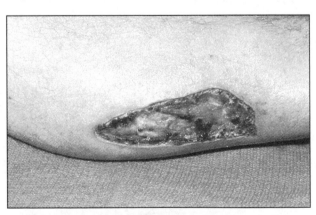

A pus-filled wound sure looks gross, but the yellow-white crust means that the body's working overtime to heal.

you have a secret weapon—special white blood cells called PHAGOCYTES (*fag-ah-sites*). These little critters love to feast on dead body cells and they especially love to eat dirt. When you are injured, millions of these guys rush to the scene to gobble up any bad bacteria. To these white blood cells, bacteria is a hot fudge sundae with extra whipped cream—completely yummy.

The phagocytes stuff themselves silly, gorging on bacteria and whatever other dirt is left behind. But alas! All that feasting is too much for them and they die. When you see a creamy, yellow-white concoction oozing from your wounds, you are looking at phagocyte corpses, a lot of dead bacteria, and used-up cells.

Pus is a good thing, but sometimes it goes a little haywire. If too much pus accumulates in a part of the body (the chest or abdominal cavities, for instance), trouble sets in. EMPYEMA (*em-pie-ee-ma*) is a disease of too much pus. It tends to affect the lungs, which get surrounded by a pus-filled fluid and then can't inflate properly.

QUICKSAND

We've all seen those tacky horror movies. A beautiful girl is all alone in the jungle. She's running. Something totally gross is chasing her. All of a sudden she's up to her ankles in something really mucky. She screams. AAAAAGGHH! It's QUICK-SAND!

Is there really such a thing? Can quicksand swallow up a whole person? And if it can, could it please swallow up that lunchroom bully who keeps stealing everyone's dessert?

Just because you're in the deserts of the Wild West doesn't mean you're safe from quicksand. Any sand can become quick if it has an underground water source.

LIVING SAND

Folks still argue about what quicksand is exactly. Some people believe that quicksand is different from beach sand—that the grains are rounder. They argue that those grains slip when pressed against each other, kind of like the ball pit in an amusement park. Water can then slip easily between the rounded grains, and lift them so they flow over each other.

But others argue that water is the culprit. A layer of ordinary sand floats on top of a layer of water (such as an underground spring). The water tries to float to the top, but the sand doesn't let it, and an imbalance is created. The sand is now "quick," an old-fashioned way of saying it's alive or moving.

Quicksand can form anywhere water and sand live side by side—in the mountains, on the plains, alongside rivers. You are most likely to find it where the ground is hilly or where there are lots of streams and wet caves. And any type of sand—powdery, rocky, or in-between—can become "quick."

I'M SINKING AND I CAN'T GET UP

Unlike in the movies, people don't step into quicksand and glug . . . glug . . . glug . . . sud-

126

denly disappear, any more than they would if they stepped into a lake. You can actually float in the stuff, and the truth is, it's easier to float in quicksand than in water.

So the next time an evil monster is chasing you and you find yourself sinking into a bog of quicksand, remember this. Move slowly. Don't flap your arms around like a turkey on the day before Thanksgiving. Try to fall on your back, and you will float easily. Stay calm and let the

THE PUTRID PAST

A person is usually able to get out of quicksand. A bigger, heavier object might not be so lucky. In the 1800s, a Kansas Pacific Railroad train had the misfortune to jump the tracks and plunge into a creek bed. Unfortunately, a recent flood had made the soil quick. The 200-ton engine sank and was never found. That'll be a great find for some archeologist some day!

sand flow around your body. Think of it as really thick water. Slowly "swim" to solid ground. Rest often and guess what? You will make it to safety.

Better yet, if you are in a place that is known to have quicksand, carry a thick stick with you. Test the ground ahead as you walk. (When a stick hits quicksand, the ground will actually make little waves.) Most important of all—for lots of reasons—don't go exploring in strange places without a buddy.

R

RASHES

Whatever you do, don't scratch!!!

Sure those painfully itchy red bumps are gross, but if you want to know more about what's truly yucky in the world of your epidermis (that's science-talk for skin), turn to SKIN ERUPTIONS on page 144.

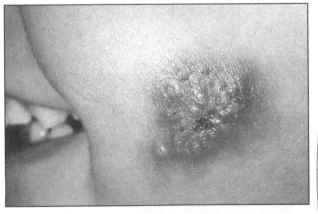

Getting a rash is bad enough, but right on the middle of your cheek? Bummer!

RATS

This is a true story. I swear it. A guy in New York City went into the bathroom, plopped down on the toilet to do his business, and opened up a book. For a few moments he sat reading and . . . well . . . dumping. Suddenly he felt something furry rubbing up against his butt. To his horror, when he leapt off the seat and looked down into the bowl, he discovered a good-sized RAT doing the backstroke in his toilet!

Impossible you say? Not for a rat! Rats have many talents, and to them, climbing through the pipes of a 16-story apartment building is no big deal.

Rat Stats

Rats can fall from a five-story building and land on their feet without ruffling a hair. They can climb up brick walls, slither up the inside of a pipe only an inch and a half thick, jump 2 feet high or 4 feet across. They can swim for days and days and days on end. They can even squeeze through a hole the size of a quarter. All this makes them pretty unstoppable.

THE RAT IN THE HAT

Fill in the blank. Mickey _____. Did you answer "mouse"? I thought so! But why not Mickey Rat? Don't tell me you fell for those stupid little shorts and those dorky white gloves. After all, mice and rats look a lot alike. They're both furry. They both have those little round ears. So how come mice get all the attention? How come rats don't have whole theme parks built around them? Huh?

A rat-infested corner of a temple in Rajasthan that honors—you guessed it—the rat.

Well, for one thing, rats have very oily fur and long, skinny tails. Brown rats just drag their tails along, but black rats can use them like a lion-tamer's whip. (Black rats are the ones with the pointier noses, in case you should happen to find yourself staring at one.)

All rats gnaw constantly and can actually chew through metal, electrical cables, and pipes. That's because their lower incisors are constantly growing. If they didn't keep wearing them down by gnawing, they would eventually grow up and start poking into the rat's brain. Pierced ears are one thing, a pierced brain is another.

Another big problem with rats is that they breed like—well, like rats! In warm climates, a mommy rat can give birth every two months; cooler climes stretch the blessed events to every four months. Mommy rats can have anywhere between 6 and 22 kids each time! (Try and get a good spot in front of the TV in a family that size!)

Four months after they are born, those

Gross but Good

Wild rats spell trouble. But domesticated rats are a whole different story. They were first bred as house pets about 100 years ago and they don't carry diseases like their wild cousins. And just as there are cat and dog breeders who raise just one kind of animal, there are rat breeders who specialize in one type of rat. Owners swear their pet rats can recognize their names, do "Rat Olympics," and even sit on command!

Man has also been able to use domesticated rats in all sorts of medical research. White rats are perfect for life in the lab because their organs—hearts and lungs and livers and such—work very much like our own. They also get many of the same diseases we do (especially cancers), and they keep making more and more rats so there's always a constant supply to experiment with!

baby rats are already ready to become Mom and Dad rats! The end result? Way too many rats! Way too many new disease carriers! And way too many rats means the rats need new places to get food. Way too many rats means the sewers where they usually live get over-crowded. Before you know it, you've got a rat doing swan dives in your toilet bowl. Talk about gross!

A TALE OF TWO RATS

Domesticated rats are harmless and actually kind of cool, but this isn't a book about cute and cuddly. So let's get down to the gross facts. There are two kinds of wild rats that are flat-out awful. BLACK and BROWN RATS are the kings of the bad rodents—super-rodents with amazing powers and the ability to destroy en-tire villages.

For starters, they carry more than 20 gross illnesses, including the plague, which is also known as the "Black Death," a disease so terrible that some historians estimate that it wiped out as much as one-third of the popula-tion of Europe in the 1300s.

A rat is like a bus for bacteria and viruses. Diseases hop on board and the rats take them for a ride, sometimes over huge distances. Other critters, such as fleas, bite the rats, then hop off and nibble on a human or two. That's when those diseases go *wild!* Before you can say "rat-a-tat-tat," you've got swellings the size of golf balls all over your body and you're heaving up your guts—literally!

The Pied Piper of Hamelin

Everyone knows the story of that little rat-infested town in Germany. "Get rid of the rats," the town elders said, "and we'll pay big bucks." Along came this weird fellow with a flute. He played like a dream, and faster than you could say "cheese," the rats were gone. But then those greedy, money-grubbing town elders stiffed him. (In other words, they wouldn't "pay the piper.")

Well, he got his revenge . . . by piping all the kids in town away, too. Like the rats, they couldn't resist his beautiful music. Legend? Maybe. But the town of Hamelin really exists. And in Hamelin, *to this day* it is forbidden to play music on the main street. (Rats are still a major bummer there, too!)

RAUNCHY RECIPES

Here's your chance to gross your family out at dinner one night. Start with some baked "bugs," move on to a warm and "wormy" delight, shock them with a "pus- or mucus-filled" main course, and end with a dessert that would make Dracula proud!

Be sure to let a grown-up in on your cool surprise, since there is some cooking involved. I'm serious, now—don't hang out near a stove or oven without an adult around and make sure an adult shows you the safest way to handle a kitchen knife. Okay? Okay! Let's cook!

BUGS ON A BRANCH

Open your guests' minds to the pleasures of eating insects with this festive hors d'oeuvre.

Foods you'll need:
6 stalks of celery
6 tablespoons
  peanut butter
½ cup raisins

Utensils you'll need:
Kitchen knife
Paper towels

What to do:
Rinse the celery stalks and then cut off the ends. (Throw the ends away.) Pat dry with paper towels. Now, spread a little peanut butter into the hollow part. Top with a parade of "ants"—those look-alike raisins.
Serves 6.

SECOND COURSE?
WARM WORM SOUP!

Straight from the corner bait-and-tackle shop. First, rummage around in the kitchen and find these items:

Foods you'll need:
8 ounces spaghetti,
  broken in half
2 cans (14 ounces
  each) chicken broth
  (not condensed)
¼ cup spinach
  leaves or parsley
  sprigs (for
  seaweed garnish)
Goldfish Crackers
  (optional)

Utensils you'll need:
Large pot
Colander
Medium-size pot
Soup bowls
Soup spoons

What to do:
In the large pot, cook spaghetti in boiling water following the directions on the package. Drain in a colander.

In the medium-size pot, heat chicken broth

and spinach over medium heat until steamy. Add pasta "worms" and serve in soup bowls. And why not serve your soup with a side dish of Goldfish Crackers to add to the theme? *Serves 6.*

PITA PIE ZITS

Go ahead. Squeeze to your heart's content. These larger-than-life pimple pizzas are yucky looking yet yummy to eat!

Foods you'll need:
6 large pita breads
(or English muffins,
split open)
1 cup tomato sauce
1 cup shredded
mozzarella cheese
½ cup ricotta
cheese
1 drop yellow food
coloring
1 package frozen peas

Utensils you'll need:
Cookie sheet
Kitchen spoons
Medium-size bowl

What to do:
Preheat the oven to 350°F. Put the pitas (or English muffins) onto a cookie sheet. Spread a little tomato sauce on each one. Mix the shredded cheese with the ricotta cheese in a medium-size bowl. Add a drop of yellow food coloring to the mixture to make a nice, gross pus effect. (Turn to PUS on page 124 if you don't know what it looks like.) Spoon lumps of the yellow cheese mixture in little piles all over the bread. Top each cheese lump with a pea as if the "zit" were coming to a head. Bake in a 350°F oven for 6 to 8 minutes. Have fun "popping" each pretend zit with your fork! Irresistible!
Serves 6.

P.S. The rest of the peas make a dandy side dish. Cook them according to package directions, drain them, and then whip them up in a blender with a heaping tablespoon or two of plain yogurt. Form the mixture into balls and call them mini mold balls, and no one will ever know the truth!

BLOODY-NOSE BURRITO

Pick at this tasty treat—it's a lot better for you than picking your nose!

Foods you'll need:
1 large tortilla
1 tablespoon butter
or margarine
2 eggs, lightly beaten
⅛ cup chopped-up
cheddar cheese
⅛ cup diced
sweet red pepper
2 tablespoons
ketchup

Utensils you'll need:
Small skillet
Pot holder (for holding
the skillet)
Spoon
Spatula
Dinner plate

What to do:
Take the tortilla and carefully poke two holes about two inches from the bottom with your little finger. Set aside.

Melt the butter or margarine in the small skillet over medium heat. Add the eggs, cheese, pepper, and ketchup and scramble with the spoon until set.

Lay the tortilla on the dinner plate, with the holes closest to you, and spoon the "bloody" mixture into the center. Fold the end with the holes up towards the center so the hole-y part forms the bottom edge. Then fold in the left and right sides so that the burrito is narrower at the top and wider at the bottom (where the "nostrils" are), like a triangle. Use the spatula to flip the tortilla over so the folded sides are underneath—your burrito should look like a big nose. Now just dig in with a fork and watch those goopy nostrils run!

Note: If you want your burrito "nose" to be super "bloody," squirt some extra ketchup onto the tortilla right before putting on the eggs, or on top of the eggs before you fold the burrito up.
Serves 1

SCAB SURPRISE

Dessert is good, this is better. Make the different parts ahead of time and put them together just before serving.

Foods you'll need:

1 box raspberry, strawberry, or cherry gelatin (to make the "coagulated blood" part)

1 pint vanilla frozen yogurt (for the "pus" part)

1 drop green food coloring

1 drop yellow food coloring

1 box vanilla wafers or other plain cookie (for the "scab" part)

Utensils you'll need:

Medium-size pot
Small cake pan
Kitchen spoon
4 to 6 small soup bowls

What to do:

In the medium-size pot, prepare the gelatin following the directions on the box, and pour it into a small cake pan. Put it in the refrigerator and let it chill for 3 or 4 hours until almost firm.

While your gelatin is firming up, take the frozen yogurt out of the freezer and let it sit until it's soft enough for you to blend in the green and yellow food coloring with a spoon.

Spoon a layer of gelatin into each of 4 to 6 small soup bowls. Top the gelatin with a layer of the frozen yogurt mixture. Now add a layer of the cookies—some crumbled, some whole—on top. Have fun picking!
Serves 6 to 8

If these dishes aren't enough to gross your family out, just read aloud to them from the sections GROSS GRUB (page 74), MISERABLE MEATS (page 99), or SICKENING SEAFOOD (page 140) while they eat. That ought to do it!

S

SCABS

You now know that you should never have tried that 360 on your skateboard, especially with your knee protectors busy protecting the shelf in your garage. The shelf is fine. Your knees, however, are totally disgusting. You took a couple of layers of your skin off. Surely there's a nicer way for skin to heal than this sorry mess growing on your knees! What on earth is going on?

THE STORY OF A SCAB

When you cut yourself or fall and break the skin, you damage your blood vessels, which start to leak. Since you don't want to lose too much of your blood supply, your body acts to stop the leak—quickly. It does this by forming a CLOT. Your blood has something called

PLATELETS (*plate-lits*), which look exactly like little plates. (See BLOOD on page 18 for more on platelets and the other nifty blood parts.) When platelets come in contact with the sharp edges of torn skin, they burst open and release special substances.

One of these substances is a protein called FIBRINOGEN (*fie-brin-ah-jin*). It makes stuff called FIBRIN (*fie-brin*), which when seen under a microscope looks exactly like that fun string that you spray out of a can. Its job is to catch all the loose blood cells, tie them together, and then anchor them to the injured surfaces. The finished product is kind of like a boat wrapped up in rope and tied up at a dock. The sides of your skin are the dock, and the clump of tied-together blood cells—the clot—is the boat.

The next step is a weird one. After the clot is formed, it begins to shrink, squeezing out the watery blood parts and pulling the sides of the wound together, kind of like a big tug-of-war in reverse. As the blood dries, it turns into a hard crust—a crust with a purpose. Because under-

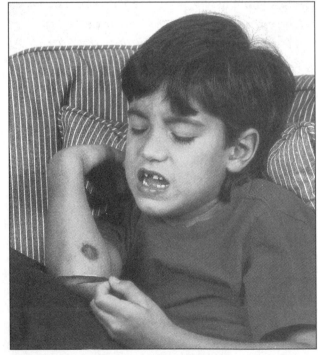

When removing a Band-Aid, the key is to peel fast!

This Sudan tribesman proudly shows off his elaborately patterned scars. In his culture, scars are a mark of bravery. This guy is obviously very brave!

neath that crust, repairs are still going on. Your body is busy making new cells to fill and cover the wound, while it also sends in white blood cells to gobble up any aliens that snuck in when the skin was cut. And where there are white blood cells, there is something truly yucky lurking . . . pus! (Read PUS on page 124 for the details on that gross substance.)

The air is busy drying the surface out. The fibrin is busy tying everything together. The white blood cells are stuffing themselves silly at a banquet of bacteria. And all this time, new skin cells are being produced to fill in the holes where the old skin used to be. Your skin has created a coat of armor for itself that an enemy sword will have a hard time piercing. You now have yourself a fine scab—one you can be proud of! That thing you are longing to pick at is a hunk of dried, clotted blood. Yuck!

Remember this, though. Picking at scabs is almost as gross as picking your nose, and it slows down the healing process. A new layer of skin has to form and hang out long enough to develop a top layer of protective dead cells. Picking and pawing at the drying blob keeps that from happening. If you pick at that scab, your wound will become a knight going to a joust dressed only in his underwear.

MARKED FOR LIFE

Sometimes, when a scab has finally dried and fallen off, you'll discover that a souvenir has been left behind—a permanent reminder of your adventure. SCARS are what happens when a wound is so big that a mere clot will not do the trick of closing it up. So an SOS goes out: "Uh, guys . . . we're leaking kinda fast here. Send *help!*"

When a wound extends down into the DERMIS (the second layer of your skin) special cells called FIBROBLASTS (*fie-brah-blasts*) rush to the rescue. They concoct something called CONNECTIVE TISSUE. Fibroblasts can reproduce really fast and they're speedy little critters, too. After all, wound-healers want to seal off the entry to bacteria as fast as they can.

You know the tough, gristly parts of a chicken drumstick? If you've ever taken a bite of that part you know it's like trying to eat a rubber band. COLLAGEN (*coll-ah-jin*)—the same stuff that makes all that gristle—is what makes a scar. The bigger and deeper the wound, the more scar tissue the body will need to make to fill the gap.

In some cultures people deliberately wound parts of their bodies just so they can get big, nasty scars. They see it as a sign of bravery. So if you happen to have a scar, wear it proudly. Maybe you can even spin a tale about how you got it tracking a lion through the jungle!

SCORPIONS

They hide under bits of broken bark and fallen logs—in closets and even in your waiting shoes. Sometimes they lurk in your folded clothes, waiting for night to fall so they can creep out and stretch their eight legs. Armed with pincers (sharp claws kind of like a lobster's) and a sac of poison topped with a sharp stinger, they are many people's worst nightmare.

The Night Was Made for Love

When a scorpion's thoughts turn to love, they dance! Their dance is called the promenade à deux (French for "a stroll for two") and it lasts for about a half an hour, during which time the male stings the female several times (ouch!). At the end of it, the male leaves a sac of baby-making cells which the female will absorb. But he doesn't stay around to watch, or to help baby-sit. If the male does not high-tail it out of there—fast—the female might decide to eat him! (Maybe that's her revenge for all that nasty dancing.)

STING FEVER

There are over 1,500 different types of scorpions. Like spiders, scorpions are ARACHNIDS (ah-rack-nidz), but they are different from spiders in many ways. For one thing, all scorpions dislike daylight. Think of them as mini-monsters of the night. In fact, scientists have recently discovered the weird fact that scorpions glow in the dark when exposed to ultraviolet light. (Those cool black lights give off ultraviolet light and nowadays, folks armed with portable black lights can spot scorpions that might be hiding in places where they should not be—like under your bed!) For another thing, unlike spiders, scorpions do not lay eggs, but give birth to live babies—as many as 25 little ones at a time. Yikes!

All scorpions are poisonous, but only about 25 species have venom strong enough to kill people. Of those 25 species, only one kind lives in the United States, and those murdering monsters live in the Southwest, so most of you are pretty safe. There are other scorpions in the United States, but their sting won't

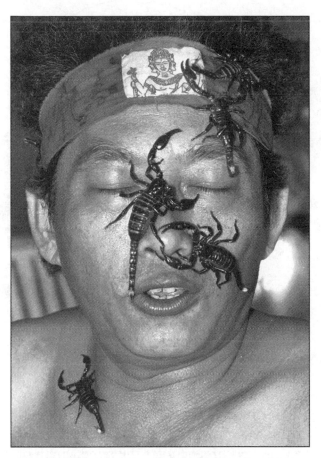

Poisonous scorpions crawl all over Malaysia's "centipede man." His secret? He says he hypnotizes the scorpions to keep them from stinging him.

with its pincers. It then pulls its stinger down over its ugly little head and plunges the sharp pointy tip into the poor victim. The venom usually paralyzes the victim, so there is no escape. The scorpion then leisurely sucks the juices out of its immobilized prey.

Scorpions have very poor eyesight, in spite of the fact that they have four eyes. They have survived since prehistoric times by stinging first and asking questions later. Fortunately, they're afraid of humans. (After all, we're a whole lot bigger.)

Scorpiana

✳ Scorpions can go for up to a year without eating.

✳ Scorpions have been around for 450 million years—before, during, and after the dinosaurs.

✳ Scorpions don't need a lot to keep them alive. Their metabolic rate (that's how much energy they use to stay alive and/or grow) is lower than that of a growing carrot or a radish.

✳ Way back when, in the dinosaur days, scorpions were big mommas—3 feet long!

✳ Scorpions do not have tails. That curving thing at the end of their ugly little body is really just an extension of the scorpion's abdomen, tipped with that nasty stinger.

✳ A scorpion can live for up to 15 years.

✳ Unlike spiders, which live for only about a year at best, scorpions take three to four years just to mature.

kill (unless you happen to have an allergic reaction to it). If you have the bad luck to be stung by one of the non-killer scorpions, it will feel like a red-hot ice pick being plunged into your skin. But that's about all there is to it. It'll hurt (understatement), but you will recover. The people who do not survive scorpion stings are usually babies, old folks, or people with high blood pressure.

By the way, the scorpion's stinger is called an ACULEUS (*ah-cue-lee-us*) and it's hollow like a hypodermic needle. (But a shot from a doctor's hypodermic hurts a lot less than a sting from an aculeus!)

The scorpion's favorite meal is a hearty helping of insects, or sometimes a juicy little mouse or lizard. When a scorpion finds something yummy to eat, it grabs hold of its victim

MOMMY DEAREST

If you think your folks are tough on you, try being a scorpion. Not only would you be pretty creepy-looking, but your own family would be downright danger-ous. Some scorpions will eat their young if they talk back and don't clean their rooms. Just kidding. But actually, they're even meaner than that! They've been known to eat their own kids just because they got in the way!

Maybe the problem is that they start so young. Think of it: If you were a scorpion, you'd be a great-grandparent by now! They have their first babies at the age of two and they can have up to 30 babies at a time. This would put most human mothers right over the edge.

Just like your mom, scorpion mommies give birth to live babies. But while your mom was pregnant for nine months, scorpions aren't always pregnant for the same length of time. If things are tough when the time comes to give birth, the preg-nant scorpion might wait a few weeks before having her babies. In fact, sometimes they seem to change their minds about having kids alto-gether, and become "unpregnant," reabsorbing their unborn children back into their bodies.

But many scientists say that scorpion moms have been given a bad rap. In fact, one scorpion expert pointed out that his friend's basset hound ate one of her babies. So there!

This yellow desert scorpion has killed a mouse with a lethal jab from his deadly stinger.

SHRUNKEN HEADS

Up until a hundred years ago, it was not a good idea to go breezing through the rain forests that wrap around the slopes of the Andes mountains in Peru and Ecuador. You might have found yourself missing an important part of your body—*your head!*

HONEY, I SHRUNK THE HEAD

There were headhunters in those hills! The Andes Mountains are home to the Jivaros (*he-var-ohs*), a tribe that once practiced head-hunting. And for all of you out there who are longing to know if there really is such a thing as a SHRUNKEN HEAD, the answer is *yes!* Here's how the Jivaros turned normal heads into shrunken ones.

First off, warriors had to capture enemies during a battle (fought with spears) and chop off their heads. (It was a major honor to bring back a head from battle.) Then, they made a vertical slit at the back of the victim's neck. The skin and flesh could now be pulled off and over the skull. The insides of the flesh were scraped out and the eyes sewn shut. The mouth was clamped shut with some wooden pins and lashed with string. The Jivaros were now ready to heat up their crock pots.

They boiled the skin from the head in a brew of herbs for two hours, which reduced its size by about half and kept the hair from falling out. Now it was sewing time once again, as they repaired the slit along the back. Then they filled the empty head with hot stones and heated sand (to help dry it) until it was nicely plumped up, and polished it to a nice golden shine!

Finally, the head was hung over a smoky fire for one entire night. Then, in the morning, it was given a final spit and polish and a few feathers and shells were added to make it look cute! When the headhunters were finished shrinking the head of

A Jivaro warrior displays his shrunken head with pride. Each one is a very real reminder of an enemy killed in battle.

SICKENING SEAFOOD

Peanut butter and jelly-fish . . . hmmm. Somehow that just doesn't sound too tasty. In fact, it sounds downright disgusting. You'd rather have lobster? Sure, why not? (Even though it's basically just a two-pound cockroach.) Squid? Well, maybe if you disguise it by calling it calamari and serve it with pasta and a whole lot of garlic bread. How about jellied eels? Seaweed stew? Raw octopus? Hey, what's the matter? I thought you said you were hungry!

an enemy, they were the proud owners of a TSANTSA *(tzan-tsa)*, and the possessor of what they believed to be an imprisoned soul.

HEAD-TOSSING

Now check this out. After all that hard work, the Jivaros didn't even keep their shrunken heads! Go figure! They'd perform some special ceremonies that were supposed to drive their enemies' souls from their puny heads, and then toss them into the forest. Well, at least they used to, until they realized that they could sell the used heads to explorers and scientists.

Some get-rich-quick artists even stole the heads of any old recently dead person (as opposed to the heads of enemies killed in bat-tle). They shrank those heads and tried to pass them off as genuine Tsantsas (a real one has to be made from a head taken in battle). So if you decide to become a Tsantsa collector, don't be fooled by cheap imitations!

SOMETHING'S FISHY

It's amazing what people will pay big bucks to eat! Raw fish eggs, also known as CAVIAR, can cost hundreds of dollars for just a few smelly spoonfuls. But it doesn't have to cost a lot to be a tummy-lurcher. There are plenty of other strange things slinking around at the bottom of the ocean that people around the world like to eat. Creepy things. Slithery things. Poison things. So pull on your lobster bib and dig in.

Garden cucumbers are crisp, green, and yummy. But a SEA CUCUMBER is just plain gross. It moves across the bottom of the ocean . . . a strange, fleshy, sausage-y thing that's alive.

Of course you already know all about the pooping parts of *your* body. (If you don't, you'd better read POOP on page 121.) But listen to this: A sea cucumber's anus is home to the pearl fish, which swims in and out of its rear end whenever the mood strikes. (Compare this to having a piece of toilet paper stuck you-know-where and you begin to get an idea of what it's like to be a sea cuke.) But a bigger problem for this poor creature is that it is a great delicacy in parts of Asia.

If you walk into a Chinese restaurant (in China) and order *"trepang,"* you will be served one of these dandy sea creatures disemboweled, boiled, and smoked. If you really want to be adventurous, have your sea cucumber stewed with soy sauce, sherry, and the webbed part of a duck's foot.

By the way, be sure to never annoy a sea cucumber. They get so rattled that they shed their digestive systems (through that same overused butt). This is important to know, because if you find yourself at the market in the Samoan islands in the Pacific, feeling a little thirsty, and you see a table with soda bottles lined up on it, be aware that they may not contain the bubbly stuff. Instead, they may contain those pooped-out sea cucumber intestines, soaking in ocean spray. And I'm talking about the real thing, not the cranberry juice. (Think I'll stick to the soda and garden cukes, thank you very much.)

Since this pearl fish makes its home inside a sea cucumber's body, his front door is the sea cuke's anus. No need to wipe your feet when visiting, I guess.

Don't try to turn this sea cucumber into a pickle. It probably won't taste too good with your ham and cheese sandwich.

GOODNESS GRACIOUS, GREAT BALLS OF SLIME

Eat JELLYFISH? Think I'm kidding? Absolutely not. In many parts of the world, jellyfish are the main course for dinner! Dried, then salted, they are high in protein and crunchy too! Even some of the poisonous ones, such as sea wasps, find their way into human bellies. Folks in the Gilbert Islands, in the Pacific, remove the ovaries (where females keep their eggs), dry them in the sun, then fry them. (In case you're wondering, I'm told they taste like cow stomach. That gives you some idea of how tasty they are, now, doesn't it?)

You can pop into most markets in Japan and China and buy some easy-to-serve dried jellyfish sheets. Take them home, soak them in cold water for about a week, and wash them well (to get the sand out). Cook 'em up with a few turnips and a scallion or two, add a drizzle of soy sauce and a little lemon and you have a fine *"Sueh Tin Yue Lopo Sala,"* a favorite in Chinese homes.

And in the Samoan Islands, pickled jellies are a sought-after snack. Take some fresh jellyfish. Hack them up into pieces. Soak 'em in vinegar or lemon juice. Pop them in your mouth—*raw*—and *bon appétit!*

(If you haven't already done so, you can find out about the nasty habits of JELLYFISH on page 85.)

Gross but Good

Seaweed can be pretty revolting stuff. It looks kind of like big clumps of snot all strung together. But did you know that you probably eat it a couple of times a day? Seaweed extracts are found in toothpaste, soft drinks, and even—surprise—ice cream. When you see CARRAGEENAN (_car_-ah-_gee_-nan) listed in the ingredients, you'll now know. You are slurping up seaweed!

QUICK! GET THE HARDWARE

Imagine! Twenty percent more protein than steak, with one quarter of the fat. The only problem is it's 3 feet long, slithers like a snake, and you need a hammer, pliers, and a blowtorch to prepare it! But for those of you who like to cook with hardware, try these handy hints for turning an EEL into a meal.

D-eel-icious! These freshly caught eels are for sale in a market in Madagascar.

First you have to catch the darn thing. But that's the easy part (you can actually catch them with bait and a fishing rod). Stun the critter by whopping it over the head with a blunt instrument (the hammer comes in handy here). Now comes the fun part. Tie a string around its neck and hang the eel from a nail. Cut the skin below the string lightly, and begin to peel it back, just like a banana. Grab a pair of pliers to get a firm grip and peel the rest of the slippery skin off. Now chop off the head and clean out the guts.

If you prepare jellied eel, which is basically eel and spices in unflavored gelatin, you will need a blowtorch to soften it enough to remove the rubbery thing from the pan. More hardware to the rescue!

And guess what? In England, there are actually eel shops, where a brisk seller is baby eel. (They're called ELVERS. Cute, huh?) You can order them up fried, grilled, smoked, roasted, baked, poached, deviled, or stuffed. So what's it gonna be?

Sick of eels? Try a LAMPREY. Folks in France think they are "_très bon_" (which means "very good"). Similar to eels . . . (like turkey is to chicken) yet tangy and different, they cook up the same, too. Of course you have to drain their blood, scald them in boiling water, scrape their skin off with a knife, cut out their spinal columns, and disembowel them before you eat them—but, hey! You got anything better to do?

(If you want to know more about these creeps, turn to EELS on page 46. Don't worry, you'll find the disgusting lamprey there, too.)

COCKLES AND MUSSELS, ALIVE, ALIVE-OH!

Remember that nursery song? Have you ever wondered what-in-the-devil a "COCKLE" is? Well, it's a cousin to the clam and a member of the MOLLUSK family. Steam them, then slurp them out of their clam-like shell. And wipe your mouth when you're done!

Sailors are always scraping BARNACLES off the bottoms of their boats. But did you know you can eat them too? Street vendors in Chile, where they have barnacles the size of a fist, offer them for sale, along with SEA URCHINS—disgusting prickly creatures that are covered with porcupine-like, sometimes-poison-ous spines. Painful to step on, but dandy to eat. The part that is eaten are the GONADS—the reproductive organs. (Eaten raw, I might add, straight from the shell, everywhere from Chile to Samoa to France to Japan.)

TASTES WEIRD.
COSTS $400 A PLATE. CAN KILL YOU!

Who in their right mind would plunk down a big fistful of cash to eat a blowfish that is loaded with a deadly poison? Lots of folks in Japan!

FUGU is a delicacy in Japan and there are restaurants there that serve nothing but. A typical meal in a fugu restaurant starts with

This blowfish uses its spines to discourage predators from eating it. Guess which predator is foolish enough to eat its potentially poisonous flesh? You guessed it—human beings.

a cocktail that comes with a cute little blow-fish fin floating in it, followed by snails the size of a small dog. The main course is served after the blowfish eyeballs are removed along with the liver and, if it's a girl blowfish, the ovaries. If those parts aren't properly pulled out, chances are good that that fugu will be your last supper, because that's where the poison lies.

Why take a chance on a fish that can make you a dead duck? People say fugu makes you feel very romantic. I guess they think it's worth eating one to have their hearts go pitter-pat. Too bad it can some-times make a heart *stop!*

SKIN ERUPTIONS

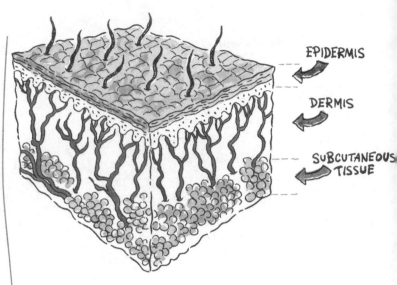

Aaargh! What are those red, raised bumps popping up all over your legs? They're itchy, too! Oh boy, are they ever itchy! So itchy that suddenly all you can think of is ripping the skin off your body. Everyone's screaming at you not to scratch, but your brain is screaming louder than all of them combined. "Go ahead," your brain yells, "scratch to your heart's content!" So, who're you gonna listen to?

THE SKINNY ON SKIN

Your skin is like a house for your body. It protects your insides from the storms of life. It keeps out the cold. It has "air conditioners" to cool you down when you get too hot. It even

has a "garbage disposal," to help whisk away all those waste products.

Skin is actually an organ, the largest organ of your body. And boy, does it work hard! Every square inch of your skin contains millions of cells, along with nerve endings that are constantly busy feeling heat, cold, and pain. It's packed with oil glands, sweat glands, and hair follicles. (For more on follicles, see DANDRUFF on page 35.)

Skin has two layers, kind of like a birthday cake. The top layer is called the epidermis (*ep-ah-der-miss*). That's the part you can see. And that part has three layers—dead skin cells at the top and two layers of growing cells underneath. The layers of cells are kind of like soldiers on the front lines. They protect your insides for a while, then they get tired and quit, only to be replaced by fresh, new troops. It takes about a month for the bottom layer of cells to move to the top.

The DERMIS (*der-miss*) lies below the epidermis. It's the biggest part of your skin. It's made up of a protein called COLLAGEN (*coll-ah-jin*) and strong fibers made of ELASTIN (*e-las-tin*). Together they make a kind of forest of elastic. That's why your skin can stretch as you grow (or eat too much Halloween candy). There are also blood vessels, muscle cells, nerve fibers, and a bunch of other neat things lurking in that elastic forest, too.

Under the dermis is SUBCUTANEOUS (*sub-cue-tay-nee-us*) TISSUE. It's mostly fat and provides insulation and protection. The roots of your oil and sweat glands hang out here.

With all that surface to protect, there are plenty of places for things to go wrong with the skin. Let's see, where to begin? There's poison ivy, prickly heat, eczema, and hives. Measles, chicken pox, and impetigo. And that's just for starters. Rashes can run the gamut from surface splotches to deep-from-inside irritations. (See PARASITES, on page 115, and ACNE, on page 1, for other skin irritations. Read VILE VEGETATION on page 180 for more on poison ivy and its pals.)

Some rashes start when your skin touches something it doesn't like—whether that something is strange leaves in the woods or cheap jewelry. This is called DERMATITIS (*der-ma-tie-tiss*). "Derma" means "skin." "Itis" means "inflammation." (You're smart, put it together!)

Before you know it, you're as pink as a strawberry shake. A "pop" history quiz can give some people hives, too, since feeling stressed out can also widen those darned blood vessels.

Many illnesses can make a mess of your skin, too—CHICKEN POX and MEASLES, for example. These two are caused by VIRUSES. Those itchy-as-heck, fluid-filled blisters scattered across the skin are actually little pockets filled

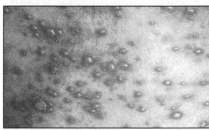

with the virus. (Turn to VIRUSES on page 184 for more on these nasty afflictions.)

Super itchy, super ugly, chicken pox is caused by a nasty virus.

ITCHING FOR EVEN MORE?

A hot summer day or an overeager gym teacher can make you scratch! Too much heat triggers too much sweat, which can keep the top layer of epidermal cells from being replaced. The cells, which are supposed to be flaking off, get bogged down and just hang around, forming a wall that keeps the fresh sweat from getting out. Trapped inside, all hot and miserable, the cells get unhappy and revolt by swelling up. Before you know it, you've got PRICKLY HEAT.

Certain foods and drugs can make your skin go wild too, by creating an allergic reaction called HIVES. The body tries to help by releasing HISTAMINES (*hiss-ta-meenz*), which widen the blood vessels. That way, the rescue crew—your white blood cells—can rush to your aid without getting stuck in slow-moving traffic. But the extra blood rushing to the area leaves its mark with raised red welts.

THE REVENGE OF THE TOO-TIGHT SNEAKERS

You just picked out some cool new shoes. But a couple of hours after putting them on, the tops of your heels feel like they have two blowtorches aimed at them. You kick off your shoes and take a peek. Arrgh! BLISTERS! Why do we get those pesky water-filled swellings?

That watery stuff is fluid released by tiny blood vessels in an area under attack from rubbing or burning. It's like a giant warning flag from your body telling whatever's rubbing you the wrong way to BACK OFF! Also, that giant balloon of fluid protects the damaged skin from further injury while repairs go on "under-skin."

To pop or not to pop? Doctors advise you not to pop a blister unless you absolutely can't move without screaming. If you do opt to pop, use a sharp sewing needle, but never heat it in a flame first. Matches leave carbon deposits and you'll end up with a permanent black stain at the spot. Instead, dip the needle in rubbing alcohol to kill any lurking germs. Then, using a bit of sterile gauze, gently press out the fluid. Always leave the leftover skin there as a kind of protective blanket. Smooth on a little antibiotic ointment and a bandage. And next time, wear socks with your new shoes!

DERMA-DRAMAS

Here are a few more things that can go wrong with your skin.

ECZEMA With a name like ECZEMA (*eggs-uh-muh*), it has to be disgusting! If your skin is dry, red, cracked, covered with blisters that ooze and get all crusty, and you have a family history of allergies, you may get to sport this crusty rash from time to time.

IMPETIGO begins with a small patch of tiny blisters. That wouldn't be so bad—but wait! It

gets worse. Soon the blisters turn into patches of red, moist, dripping skin that harden into a brown crust. This infection, which is caused by bacteria, can keep spreading and, unfortunately, since it usually shows up around your mouth and nose there's no hiding the grossness under your clothes! The good news is, doctors have magic medicines up their sleeves that will make this disappear in a jiffy.

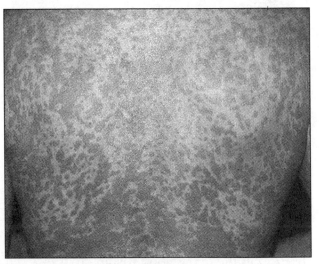

Talk about an allergic reaction. This woman broke out in a red, raw rash because she was sensitive to a prescription medicine she was taking.

MOLES Holy mole-y! Moles happen when bunches of NEVUS cells decide to hang out together. These cells have tons of MELANIN, which is what gives your skin its color, all concentrated in a small area. To add a delightfully gross touch to the event, occasionally hair will sprout out from the center like a birthday candle in the middle of your cell-cake.

PSORIASIS *(sore-eye-ah-sis)* is another skin tormentor. No one is sure why it happens but when it happens, your skin cells go nuts. The upper layer starts to grow too quickly.

Spotting the Spots

All those rashes fall into neat categories. Dazzle your friends with this bit of bizarre knowledge!

❋ A MACULE *(mack-yule)* is a flat splotch of color. Chicken pox starts out with these.

❋ A PAPULE *(pap-yule)* is round and raised a tiny bit, like a very small mosquito bite.

❋ NODULES *(nod-yules)* are big papules.

❋ A PLAQUE *(plak)* is a raised, flat patch of skin. People with conditions such as psoriasis (see above for pronunciation) have these.

❋ VESICLES *(ves-i-culs)* are small blisters filled with fluid. Chicken pox end up as vesicles.

❋ And big old BULLAE *(boo-lie)* are large, fluid-filled blisters.

Now you know why when you call your doctor and say you have a rash, she makes you come in. She needs to know if you're talking about a macule, a papule, a nodule, or a plaque attack!

This woman probably forgot to slather on her sunscreen and has discovered that bright red skin is also painful. Repeated sunburns can increase your chances of developing skin cancer later in life, so always wear a strong sunscreen and limit your time in the sun, too.

Normally, skin cells get replaced on a 30-day cycle. But psoriasis speeds the process up to every three or four days. Too much, too soon! The extra cells form thick, itchy, burning plaques on the surface. Exposure to ultraviolet (UV) light can help clear it up, along with special medicines that help your body suck up more UV rays. If you get crusty, don't despair. There *is* help!

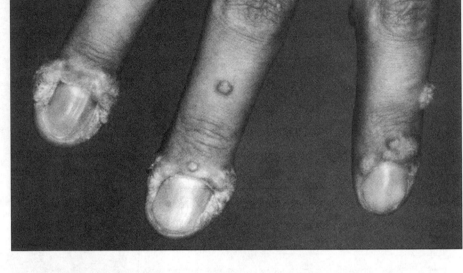

Warts gone wild. Viruses cause these generally harmless—but still nasty—skin growths.

SUNBURN Too much sun? The freshly-boiled-lobster look of SUNBURN is caused by blood rushing to the aid of your damaged skin. After the redness goes away, you get to discover the joys of peeling off whole sheets of the top layer of your epidermis, since the ultraviolet rays of the sun have pretty much destroyed it. Sunburn is no laughing matter. In the long run it makes you leathery and wrinkly and it can even kill you (by giving you skin cancer). So never mind the tanning lotion ads. Have fun in the sun but protect your skin while you're at it—cover up or wear strong sunscreen. You'll live longer, and look better, too.

GO AHEAD . . . KISS A FROG

Warts, those hard, raised, skin-colored lumps on your skin, are not caused by kissing Kermit. They are caused by a virus that confuses the skin's cell-makers. Before you can say "wart's up?" the cell factory has produced too many cells. That's what that lump is—a crowd of too many cells. If those warts happen to pop up on the soles of your feet, you've got PLANTAR'S WARTS—and if you do, poor you. Plantar's warts hurt, big-time!

You can't catch a wart from a frog, but you can sure catch them from a person. For starters, if you get a wart, don't play with it! Relax. Chances are it will go away all by itself. Sometimes they vanish in a couple of months. Sometimes it takes a year or two. If you just can't wait that long for a wart to go away by itself, here are some wart-wise tricks that may (or may not) help to speed things up. (Check with a doctor before trying these.)

❋ For finger warts, wrap three or four layers of tape around the wart and leave them on for about a week. Let the wart air out for half a day, then repeat. It might take three or four weeks, but this trick usually works.

❋ Sometimes soaking the wart in hot water for an hour or two every day will make the wart fall off faster.

❋ Crush a few tablets of vitamin C and make a paste with a little warm water. Apply it to the wart and cover it with some gauze and tape. The citric acid may irritate the wart enough to make it go away.

❋ If all else fails, try this old witches' cure. Rub your wart with a chicken gizzard when the moon is full. Then bury the gizzard in the middle of a dirt road. No promises with this one, but if you're desperate, why not give it a try?

SKUNKS

It is the king of all farts . . . an oily anal eruption so stinky that it'll make your nose want to close up shop and your eyes burn and water. You can even taste the foulness. And the bringer of all these bad tidings? A sweet, cuddly critter with a kind heart and two powerful stink-bomb glands next to its butt!

SWEET BUT SMELLY

SKUNKS are actually pretty nice little stinkers. And when they are happy, they smell just fine. But they don't like getting pushed around, and they don't like anything bigger than they are. (Unfortunately for our noses, lots of things are bigger than they are.) When skunks feel threatened, they have a not-so-secret weapon and they're not afraid to use it.

Let's say you're walking through the woods and you find yourself in a face-off with a skunk. Since you are a lot bigger than a skunk, the skunk naturally feels threatened. (Admit it. You'd feel that way too if you ran into someone who was 20 times taller than you.) The skunk hopes that you will go away. Only problem is, you're now too terrified to move.

The skunk stamps the ground with its feet. Its teeth may chatter. In skunk-talk, this all means "Get out of here, now, you idiot!" But, fool that you are, you stand there, feet still glued to the ground. So, the skunk moves on to phase two, raising its bushy tail. But the tip is still limp. What do you do? Quick! Run! There's still time!

Still too terrified to move? When the tip of the tail stiffens, you've gotten your final warning. The trick was to move away before that happened. Now you're in real trouble. So what's next? Bang-bang. You're it! You stink!

Armed with enough ammunition for four or five shots, able to shoot as far as 12 feet, the skunk lets loose with an oily, golden liquid that it keeps stored in two grape-sized

A striped skunk caught in mid-squirt. I hope this photographer used a zoom lens to take this photo since a skunk can hit a target 12 feet away.

sacs embedded in the muscle tissue on either side of its ANUS (*ay-nuss*). (You know, the little hole that poop comes out of, down between those butt cheeks.)

A little tube extends from each of these sacs to the skunk's butt. Each ends in a nipple kind of like the ones you've got on your chest. But these are inside the skunk's butt. A SPHINCTER (*sfink-ter*) muscle holds the whole thing shut. When the skunk gets scared, it "moons" its enemy, and then relaxes the sphincter muscle while tightening the muscles around the sacs, and lets go!

Out comes a stream of that oily, noxious fluid ("noxious" means "really stinky") that's so strong it can make you sick to your stomach and cause temporary blindness if it gets

in your eyes. And skunks, except for baby ones, have perfect aim. Fortunately for the next person who trips over the little fella, that skunk will not be able to "skunk" anyone else anytime soon. It takes a skunk between one and ten days to recharge. Does that make you feel any better?

Most animals figure out early on that any meeting with a skunk is basically a no-win situation. The biggest, meanest bear that comes face-to-face with a delicate little skunk will haul tail and get out of the way fast. Let's face it: A little cowardly behavior beats being temporarily blinded by a shot of skunk spray. The exception to this rule of animal behavior is the dog, who just never seems to get with the program. But what do you expect from something that drinks from the toilet bowl?

A Nasty Note

Skunk spray, which is sometimes called MUSK, is used as a base for some of the world's most expensive perfumes! Only a tiny bit is added (so people don't go around dropping from the stench). It's used because it helps the scent to last longer. (Think of how long skunk-smell can just hang in the air.)

WHAT IF YOU GET SKUNKED?

Take a bath in tomato juice, right? Wrong! That really doesn't work all that well. This strange custom started because skunk-stink is caused by a substance in the musk called MERCAPTAN (*mur-cap-tan*), a very strong BASE. A base is the chemical opposite of an acid. When you mix a base and an acid together, they sort of cancel each other out. Tomato juice has a lot of acid in it, so it seemed like it should cancel out the mercaptan, but it just doesn't work well enough. That's because the skunk's stinky stuff is also full of oil and sticks to everything it touches. So you have to break down the oily part, too.

Try this remedy instead. Fill a bathtub with warm water and a few squirts of dishwashing liquid. Add some water to half a cup of baking soda and mix it into a paste. Now toss the offending body (whether that's you, or your dog or cat) into the tub and rub

The Skunk Files

❋ Skunks are only 2 inches long when they are born. They have no hair, but their skin sports the black and white pattern that the hair will have when it grows in.

❋ A baby skunk can spray its musk by the age of 1 month.

❋ A skunk can eat live bees and wasps! The stings don't bother them.

❋ Next to cars, a skunk's most dangerous enemy is the owl. Owls lack a sense of smell so they don't give a hoot about how bad a skunk stinks.

❋ Why are there so many dead skunks on the road? Skunks simply won't run away from danger, even when that danger is a 4,000-pound pickup truck moving at 60 miles an hour. They just haven't figured out that cars don't have noses and aren't threatened by that raised tail.

❋ Skunks used to belong to the same family as ferrets, weasels, otters, and badgers. (The fancy Latin name for that fami-

ly is MUSTELID (_must-uh-lid_).) Scientists now think skunks are different enough to have their very own family, the MEPHITIDAE (_muh–fih-tih-day_), which means "foul-odored ones" in Latin.

❋ There are three main types of skunks—spotted, striped, and hog-nosed. Their markings are each a little different. But their stinkiness is the same!

the mixture all over. Follow with a vinegar rinse. Then rinse that off with soap and water. This works a whole lot better than tomato juice.

But guess what works best. A campfire! Wood smoke is a perfect natural antidote. Within minutes, the smoke will suck away all that skunky smell. The smoke works in two ways. A substance in smoke called CREOSOTE (_cree-oh-soht_) is very acidic, so it neutralizes the

base. The smoke also seeps into any organic materials—like fabric, hair, or skin—it comes in contact with. (That's why your clothes always smell so, well, smoky when you've been hanging around a campfire.) Anyway, which would you rather smell like? A campfire or a skunk butt?

SLUGS

There has just been a delightful summer shower. The air smells sweet. You can't wait to rush outside and splash in a puddle or two. You're out the door, barefoot, and onto the road. Suddenly you skid on something. Something squishy. Something that looks like a big wad of snot. Then you notice that there are squishy things oozing all over the place— crawly things, dragging things, slimy things. The dirt-dwellers have *all* come out to play . . . just like you! You are now a part of a slug-fest!

NAKED SNAILS

SLUGS are MOLLUSKS (*mol-usks*), as are clams, mussels, scallops, oysters, snails, squids, and octopuses. Slugs are just like snails, but without the shell, so you get to see them in all their gross glory. (Some slugs do have a tiny shell, but it's inside the slug's body where you can't see it.) They come in an assortment of colors—pink, brown, beige, black, and gray. Some even have spots. There are over 26,000 different types of slugs in the world, all leaving their mucousy trails behind.

Slugs are happiest when the weather is damp and humid, which is why they come crawling out from under rocks and leaves after a rain. In the north-

western parts of the United States, a place where it is often cool and cloudy, slugs can grow to the size of a small banana—up to 7 inches long! Not surprisingly, those big fellas are called BANANA SLUGS. They range in color from unripe banana (green) to rotten banana (black). But you don't want to peel one of these babies and slice it up on your cereal— unless you're in the mood for some mucus in your cornflakes.

SECRETS OF THE SLIME

What makes slugs so oozy? Well, they're covered with the same stuff that runs from your nose. But why would it want to cover itself in snot?

First of all, mucus protects the slug's skin, which is only one layer of cells deep (our skin has three layers). Without this beautiful booger-coat, the slug would quickly be invaded by bacteria and mold.

Second, a mucus-free slug would not be

able to move. That mucus, which is made in a gland just beneath a slug's head, turns the ground into a slippery ice-skating rink for the little creeper. The slime is like a red carpet on which the slug gracefully glides along.

Third, the mucus makes a slug taste disgusting. Think about it. Would you want to bite into a juicy spoonful of snot? Didn't think so! Other animals feel the same way. There aren't too many critters that would choose a slug for dinner. About the only ones that do are really hungry moles, ducks, and garter snakes.

Gross but Good

Underneath all that mucus is a creature that may help cure a deadly human disease. Cystic fibrosis is a disease that causes the body to overproduce mucus. It suffocates its victims by clogging up their lungs. Medical researchers are taking a really close look at the slug's mucus-making abilities because the mechanism that makes and regulates slug-snot is very similar to ours. If doctors can understand how to regulate mucus, they may be able to help those who suffer from this life-shortening illness. More than 30,000 people in the United States alone have the disease.

This isn't the first time healers have turned to slugs for help. Native Americans of the Pacific Northwest baked slugs and ground them into a powder, and then mixed them with bear grease. They used the concoction as a healing ointment. They also used slug-slime to soothe burns and bites.

And thousands of years ago, slugs were handy to have around for other reasons. Hunters squished and mushed slugs against their spear handles to help give them a firm grip, and folks kept their clothes on by making a slug-paste that held their garments together. Just think—no zippers to get stuck, or buttons to pop off! Kind of like a natural form of Velcro. Cool!

Spotted garden slugs sure do love tomatoes. Come to think of it, they love most anything growing in a garden.

BIG FOOT

Slugs have only one foot, but it's a biggie. The slug's foot runs the length of his body and he uses it to push himself along in his river of slime. As the mucus highway dries, it leaves a silvery trail of dried ooze behind—a road map of a slug's travels.

Slugs, like snails, are GASTROPODS (*gas-trah-pods*), which means "stomach-foot" (although they don't digest with their feet). Unlike snails, which have a shell to duck into, slugs have only a head-covering called a MANTLE, a loose flap of skin they can hide under if they get scared during a chainsaw massacre movie!

Here's a disgusting tidbit. If a slug has to hide from something, it can squeeze itself into very tight spaces by stretching to 11 times its normal length, and then pouring itself in like a liquid.

BIG APPETITE

Slugs are big eaters, too. They have ribbon-like tongues with rows of tiny teeth that they use kind of like your mom's cheese grater. Banana slugs dine on wild plants, fallen leaves, and, sometimes, dead animals. EUROPEAN SLUGS are the ones you see in most gardens. They are much smaller than the banana slugs, but boy, can they chow down! They love flowers, fruits, and veggies. In really wet years, slugs have destroyed 75 percent of the strawberry crop in parts of Washington state. But actually, a hungry slug will eat just about anything, including poison ivy, animal poop, and soap. Slugs even eat other slugs.

SLUG LOVE

Like leeches, slugs are neither girl nor boy, but both, and they are big-time baby-makers. GREAT GRAY

Slug Sports

Every year in Elma, Washington, people come from far and wide to watch the world's fastest, bravest slugs battle it out for the title of "World's Fastest Slug." These pumped-up athletes are well fed and well trained. The distance of the race is 24 inches on a tiny little racecourse, edged in salt (which slugs hate) to keep them "on track."

And the University of California at Santa Cruz has made the banana slug its school mascot. You can join a campus Slug Club or buy a cuddly stuffed slug in the college bookstore for snuggling with. Go, Slugs!

SLUGS AWAY

Here's how to keep those mounds of mucus away from your favorite garden plants and trees.

SLUGS dangle from a thick strand of snot, and twist around each other so that they can exchange the sperm they need to make more slugs! Each slug lays hundreds of eggs, which will be ready to hatch in just three weeks. Then the slug babies all head off and demolish the first garden they come to! And garden slugs have got to go—unless you want to eat Slug Shortcake for the Fourth of July!

✳ Powdered ginger sprinkled around your precious plants forms a "fence" no slug will cross. Wrapping the base of a tree with a thin strip of copper will do the same. (The copper gives off a small electric charge which zaps the slugs. They hate it!)

✳ Rotting fruit peels, left for a couple of days in water, mixed with half a packet of yeast and a half cup of beer, will go a long way toward stopping the slimers. Fill a few pie plates or shallow bowls with the mixture, press down into the soil, and come back in two days to survey the corpses! (Beer, which has long been a famous slug-slayer, works because the yeast in the beer attracts the slugs and the alcohol in it is toxic to them.) Well, we all know drinking can kill you!

❋ You can spray slugs with a combo of vinegar and hot pepper, or—if your mom doesn't mind you destroying the blender—slug juice. Make it by placing a cup or two of dead slugs in the blender. Set it on high to puree them and then pour the whole gloppy mess through a strainer. Take the leftover juice and put it in a spray bottle, adding a squeeze of lime for added destruction. (Note: Do *not* serve in a frosted glass with a little paper umbrella.)

❋ Sprinkling salt on a slug will not always kill it. Even though the slug may look like it has shriveled up and died, in time, it could absorb enough water to "re-inflate" and slither on.

SNAKES

There's something pretty creepy about SNAKES, and it's not just the way they move. From ancient times until now, people have been scared stiff of snakes—and not without reason. (Just think of what happened in the Garden of Eden.) There are 2,700 different types of snakes slithering around the globe. Most of them are horrid-looking but harmless, but some can kill you. Here's the lowdown on those creeping, crawling, tongue-flicking serpents.

HOW A SNAKE SNACKS

Snakes can smell with their tongues, see by sensing heat, and give most of us a major case of the creeps. They come in all sizes from small (about 7 inches long) to eat-an-entire-person-in-one-gulp big. In fact, 30-foot-long snakes are a common sight in the rain forests of Central and South America. But if you think the thought of a snake the length of a school bus is gross, wait until you find out what happens when the snake gets hungry!

Let's start with the PYTHON who has just ordered up a nice, plump rat for dinner (ratwurst anyone?). In less than a second, the snake will have bitten into that rat and coiled its body around it several times. The bite keeps the rat from scurrying away, but that's not what kills the furry fella. Every time the rat breathes out, the snake tightens its grip a little more. Exhale. Tighten. Exhale. Tighten some more. Finally (gasp!), the rat can't get any air into its lungs, and it suffocates. Now, *that* is a nasty death.

Next, it's chow-down time. All snakes swallow their food whole. That fat rat somehow has to fit through the snake's thin head and neck. How? Well, for one thing, a python's jaws can open 130 degrees. (Our jaws can manage only a measly 30). So as the snake's upper jaw points nearly straight upward, the lower jaw points nearly straight downward.

But that's not all. The snake's lower jaw is split in two, right down the middle, and is hinged by ligaments that are like giant rubber bands. This means that the snake can move the left side of its jaw without moving the right side. So when the snake has that rat in its mouth, it bites down on the left side and then opens the right side of its jaw, moves it forward over the rat, and bites down on that side. Then the snake does the same thing with the left side of its jaw. It keeps doing this side-by-side biting until it has the entire rat down its throat.

Other parts of a snake's skull stretch right along with the mouth. The end result? A snake that can easily swallow a critter three times larger than its own head! It's as if you could unhinge your jaw and open your mouth wide enough to swallow a basketball whole and then slide that entire basketball down your throat without chewing it. Neat trick!

PLEASE PASS THE SWEET-AND-SOUR RAT

Now, a snake can't just pick up a rat and shove it down its throat. It has no hands!

But it does have really strong cheek and throat muscles. For easy swallowing, dear, departed Ratty enters the snake's throat headfirst. (Snakes eat all sorts of things that have sticking-up parts—things like birds, porcupines, even goats with horns. So headfirst dining insures that anything sticking up will get pressed back as it enters the snake's mouth.)

Once Ratty is completely engulfed, the powerful muscles of the snake's body squeeze supper into the stomach, an event that takes several hours. Digesting an entire rat takes time too, but this presents a truly gross problem. The snake's food has to be digested before it starts to rot and give off toxic chemicals. Since it can take up to two weeks to digest Ratty (who is by now quite dead), that fresh rat can easily turn into spoiled rat. So snakes frequently end up barfing dinner, just like you might if you ate something really revolting. By the way, partially digested, week-old rat is pretty disgusting to look at!

The biggest snake meal on record? An AFRICAN ROCK PYTHON once stuffed a 130-pound antelope down its slender little throat.

The hungriest? An ASIAN RETICULATED PYTHON snacked on a 28-pound goat, was still hungry, and went back for seconds (a 39-pounder this time). A few days later, still in the mood for a little snack, it downed a 71-pound ibex. Now, that's an appetite!

Snakes *can* swallow a whole person, though probably not a linebacker. For those of you who doubt this, an entire human body was cut out of a reticulated python in Indonesia a couple of years ago, covered in slime and gastric juice.

This emerald tree boa has mastered the art of saying "ahhhh."

"Let me slip into something more comfortable." A king snake sheds his skin.

MOLTING IS REVOLTING

What if your skin wasn't able to stretch with you as you grew? It would have to rip open to make room for the new, bigger you. That's what happens to snakes. About every six weeks or so, they shed their entire outer layer of skin, from tip to tail, and slither away in a fresh new larger-size skin. It's called MOLTING. You can tell when a snake is about to molt because it gets really sluggish, its eyes get cloudy, and its skin looks dull as dirty dishwater.

Gross but Good

The pit vipers of Brazil and Argentina have a deadly venom that can both kill *and* save lives! Huh? How's that? Researchers have found a compound in the venom that has become the mainstay of medicines used to treat high blood pressure and heart failure. And the Mayan Pit Viper's venom is used in the treatment of stroke victims.

TONGUE TWISTERS

Since snakes have no hands, a fork for a tongue makes sense, right? (No, they don't actually eat with it.) In fact, the tongue is one of the most important parts of a snake's body. And while a snake can taste and feel with it, the truth is that the notch in the snake's tongue is mostly used to help them do their smelling. They don't even have to open their mouths to slide the little sniffer out. There is a slit in the upper jaw that the snake flicks its tongue through.

Snakes can smell the difference between food, fun (who was that adorable snake that just slid past?), and foes! They can even spread their tongue forks apart and smell two different things at the same time!

WELCOME TO THE SNAKE PIT!

ANACONDAS
(*ann-ah-con-das*) are the heaviest snakes around. They can weigh in at up to 235 pounds. They're the ones that are as long as a school bus! Anacondas live in or near water and they usually drown their victims

"I can't believe I ate the whole thing." This anaconda has swallowed a whole caiman.

before devouring them! (Which is probably just as well, if you think about it.) One neat thing about them is that the markings on their tails are unique, just like our fingerprints!

GARTER SNAKES are the ones you are most likely to run screaming from in the woods or in Grandma's garden, but they are harmless to

A Bit on Snake Bites

✻ Forty-five thousand people a year get bitten by snakes in the United States. Only 8,000 of the bites are from poisonous snakes. And only about a dozen people die from their bites. Bad pit vipers are usually to blame! But if you're bitten, get medical treatment within two hours and you should be okay.

✻ There are about 20 species of poisonous snakes in America, but there are four that seem to cause the most trouble—the coral, the rattler, the copperhead, and the water moccasin. Most bites occur in southern and southwestern states, but poisonous snakes have slithered into every state in the continental United States.

✻ The largest venomous snake in the world is the King Cobra, which can grow to be 18 feet long. These snakes live in India and they're the ones that have that little hood that flares out when they are feeling grouchy. Their babies are born loaded with venom and ready to kill!

✻ The head of a decapitated snake can still bite! Yikes!

✻ The best way to avoid tangling with a snake? Watch where you put your hands and feet and look before you sit or squat while enjoying the great outdoors. And never move a rock, a plank, or a log by sticking your fingers under it. Who knows what might be lurking there.

✻ Forget making an X-shaped cut on the bite and sucking the poison out. It doesn't really help. The best snakebite kit? The keys to the car . . . a car that can drive the victim to an emergency room immediately!

humans. They grow to over 4 feet and live every-where in America except the desert regions. They have stripes running down their sides, and spend their days shoving frogs and toads down their throats. Mommy garter snakes can give birth to 50 squirming, wriggling, fully

A wriggling, writhing snake pit—a garter snake mom and her many babies.

formed snakes at a time. That's a lot of birth-days to remember!

MAMBAS One of the deadliest types of slith-erers around is the MAMBA, which belongs to the same family as the COBRAS. All members of this family have fangs with deep grooves that transport a lethal venom. One bite from a mamba can make your muscles seize up so tightly that your back breaks! And Indian cobras don't even have to get their fangs on

Looks sweet. Isn't. Mambas are some of the deadliest snakes around. This green mamba likes to hang out in trees.

you to do their damage. They can rise up and "spit" venom directly into their victims' eyes, blinding them!

PIT VIPER Little beady eyes. Flaring nostrils. Head shaped like a triangle. Curving fangs, sharp as hypodermic needles. No, it's not your English teacher . . . it's a PIT VIPER! Rattlesnakes, cottonmouths, and copperheads are all members of this deadly gang. Pit vipers have well-developed pit organs (located between the eyes and nostrils) that they use to track their prey. Pit organs detect heat, so they allow the snake to "see"—and creep up on—a warm-blooded

animal in the dark. (Some other nasty snakes, such as the pythons and the boas, also have pit organs.) Vipers kill their prey by injecting poisonous venom before devouring them for dinner. (By the way, all vipers come equipped with at least three sets of extra fangs, just in case one set gets damaged!)

This green tree python has squeezed the breath—and the life—out of this unlucky mouse.

PYTHONS AND BOAS The longest snakes in the world are PYTHONS and BOAS. (Pythons tend to be a little bigger than boas.) One bush pilot in Africa swears he saw a 50-foot snake rising 10 feet up in the air, ready to strike! (But relax. Most pythons max out at about 30 feet.) These snakes suffocate their victims before stuffing them down their throats.

Best bet? If any snake starts sliding toward you, don't stand around waiting for it to introduce itself. Hightail it out of there.

Pit vipers are heat-seeking serpents. This purple-backed one lives in China.

out. They're called VIBRISSAE (*vi-briss-eye*). Their job is to trap stuff that might try to sneak in, like black soot, small bugs, evil bacteria, and alien space invaders (just kidding about that last one!). If you've ever wondered why Uncle Frank's got more hair in his nose than on his head, now you'll know that it's just his vibrissae in need of a barber.

Back to the dust in your nose. Now what? The next line of defense is the MUCOUS MEMBRANE. Imagine a damp, sticky doormat that germs and dirt have to wipe their feet on. This membrane makes a gooey liquid that's perfect for catching and destroying bacteria. It will take your body about 20 minutes to cook up a fresh batch of mucus—close to a quart a day (about the size of four glasses of milk)! What turns mucus those delightful colors? It all has to do with the type of bacteria and bacterial waste that's mixed up in it.

SNOT

It's happened to everyone. There you sit, trying to look cool, when something damp and runny decides to roll out of your nose and start dripping down your upper lip.

Snort. Sniff. Swipe. Then, when no one's looking, swallow! If you're like most of us, you've probably done your fair share of nose-mining, followed by nose-dining. What you are digging out when you do this is MUCUS (*mew-cus*), gooey stuff that is actually one of the best friends your body has. Let's nose around a bit and find out what those little boogers actually do!

I HAB A STUFFY DOSE

Pretend you are a hunk of dust that's just been sucked into a nose. You slide in through the nostrils (those two funky-looking little holes) and sneak past some coarse, wiry hairs that are supposed to keep dusty old things like you

The difference between little kids and big kids? Little kids pick their noses in public whereas big kids (and for that matter grownups) pick them on the sly.

A big ahhhh-choooo captured mid-blow by a high-speed camera shows the thousands of mucus droplets scattered by a single sneeze.

ANYONE FOR PHLEGM-A-NADE?

Can you say MUCOPOLYSACCHARIDES (_mew-koh-pol-ee-sack-ah-rides_) three times, fast? That's the stuff that's cooked up in that mucous membrane, squeezed out by special slime-makers called GOBLET CELLS. Yummy. A goblet full of mucus . . . now there's something you wouldn't want to drink. Well, surprise! You swallow well over two cups of snot each and every day! Mucus is actually 95 percent water, 2 to 3 percent salt, and 2 percent MUCIN (_mew-sin_), a special kind of protein that's actually used to make some types of glue.

When you catch a cold, those membranes go wild, making lots of extra goo to trap the enemy—

those vile viruses and bacteria. (You can read about those evil things in BACTERIA on page 6 and VIRSUSES on page 184.) Now you have a nose full of germs and dirt trapped like a bunch of dead bugs on flypaper. How does it all get out? Read on.

CILIA (_sill-ee-uh_) are tiny little hairs. How tiny? Well, you'd have to lay 25,000 cilia end to end just to stretch 1 inch! There are millions of them in your nose, waving back and forth more than a thousand times a minute. Some sweep odor molecules to the brain. Others work a bit like tiny brooms, pushing the dirt-encrusted mucus toward the exit . . . your esophagus and eventually your stomach! The digestive juices in your tummy are terrific at killing the trapped bacteria. Dinner anyone?

MUCUS, MUCUS EVERYWHERE

Guess what. Your nose isn't the only part of your body loaded with mucus. Whole parts of you wouldn't work without it! In fact, if it weren't for mucus, you wouldn't be alive today, since mucus keeps your stomach from eating itself up, and helps make making babies possible.

You also have mucus factories in your inner ears and in the airways of your lungs. Mucus made in this part of your body is called PHLEGM (_flem_). (Not to be confused with the Spanish dessert flan, though they are the same consistency.)

SUPERSONIC SNOT

For high-speed action, nothing can beat a big, wet, messy sneeze. It travels out of your body at speeds high enough to get you a ticket on the highway. Some sneezes have been clocked at more than 100 miles an

THE PUTRID PAST

"**Snot**" is the word we use to describe the mucus that lives in your nose. And although Mom and Dad might not like you calling it "snot," that was what everyone, even kings and queens, called it back in the 1600s. In the 1500s, books on manners even advised as to the proper way to pick—one finger versus two, and what to do if a stray bit fell off!

hour! Sneezes happen when the cilia get super-agitated by things such as cold germs or ALLER-GENS (*al-ur-jenz*)—plant pollen, pet dander, and other nose invaders. Your body just can't wait to get rid of these offenders the usual way, so it blows them out. And here's a thrilling thought: that spray of snot is filled with all sorts of germ-carrying particles. Some can travel across the room. Some can float in the air for almost an hour. Duck!

YOU DON'T HAVE A COLD, SO WHY IS YOUR NOSE RUNNING?

Ever wondered why your nose drips on cold days? Remember,

REMEMBER: Don't digitally manipulate your nasal vestibule!

PICKING YOUR NOSE IS DEFINITELY UNCOOL!

the mucus in your nose is 95 percent water. And kind of like dew on a chilly morning, all the water in your nose and in your breath comes together, or condenses. The condensed moisture forms big, heavy drops, which then run out of your nose, over your lips, down your chin, and onto your brand-new sweater.

But here's a neat fact. When the temperature outdoors is 10°F and you inhale that icy air through your nose, the cilia, mucous membranes, and circulating blood frantically try to warm it up. By the time the air hits the back of your nose, it'll be a much warmer 86 degrees! Too bad feet can't warm up that fast.

The Subject Was Noses

Oh those wacky scientific types! They just love giving long names to ordinary things, turning to Latin and Greek for their secret code words. *Rhin,* a word-starter that describes all things "nosy," comes from the Greek word for that pointy thing in the middle of your face!

✳ **RHINORRHEA** (*rye-no-ree-ah*) is the medical term for those lovely green and yellow fluids that run from the nose. Kind of like diarrhea of the nose.

✳ **RHINITIS** (*rye-ni-tis*) is what doctors call it when the mucous membrane in your nose is inflamed.

✳ **RHINOVIRUS** (*rye-no-vi-rus*) is what we usually call the viruses that cause a head cold.

✳ **RHINOPLASTY** (*rye-no-plas-tee*) is the ever-popular "nose job," invented in India over 1,500 years ago, where a nasty type of punishment involved cutting off someone's nose to spite his face. If you were caught stealing, your nose was snipped off as a mark of your evil deed. No one

wanted to walk around noseless, so doctors secretly figured out how to rebuild the missing part.

✳ **RHINOTILLEXOMANIA** (*rye-no-till-ex-o-may-nee-ah*) is what scientists call nose picking. (Leave it to scientists to come up with a 10-dollar word for something as lowdown and dirty as that!) There are even researchers who study nose picking, asking nosy questions like, "Do you look at what you have pulled out?" and "What do your nose pickings most taste like?"

✳ **RHINOCEROS** means "nose-horn." (Perhaps these beasts would like the name of a good rhinoplasty surgeon.)

SPIDERS

Remember the itsy-bitsy spider from your preschool days? Sounds kind of cute, doesn't it? But those big hairy guys—the ones that come crawling across your face in the middle of the night or leave those icky webs for you to get tangled up in—are a spider of a different color. And there's nothing like looking up to see a spider dangling in front of your face or finding spider-spinnings stuck in your teeth to send a chill down your spine.

ALONG CAME A SPIDER AND SAT DOWN BESIDE HER . . .

There are more than 36,000 different kinds of spiders crawling up walls and down shirt backs all over the world. Spider scientists (who, by the way, are called arachnologists) think they've only counted about half of the species that are probably out there. Some are as big as your hand. Some are so small, you can't even see them swiftly scurrying up your leg. Let's put it this way: If it has eight legs and a body with two

parts, it's probably time to hide your curds and get out of the way!

Spiders are ARTHRO-PODS (*ar-throw-pods*), which is a fancy word for critters with jointed bodies and skeletons on the outside. (Insects and crustaceans are also arthropods.)

Spiders belong to a group of arthropods called ARACHNIDS (*ah-rack-nidz*), which got their name from a Greek myth about a woman named Arachne (*ah-rack-nee*). (You can read about other disgusting arachnids in the MITES, SCORPIONS, and TICKS entries.) Arachne was a weaver who made beautiful cloth, but she also liked to brag about how talented she was. She started

Garden spiders weave intricate deathtraps for unsuspecting bugs. Read on to see if you can identify what kind of web this is.

Gross but Good

Spider silk is stronger than steel threads of the same thickness. Scientists are studying the chemistry of the silk so they can duplicate it to make parachutes and lightweight bulletproof vests.

telling everyone that she was a better weaver than the great goddess Athena (and let me tell you, competing with the Greek gods is a big no-no). So Athena got mad and turned Arachne into a tiny creature with really hairy legs, which is never a nice thing to do to a woman!

I SPY . . . A SPIDER!

There are two main types of spiders—WEB BUILDERS and WANDERING SPIDERS. Here's how to know what you're screaming at.

Spiderwebs do more than just get caught in your hair. If you are a spider, webs are perfect for snagging a snack. All spiders can make silk, but the web builders are the real pros. They have long skinny legs, perfect for tightrope walking on the thin strands of their webs, tiny eyes, and really terrible eyesight, so they depend on their legs to "see" for them by feeling ahead for danger.

Spiders can produce different kinds of silk—sticky, slippery, thin, thick—whatever it takes to catch some supper! After its web is spun, the web-spinning spider waits in the center, one leg on each spoke. They know it won't be long before a bug banquet gets stuck on the sticky silk.

Wandering spiders don't trap their food in webs. Instead, they hide under leaves or bits of tree bark, then wait for something yummy to come along. They have two huge front eyes, four smaller eyes tucked underneath, and two small eyes above—eight eyes in all. And with all those peepers, they can spot just about anything before it sees them. They have very hairy legs and each hair is like a little fingertip—very sensitive. Wanderers have two claws on each foot, with hairy pads in between so they can walk on very slippery surfaces, like the smooth bark of some trees.

Why don't spiders get caught in their own webs? Because their tiny little toesies are covered in oily secretions!

WEB STYLES

Let's pretend that you are a non-oily-footed bug. You've just gone out for a little spin, and before you know it you're all tangled up. Chances are you've gotten tangled in one of these four different spider web styles.

✳ ORB WEBS radiate out from the center in a circle shape, like spokes on a wheel.

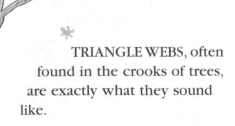

✳ TRIANGLE WEBS, often found in the crooks of trees, are exactly what they sound like.

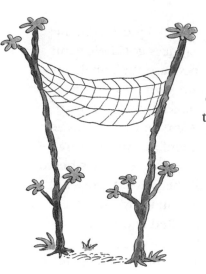

❋ SHEET WEBS look a little like a hammock. Forest-dwelling spiders like to dine in these.

❋ TANGLE WEBS are a real mess. And anyone who finds himself caught in one of these is likely to be in a real mess, too because it's the kind that black widow spiders spin. (More about them later.)

Webworks

Spider silk is made in the SPINNERET (_spin-er-et_), a special organ in the spider's abdomen. Out oozes a yucky liquid made by special glands. The ooze turns to sticky threads when it comes into contact with the air. And spider silk isn't just used to make webs—armed with those strands of silk, spiders can also whip up a parachute, a cozy cocoon, a tightrope, a fishing line, or a lifeline if they suddenly have to leap from a tall building.

It's been said that if you took 2 million spiders (and some experts estimate that 2 million can easily be found in just one small, grassy field), they would spin enough silk to circle the equator. In nine days, they could crank out enough to reach the moon!

TALK ABOUT TOSSING YOUR COOKIES. . .

Spiders don't really eat their dinner . . . they drink it! Here's how.

Let's say you are a web builder, hanging out on your web, and you feel a case of the munchies coming on. A juicy fly makes the mistake of resting on one of your sticky strands. Aha! Dinner!

First, you use your fangs to inject your victim with paralyzing juice. (Almost all spiders are venomous, but relatively few have venom powerful enough to harm a human.) Now your victim can't move, but it's still alive. Then—this is the gross part—you puke up a whole wad of digestive juice all over the victim. Your acidic throw-up dissolves the poor fellow and turns him into a mushy glob. Yum . . . an insect smoothie! Perfect when you are feeling a little peckish.

If there are no bugs on the menu and a spider gets really hungry, it can eat its web! The webs have a lot of protein and an average one takes about 30 minutes to devour.

A SAMPLING OF SLEAZY SPIDERS

Here's the scoop on some of the grossest spiders crawling around—hairy legs and all. The biggest ones have fat, furry bodies. Some have bodies 4 inches long, with inch-long fangs poking out of their mouths. Their outstretched legs can measure up to a foot in length. That's bigger than this book!

AUSTRALIAN SOCIAL SPIDERS Young AUSTRALIAN SOCIAL SPIDERS don't have to worry about good table manners. When they are born, Mom fattens herself up and turns herself into a living refrigerator. Her babies suck her blood until she gets so weak, she can't move. Then the little spiders barf all over her, turn her into mush, and eat her until there is no more Mom! Talk about ingratitude!

BIRD-EATERS The award for the flat-out grossest-looking spider will have to go to the BIRD-EATER. It's big (a 9-inch leg span and a 3-inch body), it's hairy, and it can devour a hummingbird and still have room for dessert!

BLACK WIDOWS If you happen to pick up a long, shiny black spider (and if you do, you might want to see someone about your obvious lack of *a brain!*) and notice a red, hourglass-shaped marking on its tummy, you're in for serious trouble. BLACK WIDOW SPIDERS are some of the deadliest critters around! These pain-producers can be found in every part of America, except Alaska and Hawaii. Within an hour of being bitten by one, victims will feel a lot of pain at the bite site, along with a bad headache, nausea, and vomiting. Muscles can start to go into spasms (Ever have a really bad cramp? Imagine your whole body doing that!) Very young children and very old people can die from black widow bites.

THE PUTRID PAST

Back in the days when outhouses were where you went when you had to go, spiders were what many people ended up grabbing instead of toilet paper! Spiders loved the outhouses' dark corners. They also often ended up attached to body parts that were being waved in their faces—especially boys' and men's peeing parts!

By the way, these spiders got their name because the female spiders (which are much bigger than the guys) sometimes devour their menfolk after mating.

Everyone's heard of the Black Widow, but did you know that there are Red and Brown Widow spiders, too? Their bites are just as lethal. It's best to hightail it to the emergency room if you have been bitten by a widow spider of any color.

BRAZILIAN HUNTSMANS The speediest killer award goes to the BRAZILIAN HUNTSMAN SPIDER, which has the deadliest neurotoxic venom on earth. (Neurotoxins work on the nervous system, causing paralysis.) This spider can paralyze your vital organs, leaving you unable to breathe! The good news is that these really gross spiders mostly live deep in the rain forests of Central and South America, far away from people.

BROWN RECLUSES But just because you live thousands of miles away from the nearest rain forest doesn't mean you're 100 percent safe. Another dangerous critter lurks in North America—the BROWN RECLUSE SPIDER. It likes to hide under piles—rock piles, wood piles, and even piles of clothing. If you are bitten by a spider with a dark, violin-shaped marking on its back, get to the emergency room on the double. You will start hurting in a few hours and a bloody blister will swell up at the bite site.

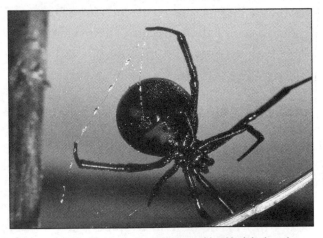

If you see a spider that looks like this one—with a black body and a red hourglass on its abdomen—scram! It's the deadly black widow!

CRABS AND BOLAS One type of spider thinks it's Dracula and another thinks it's an Argentinian cowboy. The CRAB SPIDER bites other bugs' necks and drains them completely dry of blood! And the BOLAS SPIDER spins a long thread with a big wad of shiny, sticky stuff on the end. It twirls it around so it flickers in the moonlight. Moths think it looks cool and they fly in for a closer look. Before they know what's happening, they've been lassoed, tied up, and eaten!

TARANTULAS (*ta-ranch-ah-las*) are the best known of the real baddies. These *big* hairy spiders can make your life miserable, so don't toy with their affections. When a tarantula is annoyed, the hair on its belly stiffens. Each hair is like a little barbed dart, and a tarantula has a lot of little hairs—which equals a very big ouch! Those hair-barbs can puncture and inflame your skin. Luckily, although tarantulas are annoying, they're not deadly.

Tarantulas may be furry but they're not cuddly. Their hairs are sharp and can irritate your skin. Handle with care.

TRAP-DOOR SPIDERS dig a tunnel and line it with silk. Then they close it with a movable door. When they sense the vibrations of a victim walking by, they throw open the door to "welcome" their new guest. Bugs check in . . . but they don't check out!

SPITTING

Ever have a big glob of gluey stuff stuck just at the back of your throat? You just never know quite what to do with it. Should you swallow it, snort it, or sling it out of your mouth? Well, spitting may be considered pretty gross nowadays, but a hundred years ago, it was totally cool to spit. Every elegant home had a special little container, called a SPITTOON, for folks to leave their mouth deposits in. Don't believe me? Read on!

CHEW ON THIS

It all goes back to King James II, an English ruler who lived in the late 1600s. He hated tobacco smoking so much that he made it a crime to smoke. If you were caught smoking it was off to jail with you! Ask any smoker how

Gross but Good

The fancy word for spitting is to EXPECTO-**RATE** *(ek-speck-toe-rate).* You might have heard of cough medicine with an expectorant in it. That's a fancy word for stuff that loosens phlegm and makes you cough up and spit out big globs of gray-green stuff. That's one time when spitting is good, because that big old ball of mucus will have trapped a lot of harmful germs in it. And let's face it. The only good germ is a "gone" germ.

Spit has other dandy uses too. In the army, soldiers spit-shine their boots. And deep-sea divers spit into their masks before they put them on to keep them from fogging up.

hard it is to quit, and you'll understand why for some folks, this was a real problem.

Not only did King James's rule about smoking send people into their closets to secretly light up, he ended up turning people on to other ways of getting their tobacco fix. Out of desperation, addicts discovered that if you chewed or sniffed ground up tobacco, it had pretty much the same effect as smoking it. SNUFF users would grab a pinch of ground-up tobacco, hold it under their nose and inhale sharply! That made them sneeze quite violently and yet, oddly, they seemed to enjoy it. And, worse still, people ended up as quidders—the old English word for people who liked to quid, or chew, tobacco. (Too bad they didn't just "quid" altogether—they'd have lived longer!)

Now, if you swallow the juice that's created from chewing tobacco, you will get very sick. In fact, you will most likely hurl. So you have to spit the juice out someplace. That's why the spittoon (also called a cuspidor) was created.

By the early 1800s, everybody, not just in

England, but all over Europe and in America, chewed tobacco, from sweet old grandmas to young teenagers. Of course, in those days, the average age to kick the bucket was around 40. And chewing tobacco was probably one of the reasons people didn't live very long, since, as we all know now, tobacco is very bad for your health!

Every home, every train station, every church, every tiny shack, and every room of every beautiful mansion had a cuspidor. In fact, the very first official act of President Andrew Jackson was the purchase of 20 spittoons for the White House! People even had easy chairs with a little drawer on the side to deposit their spit in. Trust me on this. I'm not quidding!

Everybody was chewing and spitting up a storm. Naturally, people wanted to be considered good at whatever it was they were doing. So spitting became something of an art form. Creating a good-sized "pinger" (so named for the sound a wad of tobacco made when it hit the side of a spittoon) became a skill to be envied.

No doubt about it. Spitting was hot stuff a hundred years ago. That's why in the movie *Titanic,* Leonardo DiCaprio teaches Kate Winslet how to let loose a loogie. I'm telling you, *everyone* was doing it!

GREAT BALLS OF SPIT

Mom, apple pie, and baseball. A big chunk of what makes America great, right? But no matter which team you're rooting for, it's a sure bet that most baseball players are champions at one sport—hawking those loogies. Spitting and baseball became linked because many players chewed tobacco to ease the stress and pressure of playing. Nowadays, they often chew on other things, like pumpkin seeds or gum, but nervousness can still make for a mouthful of saliva.

Just like there are rules for baseball, there

are rules for spitting in baseball. Spitting in the dugout? If you must. But spitting on someone's face is a big no-no! So when one well-known ballplayer lost his temper and let one fly in the face of an umpire, all spit broke loose. Spitting became front-page news and one New York City radio station thought it would be downright sporting to present that saliva-rich player with a big jar filled with gobs of the stuff (just in case his mouth got dry the next time an umpire annoyed him). So, while fans lined up to buy play-off tickets, they invited folks to step right up and spit. Their goal? To give the spitter a filled-to-the-rim jar of that gross white stuff! And many a fan made a contribution to the spit jar!

Baseball also gave us the word "spitballs," which nowadays are considered a baseball no-no, but at one time were A-OK. Back in 1902, an outfielder named George Hildebrand shared a radical discovery with a pitcher named Elmer Strickland. If you hawked a loogie onto a baseball, the ball would do all sorts of weird things when you threw it. It would wobble so much that the batter couldn't figure out where it was going to end up.

Most pitched balls follow a predictable arc. Curveballs do one thing. Split-fingered fastballs twist another way. But all pitches have one thing in common. The ball spins as it's thrown. Spit on a ball reduces air friction and keeps it from spinning as it's thrown (not to mention being extremely gross for the batter and the catcher!). With a glob of spit on a ball the arc becomes completely unpredictable. The ball dips and sways from side to side—sometimes as much as 11 feet. Batters can't figure out where the ball is going to end up as they watch it coming at them.

Throwing a spitball in a baseball game can get you in trouble. And guess what? Throwing that other kind of spitball—a wadded-up, chewed-on piece of paper—in the classroom can send you arcing toward the principal's office like a well-thrown spitball!

LOOGIE LAND

Nowadays, in the United States, it's considered both unhealthy and uncool to spit in public. But there are some parts of the world where everybody still spits. In China, for example, both men and women don't hesitate to let one fly on the finest floors—in banks, department stores, wherever and whenever they clear their throats, leaving trails of white globs behind them. And this happens fairly frequently because the air is so polluted in China that their poor bodies have to keep producing massive amounts of mucus just to trap all the soot and dirt trying to get into their lungs. So, a word to the wise: If you find yourself in China, watch where you walk!

In many places, spitting has become a sport! All across the world—at country fairs, church picnics, and sleep-away camps—people hold contests to see who can spit a watermelon seed the farthest. A man in Texas named Lee Wheelis claims to have spit a seed 68 feet, 9 1/4 inches.

So next time you have watermelon for dessert, why not practice becoming a world champion? Get out that tape measure and let those seeds rip. It's the only spitting that will actually get you into the *Guinness Book of Records*.

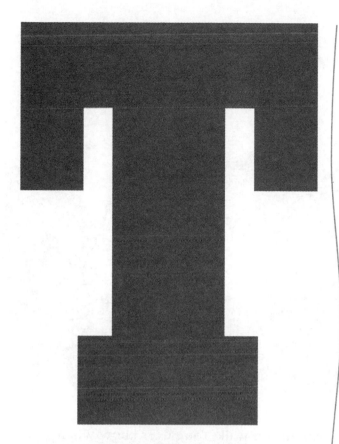

TAR PITS

Ever gone out for a walk along a blacktop road on a really hot day? Remember how that pavement felt—sort of soft and mushy? Maybe it got so soft you could even leave a footprint? Now, picture pools of soupy, sticky, gummy black tar. Imagine that leaves and dirt and dust have blown on top and are hiding the goo. Imagine being a not-too-bright animal and you've now got an idea about what a treacherous trap a TAR PIT can be.

RANCH OF TAR

That's what Rancho La Brea means in Spanish. And that's where California's La Brea Tar Pits are. Trapped within the pits' thick black gunk, scientists have found a treasure trove of skeletons of creatures long gone from the earth.

About 2 million years ago, thick oil from deep down in the rocky depths oozed up to form pools in crevices and cracks in the rocks on the surface. Once there, the oil's consistency changed. It got thick and very gluey. And it wasn't long before the first animals started getting that stuck-in-the-pit feeling.

HERBIVORES (*er-buh-vores*)—animals such as horses, bison, and camels that snacked on the grasses and grains that grew in the area—stumbled in and got trapped. Sensing a quick and easy kill, the CARNIVORES, greedy meat-eaters, closed in. But they also found themselves stuck, and stuck tight!

During the winter, cooler temperatures hardened the tar, and during the rainy season, swollen streams washed a layer of dirt and sediment over the rotting corpses. Then, as the warm summer weather returned, the whole fun-filled cycle repeated itself.

Many people think that there are dinosaurs trapped in the muck of La Brea. But this pit was an Ice Age creation, dating from about 2.5 million years ago. Dinosaurs were

If you visit the La Brea Tar Pits, you'll see this mastdon trapped in the tar. Don't feel too sorry for it, though—it's only a sculpture.

long dead by then. They kicked the bucket back in the Cenozoic era, about 65 million years ago.

Still, some really hefty animals are tucked away in there, ones that are bigger than the critters of today. Why? It's a basic law of nature: only the fittest survive. But "fit" is a relative term. A tyrannosaurus is stronger than a cockroach, but which one is still alive and kicking? Although, big sometimes is better, big needs more food. When food becomes scarce, like it was during the Ice Age, who wins? They who eat light!

Among the finds in the tar: giant lions (a head taller than the ones that prowl today), a 12-foot-tall mammoth (an elephant cousin) with 8-foot-long tusks, saber-toothed cats, and birds the size of big Buicks!

There's still tar (and a nasty, oily smell) in those pits. You can visit them and see for yourself, just seven miles from downtown Los Angeles in Hancock Park. And active tar pits still exist all over the world. Just watch

where you walk. You never know when you might end up with your feet glued to the ground!

A Nasty Note

In the late 1700s, Spanish explorers hiking through California found a tribe of Native Americans using asphalt (which is basically soft tar mixed with sand or gravel). The Yokut Indians had lots of uses for the tar. They patched roofs with it, made artworks from it, and used fist-sized balls of tar as a kind of money.

But getting the tar from the pits was one of the nastiest jobs around. The temperatures in the area hovered at around 120 degrees, and in the tar pits, the temperature was as high as 140 degrees. Working a tar seam was hot, horrible work. Men worked in their birthday suits and then had to be scraped off with a special knife at the end of the day. OUCH!

TICKS

Let's see. There's Lyme Disease. Rocky Mountain Spotted Fever. Russian Encephalitis. Bhanja Virus. Nairobi Sheep Disease. Omsk Hemorrhagic Fever. And the list goes on. A whole slew of diseases spread by one little creature can spell big trouble for people. So, how are you feeling? A little warm, did you say? Feel like you're coming down with something? Pick anything small and dark off your body lately? Had any close encounters with a TICK?

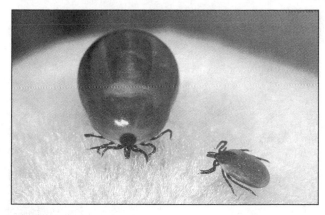

"Oooh, I think I ate too much." The eastern wood tick on the left has just had a good, long blood feast. The fellow on the right is ready for a meal.

TICK TOCK

Ticks are bloodthirsty little devils who can leave you anywhere from a little itchy to a lot dead! Like spiders, scorpions, and mites, ticks are ARACHNIDS (*ah-rack-nidz*), and there are about 800 different kinds of them worldwide. About 100 of those carry diseases, so you can see why they're not very popular.

Ticks are parasites. Of course, you know that parasites are too lazy to get a job, earn some money, and buy their own food at a proper grocery store like the rest of us. Instead, they simply drop on board some poor, unsuspecting creature, like a dog or a mouse or you, and make themselves at home. (See PARASITES on page 115 for more on these disgusting freeloaders.)

Ticks are lazy little dudes. They don't like to work too hard to find a host. A tick is willing to hang around on the tip of a blade of grass for a week, a month, even a year, just waiting for something tasty to cross its path. (This hanging around and waiting, by the way, is called QUESTING BEHAVIOR.) Ticks are nothing if not patient.

Ticks find their hunk-of-host by using their extreme sensitivity to carbon dioxide, the gas we mammals give off as we exhale. And since humans can't walk around holding their breath forever, it's only a matter of time before a tick hitches a ride on one.

Let's say you've gone for a walk in the woods and brushed up against a weed, and a hungry tick has grabbed onto your calf. Now what? That little bloodsucker is happier than a pig in mud, because it's just landed on an all-you-can-eat buffet. That tick will bury its mouthparts into your skin and grab on to you with its creepy little legs. The center part of its mouth, called the HYPOSTOME (*high-po-stome*), is shaped like a blunt harpoon. It's flat on the top, curved and barbed on the bottom,

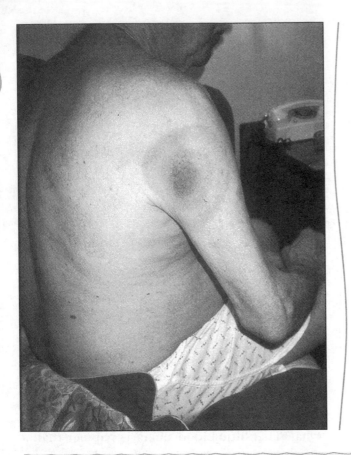

with sharp teeth at the front.

Those barbs are what anchor ticks tight to your flesh. Some ticks even make a cement-like substance that helps them grip even tighter. Settled comfortably in, it's time for a little bite. Their sharp teeth cut the blood vessels just below the skin, and a little swimming pool of blood forms. The tick starts sucking, swelling bigger and bigger until it's bloated and fat.

Why can't you feel a tick bite? Well, it's kind of like when you have a cavity and you go to the dentist. He injects something called an ANESTHETIC *(an-ess-thet-ic)* that puts your nerve endings to sleep so those screaming-in-agony pain messages just can't make it to the brain. Ticks have their own private supply of anesthetic, and they let loose with a little just before they dig in. So you feel nothing until it's too late.

Bull's-eye rashes are a warning sign of Lyme disease, a bacterial illness spread by tick bites.

Tick Alert

After screaming your head off when you make the gruesome discovery that a tick has moved in, here's what you should and should not do next.

✳ DON'T try to dig the tick out with your fingernails. It will break apart and leave body parts lodged in your skin. This can cause a serious infection.

✳ DON'T panic. Not every tick carries illness, and a tick has to be embedded for well over 24 hours to do any damage.

✳ DO tell your parents. And also tell your parents that this is the correct way to remove the critter. You'll need a pair of tweezers. Carefully grasp the head (not the body) of the tick with the tweezers. Pull firmly and steadily until the tick lets go; don't tug or jerk on the tick or the head might break off inside your skin. If you live in an area where tick-borne diseases are a problem, put the varmint in an empty jar and bring it to your local Board of Health or a doctor. They will test it to see what's up.

✳ DO be aware that some ticks are really tiny, about the size of the period at the end of this sentence. So always be on the lookout for "freckles" or "dirt specks" where there shouldn't be any. And DO wear light-colored long pants with socks pulled up over the cuffs if you're going to be out in the woods or walking through a field of tall grass.

✳ DON'T ignore a funny rash, a strange achy feeling in your joints, or something that feels like the flu. These can be the vague first symptoms of LYME DISEASE. If you have any of these symptoms, especially after having been in known tick territory, you'd better go to a doctor and get checked out.

The tick sucks and sucks and sucks some more. At the same time, it squirts out saliva mixed with an ANTICOAGULANT (*an-tee-co-ag-u-lent*) to keep your blood from getting clumpy and lumpy. And that's where the trouble begins. (By the way, ticks aren't the only ones to use an anesthetic and anticoagulant while sucking blood; LEECHES do, too. Read about them on page 88.)

DEADLY DROOL

Why are ticks so deadly? Well, the problem is they infect us with germs for which we have no IMMUNITY (*im-you-nit-ee*). All creatures, including humans, carry teeny organisms in their bodies. We have immunities to many of the microbes that live in us, such as the ones that help us digest our food.

What exactly is immunity? Well, imagine this. You see a really repulsive horror movie. You've screamed for an hour, gnawed your fingernails down to the nub, and generally felt like hurling through the whole thing. But you decide to watch it again anyway. In fact, you rent the video and watch it over and over and over, until the grossest scenes don't bother you at all. They even begin to seem a little silly. Immunities in your body work the same way. Your body gets used to whatever is upsetting it, and isn't bothered by it anymore.

But when a tick bites, it put alien animal germs in a new place, a place where they have never been before. Tick saliva can be filled with bacteria, viruses, and protozoans (tiny one-celled animals) that the tick picked up while it was slurping up the blood of its last victim. Say a tick last dined on a mouse, then a deer. Then it latches on to you. The tick brings mouse organisms and deer organisms into your bloodstream when they feast. People have no immunity to these new diseases, and so we can get very sick.

TOILETS

You've got to go to the bathroom. You lock the door and take your seat. You read a comic book or two. You inspect your belly button for interesting items. You wipe. (You use WAY too much paper.) You flush. The water pours in from the tank and swirls round and round, before it all gets sucked away. Done!

For all of you out there who have ever wondered how the TOILET came to be, or where it all goes when you go, here goes.

THE HISTORY OF TOILETS

One day, long, long ago, some lucky fellow happened to get the urge to take a dump when he was wading across a stream. When

For the person who has everything: A 24-karat-gold potty seat encrusted with diamonds, rubies, and sapphires.

he did, he noticed that his leftovers simply washed away. No muss, no fuss! Most importantly—no nasty smell!

From that moment on, water and bathrooms were forever linked!

About 5,000 years ago, the first in-home potties were invented. Cold weather was probably the reason. Imagine this. You live in northern Scotland, a place where it rains just about every day of the year. It's cold and damp. The wind is howling and it's the middle of the night. All of a sudden, you've gotta go. Feel like going outside? Didn't think so. So some clever person devised a drain that led from the hut down into a pit.

By 2500 B.C., some of the cities of the great ancient civilizations (places in China, India, and the Middle East) had crude sewage systems—drains that led from each house to a big common pit, called a CESSPOOL. The cesspool had to be emptied on a regular basis and the stuff hauled away from the city and dumped somewhere.

But all too often, in most parts of the world—small villages and tiny towns—you just pooped into a pot and then dumped it out in the backyard (or out onto the street). Or maybe you dug a big hole and slowly filled it in. To get some idea of how absolutely vile that was, imagine the average cow pasture. Lots of big, mushy cow patties just waiting to be stepped in. Now, imagine walking through towns whose streets were just like those cow pastures. Back then, you had to *really* remember to wipe your feet when you came home at night!

The first-known flush toilet made its appearance in Greece on the isle of Crete about 3,700 years ago! Naturally, it belonged to the queen. It had a wooden seat, an earthenware pan, and a whole mess of drains and pipes that "flushed" the wastes away when water was poured into the system.

As Greek civilization rose, the toilet was improved upon. They invented group potties! That way, more than just one person could have a go at it. Marble benches with a few separate holes led to a ditch with water running through it.

In ancient Rome, around 50 B.C., "toilet

paper" was invented, except that it wasn't really paper. It worked like this. Next to each latrine, there was a bucket filled with saltwater. Stuck in this bucket was a stick with a sponge tied to the end of it. You used the spongy end, then put it back in the salty water. Ever heard the expression "getting the wrong end of the stick"? Well, now you know where it comes from!

There was a big, big problem in Rome, though. They made metal pipes to carry water in and out of the home. Those pipes were made from lead, because lead was easy to curve and bend. Only one problem. As you all know, lead is a

THE PUTRID PAST

In the mid-1500s, the King of France ruled that there was to be no more peeing or pooping in the streets. A proper cesspool was now required. But eventually those tanks got filled up. So what happened then?

The French simply called upon their local Maître Fi-Fis. (Sounds like a poodle groomer, no? NOT!) These guys visited the cesspools in the still of the night, carrying ladles and buckets and pulleys and ladders. They skimmed the liquid portions off the top using buckets, then climbed on in and shoveled out the harder-to-get-at hunks.

Naturally, this was not considered a particularly cool job. But it had to get done, so it paid pretty well. And since everyone knew that failure to pay up promptly might lead to the smearing of the Fi-Fi's buckets on the sides of the house, Fi-Fis rarely had trouble collecting their fees.

no-no because it's poisonous. The same pipes that carried waste out of the house were bringing in drinking water that was full of lead. Some say that one of the reasons the Roman Empire crumbled was because everyone went ga-ga from lead poisoning.

DOWN THE DRAIN

When Rome fell to invaders in A.D. 476, so did the potty. During the Middle Ages, also called the Dark Ages (from A.D. 500 to A.D. 1400), when knights were bold and wore those clunky suits of armor, plumbing took a nosedive. You know those moats that circled the castles? There's another reason they kept invading armies out. Yup, you guessed it. They doubled as a giant toilet.

Those were dark times, the Dark Ages. For those 900 or so years in Europe, people pooped and peed in pots kept near their beds, called CHAMBER POTS. When they were filled to the rim, some lucky person would walk over to the window, and shout "gardez l'eau!" *(garday low),* which means "watch out for the water." The French, being polite, invented the expression, but the English picked it up and mispronounced it as "gardy loo." (To this day a toilet is called a "loo" in England.) The only problem with this polite warning is that it was shouted out at approximately the same second the pot's contents were land-

PLEASE DON'T SQUEEZE THE SPONGES

Space Dumping

How do astronauts manage to "go" in space? Without gravity to weigh things down, pee and poop simply float around in the air. This is not something you want to see hovering in the spacecraft around you. Here are a few facts about space toiletry.

❄ The first astronauts used plastic bags with sticky strips to attach them to their rumps. They did their duty in the bag, then they froze the poop in the bags and returned them to earth for scientific study. Wow! Poop-sicles!

❄ Nowadays, astronauts have to buckle up before they can take a dump. They have special thigh seatbelts to keep them firmly attached to the toilet. You know how Mom's vacuum cleaner sucks up dirt? Outer space potties have a vacuum in them to suck away the poop. The seats are also designed to form a tight seal around an astronaut's bottom so nothing can accidentally float away.

❄ The astronauts aboard *Apollo 13* referred to peeing as "visiting the constellation U-ri-ine." (You, of course, know the constellation is really called Orion.) They peed into little baggies, then sent the contents through an airlock to be sprayed out into outer space. Bet our as-yet-undiscovered pals from other planets really appreciate that!

❄ Some spacesuits have a built-in pee-collector inside. It catches and stores the pee for later dumping in the shuttle or space station waste management system.

❄ The *Endeavor* space shuttle has a 23-million-dollar restroom! Everything slides into neat easy-to-replace canisters. (The older-style potties sometimes found the astronauts mashing their poops down into special containers with a spatula!)

ing in the street. You had to walk fast and carry a big umbrella in those days!

Everyone thinks that a man named Thomas Crapper invented the modern flush toilet. Well, they're wrong! It was a fellow named John Harrington. He built it for his godmother Queen Elizabeth I of England in the late 1500s. That's why the bathroom is sometimes called the "john." But it didn't catch on for a couple of hundred years. Crapper's contribution was merely one of improving on Harrington's idea. In the late 1800s, he invented all sorts of plumbing-related products, such as pipe joints, drains, and the little tanks that hold the water above the potty seat.

IN CASE YOU'VE WONDERED...

Reading on the can is a pretty common habit, but I'll bet you don't know how that activity got started. In the 1700s, American colonists built outhouses—little buildings with a wooden seat over a pit or a big bucket. Old newspapers were kept out there and recycled. It was very practical. You could read a page, rip it out, and then use it as toilet paper! (Warning! Newspaper can be a bit rough on tender spots, if you know what I mean.)

FOLLOW THAT FLUSH!

Your dirty bathwater, the suds in the washing machine that just soaked your skivvies, that trip to the can in the middle of the night. It's all just one big happy family when it's time to leave the building. To a thirsty sewer pipe, it's all just waste water.

In big cities and bigger towns, every house has pipes that hook up with an underground maze of big and little pipes called sewers. If you could peel back the concrete and look beneath the streets, you'd be amazed at the intricate web of main pipes and branch pipes, lateral drains and sub-mains, trunks and outfalls. It's really something!

Where does it all go? Let's follow the flush in a typical big city. Let's pretend you are a piece of t.p. that has just wiped a butt and been tossed into the toilet. The handle is flicked . . . and you are swished, sloshed, and sucked away. After sinking lower and lower through a series of pipes, you will end up in a sewage treatment plant.

An average big-city treatment plant will process about 72 Olympic-sized swimming pools worth of poop, pee, and other wastes daily. (Couple of laps, anyone?) Using bacteria, chemicals, and machines, the crud is broken down and separated into liquids and solids. The treated liquid stuff is called effluent (*ef-lu-ent*), and it will be dumped into the nearest waterway. (Yes, it's true!) The smelly solid leftovers are called SLUDGE, which is either dumped in landfills or burned in huge furnaces.

In rural areas, the flushed toilet paper will not have to travel so far. Every house has a SEPTIC TANK, a huge, drum-shaped concrete container buried out in the backyard. The solids sink to the bottom of the tank and must be pumped out every couple of years. The rest ends up flowing into the ground under the yard, an area called a LEACH FIELD (not to be confused with a field of leeches) where it seeps into the dirt.

So remember, a flush is only the beginning. . . .

URINE

It's happened to all of us. One minute you're dry as a desert, the next you're wet from thigh to toe. Maybe you were laughing uncontrollably. Or maybe that mean math teacher wouldn't let you go to the bathroom. Either way, the stuff that made you a soggy mess is urine. To learn more about It, see PEE on page 117.

VILE VEGETATION

There's nothing like a beautiful bouquet of flowers to make someone feel special. And while a dozen long-stemmed roses are awfully nice, if you really want to get someone's attention, how about sending them a nice bug-eating plant? Feeling even more devilish? How about one that reeks of rotting flesh?

I SMELL SWEET. I EAT MEAT.

North Carolina legend has it that the first VENUS FLYTRAPS came from outer space aboard meteors hurtling toward earth. After all, they are native to only one spot—the sandy, boggy soil of North and South Carolina that happens to surround an ancient meteor crater.

Venus flytraps are CARNIVOROUS (*car-niv-ah-rus*) plants—plants that eat flesh. Venus flytraps love to dine on crawling critters such as ants, spiders, and other meaty bugs. Flies, which are like a pint of chocolate ice cream to a flytrap, are harder to come by. Still, a flytrap can always hope. . . .

At the tip of each flytrap leaf is—you guessed it—a trap. The trap is divided in half and looks kind of like a gaping jaw. The two halves are hinged like a door and are edged with stiff, bristly hairs. Each half of the trap also has three "trigger" hairs that, when touched, make the two halves of the trap swing shut.

Let's say some innocent little ant goes out for a sunset stroll across an open flytrap leaf. It accidentally brushes against the trigger hairs and, faster than you can say "breakfast on a branch," the leaf snaps shut. The ant is now

Snap. Crackle. Pop. A fly on the leaf of a Venus fly-trap is about to become breakfast.

lives in America's slimiest bogs and muckiest marshes. (Carnivorous plants developed the ability to eat bugs because the soil in the places they live has so few nutrients in it.) Pitcher plants devour bugs. Each of its leaves is shaped like a jug, with a slippery rim lined with stiff hairs that point downward into the leaf. When an insect lands on the inviting, but slippery, edge of the leaf, it slips downward. When it tries to turn back to escape, all those hairs push the poor bug back down into a pool of thick digestive juice that waits at the bottom. How hungry is this plant? Well, in a two-week period, one 2-foot tall specimen ate 73 cockroaches!

Oddly enough, the larvae of some fly and mosquito species love these putrid pools of bug puree, and hang out there eating the partially digested bug remains.

California's boggy wetlands are the home of a plant that thinks

trapped. But its journey to the dinner table has only just begun.

The plant waits about an hour (good food takes time) before it floods the bug's tiny prison with digestive juices. The ant soaks in the vile liquid until its body gets soft and mushy and can be absorbed by the plant. It will take 10 days for this splendid meal to be digested. At that point, the trap swings open, ready to snag some more supper.

But flytraps aren't the only bug-loving blooms out there. No sirree. . .

BUG CRUNCHERS

Flytraps have company when it comes to plants that like something more than soil and water to snack on. BUTTERWORTS have sticky glands all over their leaves. Insects crawl onto the leaves or land on them and get glued in place. (They are like those glue traps for mice.) The leaves—sensing a meal—then roll up on the poor bugs, unrolling only after the bugs have been completely dissolved by the plant's digestive juices.

And then there's the PITCHER PLANT. It

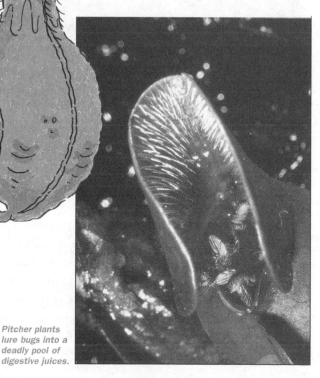

Pitcher plants lure bugs into a deadly pool of digestive juices.

it's a snake. The COBRA PLANT has leaves that look like the heads of snakes with big, red forked "tongues" covered in spiky, slanted hairs. You know those spikes that stick out of the ground in parking garages and make it impossible to back up without ripping apart the car's tires? These hairs work the same way. Bugs that try to crawl backward get pricked by them, and so they have no choice but to move forward into the digestive soup in the bottom of the leaf. There they'll be slowly digested.

The SUNDEW is the octopus of the plant world. Its leaves are covered with tentacles, each of which has a small, shiny drop of a super-sticky substance on it. Insects whizzing by see those glistening droplets and think, "Oh, yum! Snack food!" But the bug making this blunder will end up trapped—stuck fast with no way out. The tentacles hold the poor creature tightly in the leaf. Escape is impossible! As the victim struggles helplessly, enzymes produced by the glands in the leaf begin to slowly digest its body. What a way to die!

FISHING FOR COMPLIMENTS?

Try fishing for food! BLADDERWORTS are carnivorous plants that live in swamps or slow-moving streams. These green gobblers wait, drooling a substance that lures their tiny prey. Each stem has many small, bladder-like containers, each with a trapdoor that opens inward. Each trap also has tiny "trigger" hairs that cause the trapdoor to open and then shut. When a victim swims up and brushes against one of the hairs, the door springs open. The doomed little water bug or tiny shrimp is sucked in like dust into a vacuum cleaner. By the way, bladderworts are fast eaters. Thirty minutes later, the trap is reset and hungry for another snack.

BIG FLOWER! BIG STINK!

GINKGO TREES come in male and female versions. Female ginkgos produce a seed that looks like a small cherry. When these fall off the tree, the coating rots and gives off an acid that reeks of rancid butter.

But they're not the only stinkers around. In the rain forests of Southeast Asia, a parasite that grows on a vine produces the world's largest flower. It's called the RAFFLESIA (*rah-flee-zhee-uh*), and each individual blossom can measure up to 3 feet in diameter. However, if you're thinking of surprising someone with one of these monster blooms, be warned. The flower smells like 10-day-old dead cat, a stink that insects in the area adore. (Locals call it the "corpse flower" because it smells like death.)

There's also the SKUNK CABBAGE, which is one of the first plants to flower each year. Named after the grand stinker of the animal kingdom, it sends out a springtime stink-alarm—a foul smell that wakes up all the hiber-

Get a whiff of this. The Rafflesia, the world's largest flower, is a one-bud bouquet of stench.

clusters of 7 to 13 poisonous leaves, not 3. Toxic oils in the leaves are the culprits in all three plants. Although there are medicines that can help soothe the nasty rashes caused by these plants, the best thing is to do everything possible to avoid touching them in the first place. So look out! No matter where you are in America, there's a poison something growing nearby. Learn to recognize the enemy, and keep your eyes open!

And watch out for SPURGES, a plant family that includes those pretty Christmas POINSETTIAS. Spurges grow all over the world and most contain a bitter, milky sap that can burn your skin and is poisonous if eaten. One spurge called SNOW-ON-THE-MOUNTAIN is so toxic that the bees that visit its flowers produce poison honey!

And speaking of Christmas . . . resist the urge to snack on the HOLLY and MISTLETOE hanging from the mantel. They are both poisonous!

nating flies and gnats that are still snoozing under dead leaves. Look for them in wet, swampy areas, but steer clear. The leaves and roots contain crystals that can burn your throat and stomach if you get any in your mouth. A weird thing, though . . . black bears dig up and eat the toxic roots in the spring to unplug their intestines after the long winter fast! Bet you didn't know there were bear laxatives!

And let's not forget STINKING BENJAMIN, which grows in the woodlands east of the Mississippi and has beautiful white petals—that smell like dirty socks.

PRETTY POISON

Ever heard the warning, "Leaves of three, let them be?" Ivy is pretty. But POISON IVY can leave you so that you'll want to rip your own skin off. POISON OAK is a very close relative of that bad ivy—they're the same species. The only difference is that one grows in moist, shady forests, and the other sprouts in drier, sunnier places. POISON SUMAC is another plant that will make your flesh crawl. It has

VIRUSES

If you think a big, scary monster is dangerous, wait until you find out what a tiny, little VIRUS can do to you. Take EBOLA VIRUS—something that makes grown men shake with fear. Within seven days of exposure, it will have destroyed most of the body's blood vessels. People bleed to death through every opening in their bodies, even their eyeballs. The disease has been limited to remote areas in Africa, and the happy news is that this particular virus is not a good traveler.

OUTBREAK!

No doubt about it. Viruses are troublemakers, big-time. There are more than 4,000 of them, and they bring us colds, the mumps, AIDS, and even some cancers when they invade our bodies. And it's hard to figure out a way to combat them, since they're slippery little devils—able to mutate slightly, always changing just a little bit—enough to evade our efforts to outsmart them. How do they do their dirty work? Let's get "up close and personal" with a virus!

INVASION OF THE BODY SNATCHERS

They're airborne, almost-invisible chemicals coated with protein. They can sneak into your cells, grab the plans to that cell's structure, and start changing things. Instead of working normally, the cell starts making copies of the enemy invader. It's kind of like sneaking over to the photocopier and making a thousand copies of your science teacher without his toupee, then circulating it all over school.

Think of the chaos! Think of the pain when you get caught! That's a virus for you!

If you took 2 million viruses and told them to stand in a straight line, they would take up less than a half inch! They need help to do mischief, though—help that comes when they move into another living cell. You might say they're freeloaders, using up the host cell's food and energy.

Each virus has a coat made of protein, called a VIRAL CAPSID. Inside the protein coat is a dab of nucleic acid that holds the virus's genetic material. The virus sneaks into our bodies through one or more of our handy "openings" (mouths and noses mostly). Once inside, the virus spears healthy cells and injects its nucleic acid, which is used as a blueprint for building more virus. Then, like that out-of-control copying machine, the captive cell starts making copy after copy after copy of the virus until it finally runs out of space and bursts apart. Smallpox. Chicken pox. Cold sores. The flu. Warts. The destruction and

vandalism never stop when you are a virus! If you touch someone with a wart, chances are you'll find that virus has hitched a ride onto *your* body and soon you might have a wart. But you don't have to make direct physical contact to become infected. One sneeze from a person with a cold and millions of virus particles go spraying into the air. (If you don't believe me, see page 161.) You might find yourself with a cold, too. Animal and insect bites can deliver hefty doses of viruses that can kill, such as RABIES and YELLOW FEVER. And viruses such as HEPATITIS can hang out in shellfish we eat. So how *do* you stop them?

FIGHT! FIGHT! FIGHT!

Our bodies aren't going to take an invasion like that without a struggle. This is war! So the body's immune system calls up a bunch of natural defenses. Out march the ANTIBODIES, which are produced by the white blood cells. These specialized killers rip the virus apart or blast the infected host cells. With nowhere to live, the virus finally dies.

Our bodies have another protecting-trick up their sleeves. Once certain viruses have done their dirty work in a body, they'll never be let back in again. It's called IMMUNITY

(im-you-nit-ee) and it's why we get chicken pox only once in a lifetime. Let's say that a big, ugly dog moves in next door. The first time you try to pet it, it snarls like a banshee and tries to take a small chunk out of your rear end. So the next time you have to walk past that growling hunk of foul fur, you are prepared. You blow a dog whistle that sends him cowering into his doghouse with his paws over his ears. You fight back because you recognize danger when you see it. Your body works the same way. It recognizes an evil virus the second time around, knows it will cause trouble, and attacks it before it has a chance to do its cellular mischief again.

So why do we get the "common cold" over and over (and over)? Because that runny nose and tingling throat is not caused by just one virus, but by one of at least 200 very different viruses. So you'll never get sick from exactly the same cold virus twice. Still, even though they're very different, when you're blowing your raw, red nose for the umpteenth time in a day, it doesn't feel very different. Our only lucky break in the war against viruses comes from the fact that viruses tend to have trouble surviving in dirt or dust and can't live for more than about 48 hours without a host cell.

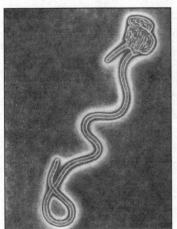 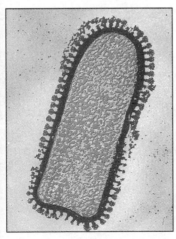 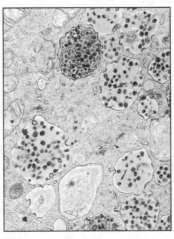 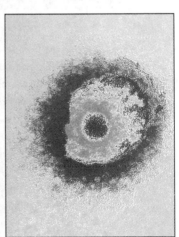

Get to know your viruses. At the far left lurks the deadly Ebola virus. Next to it, a rabies virus is caught in the act of invading a cell. Third from the left is the virus that causes AIDS. And on the right is herpes simplex, the virus that causes cold sores.

THIS WILL ONLY HURT FOR A SECOND

Annual checkup time. The doctor is coming at you with a needle the size of the Empire State Building. But inside that vial lies something that will keep certain viruses from ever taking hold in your body. VACCINES provide the same immunity you would develop if you'd had a disease already. But they provide it *before* you ever get the disease. A vaccine delivers a slightly modified version of the virus—different enough to keep us from getting sick, but similar enough so our bodies will go into "attack" mode the next time something like it appears. Our bodies can now fight off those deadly invasions.

Luckily for us, several of the nastiest viruses have been conquered by vaccines. POLIO, which can cause paralysis and make the muscles waste away, has been almost completely eliminated from human populations. SMALLPOX, which wiped out three-quarters of the Native American population when they were first exposed to it no longer exists in the world (except for some heavily guarded samples that are kept for research by the U.S. and Russian governments). Measles, mumps,

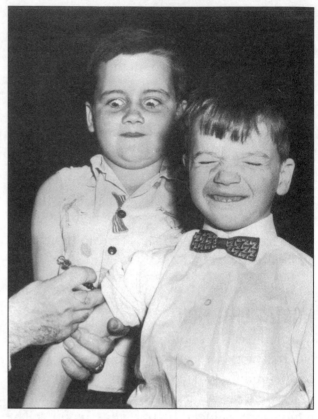

Ouch! Vaccinations may hurt, but they can protect us against many viruses. No pain, no gain!

and rubella, commonly thought of as "childhood diseases," are now also, for the most part, a thing of the past, thanks to vaccines. And even though these diseases are not life-threatening, in most cases they're not much fun, either. Doctors are trying to develop a vaccine for the dreaded disease AIDS (Acquired Immune Deficiency Syndrome). It's caused by a virus called human immunodeficiency virus (or HIV, for short), which attacks the body's natural defense system. In its weakened state, the body can't fight off diseases caused by bacteria, fungi, or other viruses. But doctors are working hard to find drugs that will make the immune system stronger. New treatments are offering hope for an almost-normal life to people living with the disease.

Gross but Good

Genetic engineers hope that very soon they may be able to send special, genetically altered and "improved" cancer-killing viruses into the body to attack cancer cells. The plan is that these viruses will invade the cancer cells but leave healthy cells alone. Armed with new instructions, the cells will produce more cancer-killing viruses until the cancer is eliminated. Maybe bad guys can become good guys!

VOMIT

Bet you know the feeling all too well. It may start with a headache. Then you start sweating. Soon, you're swallowing wads of saliva. Then, your tummy gets this "oh-no" feeling. That's when you *know* it's just a matter of moments before that chili dog you had for lunch ends up on the gym floor. But do you know why you throw up? Grab a barf bag and let's find out!

WHAT'S UP WHEN YOU UPCHUCK?

You might think that your stomach is the guilty party when you throw up. But the real culprit is the MEDULLA OBLONGATA *(ma-dull-ah- ob-lon-got-ah)*, a major player up in your brain. Think of it as "vomiting central," the part of your body that decides when you should heave your hot dog.

When you eat food that has harmful bacteria in it, eat too much food all at once (you now know you should have skipped that fifth slice of pepperoni pizza), or take a couple of spins on the Tilt-a-Whirl after stuffing your face with cotton candy, your brain sends out an SOS.

The brain gets really bossy, telling your DIAPHRAGM *(die-ah-fram)*, a strong sheet of muscle that separates your chest from the abdomen, to press down hard on the stomach. At the same time, it tells your ESOPHAGUS *(eh-saf-ah-gus)*, also known as your "food pipe," to relax. It also instructs the lower valve of your stomach, where it connects to your intestines (the valve is called the PYLORIC SPHINCTER—*pie-lor-ick sfinkter*—for all you curious types), to *slam the door and lock it up!* The strong muscles of the tummy go wild, squishing and squashing. That food has nowhere to go but up.

But there's more. To keep that upwardly mobile food from being inhaled into your lungs, one more switch is thrown. The EPIGLOTTIS *(ep-ah-glot-is)*, which is kind of like a lid for your windpipe, is pulled down and the windpipe is sealed off. After all, pepperoni pizza has no place in your lungs.

Finally, that disgusting mess is out of your mouth and into the toilet bowl. That is, if you made it to the "can" in time!

WHO PUT THE ACHE IN STOM-ACH(E)?

First off, let's get something straight. Your stomach is *not* behind your belly button. It sits much higher up, the top part hiding just a hair under your heart. In fact, most of your stomach lies behind your rib cage on the left side of your body. Bet even your folks don't know that!

GRIND!
KACHUNK!

GURGLE! GURGLE! GURGLE!

The stomach's job is to break down the food you eat into stuff your body can absorb into the bloodstream. Obviously, that burger can't slide through your arteries and veins as it is, now, can it? There's more work to be done.

CHYME TIME

The stomach turns your food into something called CHYME *(kime)*. What's the recipe for this soupy-looking stuff? Take a little food and stir in some GASTRIC JUICE, which is made fresh daily by the 35 million glands that line your tum-tum. And what are the main ingredi-

ents in that juice? Gastric enzymes and *acid!* Hydrochloric acid to be exact—acid so corrosive it can dissolve a piece of metal!

You might be wondering how come your stomach doesn't get dissolved by all that acid. The answer is in that marvel of magnificence—mighty mucus! The same stuff that drips from your nose also lines your stomach and helps takes the "aaagh" out of the acid! Also, the food in your stomach dilutes the acid. But here's the neatest fact of all. The lining of the stomach sheds its cells at the rate of half a million every minute. Your stomach gets a brand-new lining every three days!

NOW, BACK TO THOSE TOSSED COOKIES . . .

You're losing the battle against barfing. Any second, you're gonna blow! After you've raced to the bathroom and dumped your partially-digested dinner into the potty, you might wonder why that mess doesn't look like what you just ate. Or taste like it, either. . .

That nasty taste in your mouth is your stomach acid. And the vile smell is food that has already been attacked by the enzymes that live in your tummy, mixed with that wicked acid. What you see depends on how long ago you ate, and how far into the digestive process your meal got. Big chunks haven't been down the hatch very long. Soupy slime has been there longer. Occasionally, you might

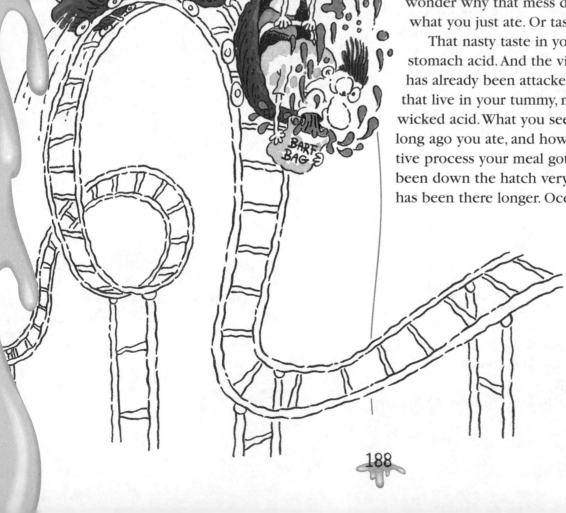

RESTROOMS

Fifteen Clever Ways to Say . . . "Throwing Up!"

1. Upchucking
2. Hurling
3. Barfing
4. Worshiping the porcelain god
5. Blowing chunks
6. Buying the Buick
7. Spewing
8. Doing the Technicolor yawn
9. Puking
10. Heaving
11. Ralphing
12. Driving the porcelain bus
13. Tossing your cookies
14. Running the stew-master

and the proper medical terms:

15. Vomiting (from the Latin for "to expel") and emesis.

upchuck some really nasty, greenish, yellowish, brownish puke. That comes from just below the stomach, from the top part of the small intestine. It's mixed with BILE, which is truly vile. Bile is a bitter alkaline fluid that's made by the liver and helps to digest fat.

RIDING THE VOMIT COMET

It makes sense that our bodies would want to protect us from disgusting food. But why torment us just for trying to go on a school field trip or a visit to Granny's? Bus rides. Boat rides. Bouncy airplane rides. Roller-coaster rides. Why does MOTION SICKNESS happen?

In this case, the culprit is our ears—especially the SEMICIRCULAR CANALS. Our ability to balance is controlled by these canals located in the inner ear. Sudden turning movements or sudden changes in our vertical position (such as when an elevator levels off too quickly or a car swerves from side to side) can

upset the workings of these delicate parts. They get all bent out of shape, and have a complete hissy fit! Our ears know

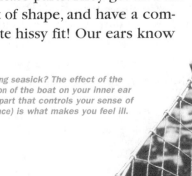

Feeling seasick? The effect of the motion of the boat on your inner ear (the part that controls your sense of balance) is what makes you feel ill.

something's up. But our eyes usually are looking at an unchanging scene—the inside of the school bus or an airplane cabin, for example. The brain spazzes out because it gets confused by these mixed signals. ("Are we moving, or aren't we?") It says "time to blow chunks" and the tummy pays the price.

BARFING AND BABIES

Imagine waking up every day, day after day, and puking several times before lunch. That's what some expectant moms can look forward to in the beginning months of pregnancy. Their bodies have to change in order to nourish and hold the growing baby. Hormones help the body make those changes. Unfortunately, those same hormones sometimes bring on MORNING SICKNESS, which, in spite of its name, frequently lasts all day.

And new babies, whose tummies aren't quite used to the job at hand, are also world-class pukers. They spit up cheesy stuff all the time. Moms call it spit-up, rather than barf, but it's the same stuff. Some can send a wad clear across the room! That's called PROJECTILE VOMITING and it's a definite danger sign—a sign that something may be blocking the baby's intestines.

Gross but Good

"**G**ag me with a spoon!" Know that nasty feeling you get when a doctor's wooden tongue depressor hits the back of your throat? It can save your life. It's called the GAG REFLEX and it happens when certain nerves in the area between your mouth and throat are touched. It closes off the route to your airways so you don't get unwanted substances in your lungs.

FIRST COURSE, SALAD—SECOND COURSE, BARF

If you think throwing up is gross, be glad you're not a cow. Cows are kind of sweet. Those big, sad, brown eyes. That swishy tail. Without them we wouldn't have milk—or ice cream for that matter. But leave it to those divine bovines to do something particularly yucky. They digest their grass salad by swallowing it, then upchucking it and eating it all over again! It's called CUD and trust me—it's not a cow by-product you would want to eat. Cud sundae with whipped cream anyone? Didn't think so!

The cow belongs to a group of animals called RUMINANTS *(roo-muh-nintz),* along with sheep, deer, goats, buffaloes, giraffes, yaks, antelopes, and chamois. They all have amazing tummies. We have just one stomach. They have four. Each does a different part of the digesting and each has different enzymes in it. Let's pretend that you are a big mouthful of grass. You have just been swallowed by a gassy, old cow. Here's what happens.

The cow starts to chew you, only she doesn't do a really good job and swallows you still looking like grass. The RUMEN, the first

THE PUTRID PAST

There were folks in ancient Rome whose job it was to clean up the barfy mess from the floors, tables, and dining couches after big fancy dinners. People ate so much, and puking after dinner was so common, that the Romans had a special room to do it in . . . the VOMITORIUM.

part of the stomach, is where you'll get good and wet until all the cellulose in you starts to break down. The cow will barf you up and chew you some more, then swallow again. This time, you'll skip stomach number one and head on to tummy two—the RETICULUM. Here, you'll get broken down even more. Next, you'll slide into the OMASUM where all the water will be sucked out. Finally, it's off to the ABOMASUM where the last stages of digestion take place.

Now, the cow's fourth stomach produces an enzyme called RENNET *(ren-it)* that is needed to make cheese. Cheese makers get the necessary ingredient by soaking that fourth stomach in water until it's all soft and mushy. Then they mix it up with a harmless-to-humans bacteria. They add it to milk at the beginning of the cheese-making process—it

Anti-Spewing Strategies

❋ If you feel sick after a carnival ride, try sipping ginger ale. Not only is ginger an ancient Chinese remedy for settling stomachs, but the bubbles will help you burp, which will release some of the volcanic pressure building up in your insides.

❋ Another thing that you can try is pressing your thumbs on a point on your wrist about two thumbs'-width above the edge of your palm. These pressure points can short-circuit the brain's barfing signals.

❋ Long bus ride ahead? Try eating some plain crackers or dry toast about an hour ahead of the

ride. It's better to have a little something in your stomach than nothing at all.

❋ If you get a stomach virus that leads to a lot of barfing, try a BRAT diet. And no—that doesn't mean whining and complaining about your food every time you eat, nor does it mean bratwurst. It stands for Bananas, Rice, Applesauce, and Toast.

❋ To keep the inner ear from throwing out a throw-up request when you're riding in a car (or other vehicle), stare at something outside so the brain can register that you are moving. For example, if you are in a car, keep your eyes on the road ahead; if you're in a boat, keep your eyes on the horizon.

Warning! Danger Ahead!

Sometimes, throwing up can be a warning sign of great danger—of serious brain injury. When there is pressure directly on, or activity near, the medulla oblongata, usually after a head injury (are you wearing that helmet when you ride your bike?), you could end up barfing without any of the usual warning signs. Strokes and severe migraine headaches can have the same effect. If you feel sick to your stomach after hitting your head, tell your parents *immediately*.

And if someone vomits blood that's a big "uh-oh." It's called HEMATEMISIS (*he-muh-tem-ih-sis*). Vomited blood can be dark red, black, or look like coffee grounds and it's a sign of a serious problem in the esophagus, stomach, or duodenum. Things such as ulcers, which eat away at the stomach's lining, can cause hematemisis.

helps the milk to form curds. and leave it to harden. Hard to look at a cheese sandwich in quite the same way when you know that!

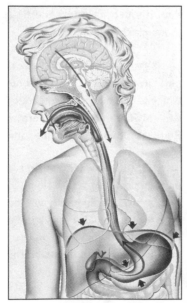

Anatomy of an upchuck. The brain sends messages to the stomach, diaphragm, and abdominal wall. Watch out, it's time to hurl!

VULTURES

"Decisions, decisions. Should I go for that lovely raccoon that just got creamed by a truck on the highway, or perhaps the elderly deer that just kicked the bucket near that big oak? Or maybe I should be a complete pig and have both. Oh, the difficult choices a VULTURE has to make!"

CHOW-DOWN TIME AT THE ROADKILL CAFÉ

Mention vultures to most people and they get kind of weak in the knees. We've all seen those movies where some guy is dragging himself through the desert, slower and slower. The sun is huge, and you know the guy's a goner. And he knows it too, because those birds—those dreaded vultures—are circling overhead, counting the seconds till he topples over and their dinner can finally begin.

But vultures are very polite. They will almost always wait until their dinner is dead before they dine!

CAUTION: NOT FOR THE WEAK OF STOMACH!

To tell the truth, the real reason vultures wait is not because they have such good table manners. A vulture's beak is not very strong, nor are its feet. This adds to vultures' delightful awfulness, because they have to wait for their food to be a bit rotten before they can dig in.

As an appetizer, they'll usually pop out an eyeball or two. When the main course is rotted enough, they peck through the stomach and make a beeline for the intestines—and all that's in them—before moving on to the rest.

Vultures are complete porkers. They just

don't know when to stop eating. They have a tendency to eat so much at one meal that they can hardly move when they're done stuffing themselves. So, when it's time for takeoff, and their big bellies are dragging them down, vultures simply toss their cookies (or their raccoon).

I SMELL A RAT . . . AND OTHER VULTURE STATS!

SOUTH AMERICAN VULTURES can smell food from miles away. Since they have to hunt over dense rain forests, their sense of smell is incredibly sharp. Think about it. You're a vulture. You can't see anything except leaves—lots of leaves, and you don't really like leaves. So you can be sure these birds have managed to get their noses tuned to supersonic frequencies, able to pick out a nice, rotting corpse from far away.

TURKEY VULTURES have a real sweet tooth, but not for candy. Their favorite snack food is a nice, fresh pile of sea lion poop.

Vultures are very clever fellows. In fact, one of the largest, the LAMMERGEIER (*lam-er-guy-er*), will take a leg bone up into the air, then let it go and watch it smash on the rocks below just so it can get to the tasty bone marrow inside. There is even a species of vulture that is one of the few known "tool-users" in the bird world. The EGYPTIAN VULTURE drops rocks on ostrich eggs for a quick omelet fix.

There are vultures on just about every continent. And they've been around practically forever. In fact, vulture bones were discovered in the La Brea Tar Pits in California, cuddling up with the woolly mammoths. They were big suckers in those days, having 16-foot wingspans.

White-backed vultures have good manners and are usually willing to share a snack.

CUTER THAN A VULTURE. STILL SOMETIMES NASTY!

EGRETS Adorable little BABY EGRETS have a dark side. When mommy and daddy bird aren't looking, they shove their smaller brothers and sisters right out of the nest. Since their little siblings haven't learned to fly yet they end up smooshed on the ground below. Pelicans do the same. It's one way to get out of sharing stuff!

OWLS Owls are wise, right? So how come they drag skunks, geese, and porcupines, along with munchy little moles, mice, and rats, up to their feeding roost? How come they stuff the whole animal—fur, feathers, bones, and all down their throats? And if that weren't bad enough, when they're done, they upchuck big, felty wads of stuff. Those pellets are full of all the leftover bits they couldn't digest—things like animal teeth and claws. Folks who study owls actually collect them. Imagine collecting wads of dried old barf! Now there's a hobby for you.

Owls have incredibly acute night vision, which helps them to find their prey in the dark.

How to Pick a Vulture Out of a Police Lineup

❋ First off, they're ugly.

❋ Second, they have a big hole through their bills (actually called a "perforate nasal septum," if you want to get fancy).

❋ Talk about a big bird. . . . Vultures can grow to huge sizes, with wingspans of 8 or 9 feet (that's the equivalent of Michael Jordan with a 12-inch ruler stuck on top of his head, flying sideways through the sky). They belong to a family called FALCONIFORMES (fal-_con_-ah-forms), along with hawks, eagles, condors, and—oh, you're so smart—falcons.

❋ They stand between 2 and 4 feet tall, about the size of a typical nursery-school kid.

❋ Vulture feathers are usually brown or black, with the exception of "King" vultures, which look like Elvis Presley. (Sorry, just joking!) Kings have cream-colored backs, with elaborately patterned, colorful heads and black, hair-like feathers. Come to think of it, they do look a little like Elvis!

❋ Vulture faces come in three designer colors: red, yellow, and black. Perfect color coordination with bloody, rotting flesh.

❋ Vultures don't have feathers on their faces or necks. How come? It's tidier when you plunge your face into someone's guts. Less cleanup.

PENGUINS What's black and white, fat and fabulously adorable, and waddles around while searching through leftover dried-up old poop for tasty bits of shellfish?

Would you believe hungry PENGUINS? Yup. They pass their time by pecking away at frozen guano (that's poop), looking for krill (a small crustacean). Penguins love the taste of krill so much that they frequently barf it all up, just so they can eat it again. Penguin parents also puke into their babies' mouths. Guess there isn't much else to do out there in the frozen Antarctic wastelands.

SWIFTS And while we're back on the subject of birds, those adorable little nests they weave for their newborn babies can be made out of some pretty strange stuff. Take the GREAT SWALLOWTAILED SWIFT. Their nests are held together with globs of bird saliva. But they've got nothing on the the SWIFTLET, who builds its nest almost entirely out of spit! The spit hardens like cement. But for a truly gross twist on the whole subject, those spit-nests are considered a food delicacy in China. They make soup with them!

THE KING

OH, YUCK!

W

WORMS

"Goin' fishin'?" Sounds like fun—until the moment arrives when you have to attach a live, wriggling, squirming, slithering WORM to a sharp metal hook. Guts gush out all over your hands. And another worm bites the dust.

There are at least 20,000 different types of worms on this planet. There are worms that like to eat parts of people and worms that prefer the flavor of garbage, poop, and mud. Some are microscopic; some can be 40 feet long! Which worm is which? Read on!

DIRTY WORDS

EARTHWORMS are eaters of dirt, dwellers in dirt, and all-around dirt-lovers. These slimy worms belong to a family called the ANNELIDS *(an-uh-lidz)*. Once you get over their yucky ooziness, you'll be surprised at how awesome they are.

Annelids are segmented worms. That means they come in lots of attached pieces, or segments. (Those bloodthirsty LEECHES back on page 88 are another type of annelid, and lots of marine worms are annelids too.) But unlike the leech, earthworms enjoy a rougher, tougher diet. They will eat anything that was once alive—including newspaper (once a tree) and T-shirts (once a cotton plant).

Your typical earthworm measures in at between 3/4 inch and 8 inches, but there are some in Australia that are over 10 feet long. Try sticking that on a fish hook!

Despite their yuckiness, earthworms have been called one of the most valuable creatures on earth. As they burrow through the soil they bring air deep into the dirt's layers and fertilize it from within with their endless pooping. That in turn makes the soil richer and sweeter. Plants and trees grow better in that rich soil. Fruits

196

and veggies grow bigger. Everyone is happy.

But alas, an earthworm's life is a difficult one. You might think they're pretty disgusting, but birds don't. Worms are just about a bird's favorite food. That's because 70 percent of an earthworm is protein—a thick, juicy steak for your average robin. Moles, who live underground, too, like it there because their favorite food—worm—is down there with them.

Lugworms are another icky underground annelid. These blood-red tubes of slime live in U-shaped burrows on beaches. The tops of the U are at the surface and the entire tunnel is lined with mucus to keep it from caving in (and for swifter sliding). When a lugworm wants to take a dump, it moves backward through its snotty tunnel until its tail reaches the surface. Then its propels its poop out onto the ground. If you see something that looks like squeezes of brown toothpaste on the ground, what you're seeing is lugworm poop.

HANGING AROUND WITH A ROUNDWORM

Worms that are slippery-smooth are called NEMATODES (*nem-uh-toadz*). This group includes roundworms, hookworms, and threadworms. Many nematodes are parasites and like to live inside our bodies or in animals. Ascaris, for example, is a roundworm that makes its home in our intestines, or sometimes those of pigs and horses. The female may grow to be 16 inches long and reproduces by laying eggs—as many as 200,000 a day. The eggs can sometimes be found on unwashed vegetables (so wash 'em up!). If swallowed they can hatch inside you. Imagine 200,000 roundworm babies wriggling inside you! Nematodes can also be found on the forest floor and in fresh

water and the sea. Flatworms are another wormy type. They have flat (surprise, surprise), ribbon or leaf-shaped bodies with a pair of tiny eyes at the front. Many are parasitic, including the lovely tapeworm (for more about this intestine-loving flatworm, see page 116).

Wormy Wonders
(or a few things I bet you didn't know about worms.)

※ You can freeze an earthworm solid and it will not die as long as you thaw it slowly.

※ Earthworms are he/she critters. Every worm has both male and female organs and they mate when one worm's head touches another's tail.

※ Earthworms do not crawl out of the ground when it rains because they are afraid of drowning. They are actually cruising for someone to love. Think about it. It's hard to find a husband or wife when you are living in a thin tunnel of dirt all by yourself. Since they don't have to worry about drying out in the open air when it's raining, they can go looking for love.

※ Earthworms are powerful pee-ers. They produce 60 percent of their body's weight in urine every day. Let's say you weigh 100 pounds and you are an earthworm. You would pee 60 pounds' worth of urine in 24 hours. You'd probably never leave the toilet!

X-PERIMENTS

Make the world a gross-er place! Feeling completely devilish now? Ready to add to the overall awfulness of the world around you? Well, here's your chance to build your own exploding pimple, mix up a vat of slimy make-believe mucus, and make a set of spore print greeting cards and mail a little mold to someone you love! It's all as easy as pie!

THE AMAZING EXPLODING ZIT

At last! a pimple you can squeeze. "Don't touch it! Don't pick at it! Leave it alone and it will go away." Nag, nag, nag. Real pimples are never fun, but this exploding zit will spew forth

all sorts of nasty stuff. And you can pick at it as much as you want. Best to do this in the kitchen sink or in the bathtub. If you do, you won't need the cookie sheet for eruption protection.

What you'll need:

Toothpick

Green and yellow food coloring

1 small paper cup

Funnel

Empty plastic bottle (a 1-liter soda bottle works well)

1 box of baking soda

1 squirt of whipped cream in a can

Pot deep enough to fit the plastic bottle

Cookie sheet or tray

Enough dirt or fine gravel to make a mound around your bottle

2 cups of sand

1 cup of white vinegar

What to do:

Use a toothpick to mix a drop of green food coloring with two or three drops of the yellow in the paper cup and set aside. You're aiming for that perfect pus color. Using the funnel, fill the plastic bottle halfway with the baking soda. Add the food coloring and a tiny squirt of whipped cream. Place the pot on the cookie sheet and place the bottle in the middle of the pot. Pour the dirt or gravel into the bowl and mound it up around the bottle, shaping it into well . . . a . . . big pimple. Leave the top of the bottle peeking out. Now top the whole thing with sand. (Pretend that's the top layer of skin.)

You are now ready to witness the eruption of Mount Zit. Quickly pour the vinegar into the bottle and stand back 'cause thar she blows!

MAKE A MOUND OF MAKE-BELIEVE MUCUS

Since it's not polite to play with all that neat stuff that drips from your nose, this is the next best thing. And if you really want to gross your buddies out, you can always stick a glob 'neath your schnozz for that truly sicko effect.

What you'll need:

Newspapers (So you don't get creamed for making a mess in the kitchen.)
2 Popsicle sticks
1/2 teaspoon borax powder (You can find this in the detergent section of your supermarket.)
2 cups of distilled water (You can buy this in the supermarket, too.)
1 bottle (4 ounces) of white school glue
Drop of green food coloring
2 empty 8-ounce jars, washed and dried
1 empty 8-ounce yogurt container, washed and dried
Ziploc plastic bag

What to do:

Spread the newspapers out over the table. Use a Popsicle stick to mix the borax and 1 cup of distilled water in one of the jars. Place the glue, the food coloring, and the rest of the water in the second jar and stir with a Popsicle stick until thoroughly blended.

Pour about a quarter of the mixture of each bottle into the empty yogurt container and mix well with the stick until it has a nice gooey, gluey feel to it. Drape in an appropriate spot under your nose.

You now have a fluid that's not quite a liquid and not quite a solid. You can store your newly made slime in a Ziploc plastic bag for further fun. Tightly cap the remaining borax/water and glue/food coloring/water jars and save for a rainy day.

EERIE EARS

What sorts of weird things does a doctor see when he pokes that little flashlight thingy in your ears? (And, by the way, it is not called an inner-ear-looker-atter!) Its real name is an OTOSCOPE, and you can make your own version and take a peek for yourself.

What you'll need:

Small piece of paper, about 5- x 7-inches
Tape
Scissors
A dark room
A good friend
Bright penlight

What to do:

Roll the paper into a cone and tape it so it stays closed. Snip off the smaller end so it *isn't* sharp and pokey. One opening should measure about 1/2 inch across, the other 1/8 inch across. You now have a basic otoscope (or "ear-o-scope" for you goofy types).

Go into a dark room or a closet with someone you like, preferably someone who isn't too ticklish. Position the cone *slowly* and *gently* into the opening of that person's ear. (Never poke anything sharp into any ear *ever*!)

Ask them to tug down gently on their earlobe a bit, moving it this way and that. Aim the light into the opening of the cone.
What will you see? It depends. You may see enough wax to put a high shine on a '57 Chevy, in which case you get to say, "Ooooh. Disgusting! You really should clean your ears every century or so!" But if there is only a tiny bit of wax—and remember, we all have some in there—you should be able to see the eardrum. The eardrum, when it is healthy, is a pretty, pearly gray, the color of an elephant's tummy. It's smooth and should be as flat as a day-old pancake.

If it is red or pink, that's a sign of an infec-

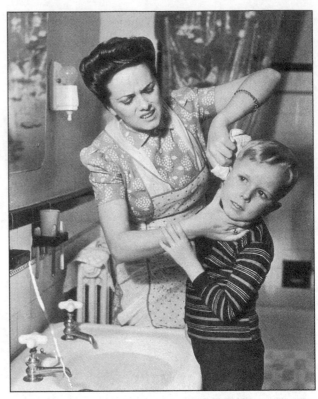

Don't let your mom see inside your ear or she might drag you to the bathroom for a scrub.

tion brewing. Is the eardrum curving outward? That could be a sign of pus pressing on the other side. Gross! And very uncomfortable, too.

THE INSIDE-OUTSIDE STOMACH

About 170 years ago, U.S. Army surgeon Captain William Beaumont took care of a man named Alexis St. Martin, an unfortunate young fellow who had been shot in the stomach. The wound never healed properly and St. Martin was left with a good-sized hole in his tummy, a hole that tended to leak. Beaumont rigged a bandage to keep everything from sloshing out. But at the same time he realized that he had a perfect peephole for viewing the secret workings of the tum.

The good doctor used that stomach opening to perform over 288 experiments, including dangling a piece of meat on a string in St. Martin's stomach and watching it get flooded by gastric juices, then siphoning the juice out to examine under a microscope. Well, guess what? You do not need a person with a gaping hole in an important part of their body to see digestion at work. Try this. It should be fun. It involves rubbing food on your clothing.

What you'll need:

Scissors
*1 totally dreadful old white T-shirt, or
    other white cotton rag*
Kitchen spoon
1 cooked, scrambled egg
Measuring spoons
*Plain old laundry soap, such as Ivory
    Snow, either liquid or powder*
2 small glass bowls
Pencil
Sticky labels or plain paper
Laundry soap with enzymes, such as Tide
Warm water

Use scissors to cut two scraps of fabric from your rattiest, raggiest, white T-shirt, each about 2 or 3 inches square. Rub a spoonful of scrambled egg into each piece of cloth and let them dry. This will take about an hour. Add a tablespoonful of the plain laundry soap to one bowl and label it. Put a tablespoon of the detergent with enzymes in the other bowl and label that one as well. Then add warm water to each of the bowls until almost full and stir. Put a piece of egg-blobbed material in each bowl and watch what happens!

What you'll see:

Enzymes work by blasting big molecules into smaller ones. The detergent with enzymes will speed the "digestion" of the egg by forcing its molecules into tiny pieces that can be absorbed by the liquid. A person's stomach doesn't have detergent and water, but it does have other enzymes that do an even better job of breaking down an egg!

MAIL A MOLD TO SOMEONE YOU LOVE

Show someone how much you really care by sharing the secrets of a fungus. The underside of a mushroom has a weird and funky "personality" all its own. Make some prints of the underside of a mushroom cap and see what comes up. You may be surprised at some of the strange colors and patterns you'll see. But promise me that before you start you will read the FUNGI section on page 71.

What you'll need:

*A large portobello mushroom from the
    grocery store*
*Some dark colored paper (Dark blue, pur-
    ple, or black heavy-weight construction
    paper folded in half works fine.)*
Large bowl
Nonaerosol hair spray or artist's fixative

The spores of a lacy stinkhorn would be a lovely gift. Too bad they live in the South American rainforest.

Let the mold-printing begin:

Snap off the stem of the mushroom and throw it away. Gently press the cap down onto the paper to flatten it. Leave it there. Don't try to move it after you place it.

Cover the mushroom by placing the bowl upside down over it to make a little dome.

Now go away. Play, eat, sleep, or ride

your bike. Leave your mushroom alone for 24 hours.

Remove the bowl and very carefully lift the mushroom cap off the paper and throw it out. Don't touch your print or it will smear. Gently carry your print to a room with a lot of circulating air, or better still, go outside. Spray your print with the hairspray or fixative and let it dry for about 15 minutes.

Wash your hands and write a few lines of gross poetry on the other side, then mail that mold to someone special.

What you'll see:

Mushrooms—at least the ones you'll be using—have gills that hold the mushroom's spores. The spores will fall onto the paper in the radial pattern of the gills. It'll look like a drawing of a wheel with a *lot* of spokes.

EXPLORE THE REAL WORLD WIDE WEB

Forget your computer's world wide web. Go out and capture something truly interesting with this surefire way to tap into the WEB. You are now spider-savvy (if you're not, go read SPIDERS on page 163), so why not learn how to round up a collection of web prints. But before you do that, try this simple experiment that shows why spiders don't stick to their own webs.

Take a piece of cellophane tape and wrap

it into a ring with the sticky side out, then press it on to a piece of paper. Try to walk your fingertips across the sticky surface. Hard, huh? Now dip your fingertips in a little vegetable oil. Try it again. You now have spider-feet fingertips! Now, onto that web-snatching. . .

What you'll need:

The common sense not to mess with any spider hanging on a web
Water-based spray paint that is darker or lighter than the paper you've chosen
Heavy construction paper or light cardboard

What to do:

Find a spiderweb away from your house or in the park—and promise me you'll check for spiders first. Make sure there isn't a spider on the web when you find one. Gently spray the web with the spray paint. Do this with a very light touch. If you spray too hard or too close the web will break apart.

Take two sheets of paper and position one on one side of the web and the other on the other side. Sandwich the two together, then gently peel them apart. The paint will stick to the web and the web will stick to your paper.

Try to collect all the different types of web. You can use your prints to make greeting cards or frame them and hang them up. Who knows . . . maybe your print webs will attract some insect action!

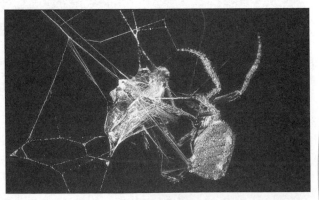

This garden orb web spider is preparing lunch—an unfortunate cricket.

ZITS

What better finale to a book of yuckiness than spewing, pus-filled ZITS? Maybe there is something yuckier, but you won't find it here. Look for information about those human volcanoes under their more proper name, ACNE (see page 1).

BIBLIOGRAPHY

Books, Periodicals, and Websites

Aaseng, Nathan. *Poisonous Creatures (Scientific American Sourcebooks)*. New York: Twenty-First Century Books, 1997.

The American Medical Association. *The American Medical Association Home Medical Encyclopedia*. New York: Random House, 1989.

Attenborough, David. *The Private Life of Plants*. London: BBC Books, 1995.

Attenborough, David. *The Trials of Life: A Natural History of Animal Behavior*. Boston: Little, Brown, 1990.

Barry, Dave. "Dining Tip: Try the Poison Blowfish." *Detroit Free Press*, February 9, 1998.

Berenbaum, May R. *Ninety-nine Gnats, Nits, and Nibblers*. Urbana and Chicago: University of Illinois Press, 1989.

Berenbaum, May R. *Ninety-nine More Maggots, Mites, and Nibblers*. Urbana and Chicago: University of Illinois Press, 1993.

Borror, Donald J., and Richard E. White. *A Field Guide to Insects (Peterson Field Guides)*. Shelburne, Vt.: Chapters Publishing, Ltd., 1998.

"Breast Cancer and Environmental Risk Factors in New York State." Ithaca, N.Y.: Cornell University Press, 1996.

Britannica Online, Vers. 97.1.1. Encyclopedia Brittanica, March 1997.

Burnie, David. *The Concise Encyclopedia of the Human Body*. London: Dorling Kindersley, 1995.

Chinery, Michael (editor). *The Kingfisher Illustrated Encyclopedia of Animals*. London: Kingfisher Books, 1992.

Clayman, Charles (editor). *The Human Body: An Illustrated Guide to Its Structure, Function, and Disorders*. London: Dorling Kindersley, 1995.

Cutler, Kit. "Tarnished: The Ups and Downs of the Spitball Pitch." (online) http://www.princeton.edu/"ccutler/spitball.html

D'Amato, Peter. *The Savage Garden: Cultivating Carnivorous Plants*. Berkeley, Calif.: Ten Speed Press, 1998.

Deary, Terry, and Peter Hepplewhite. *The Awesome Egyptians (Horrible Histories)*. London: Scholastic Children's Books, 1993.

Deem, James M. *How to Make a Mummy Talk*. New York: Bantam Doubleday Dell Books for Young Readers, 1995.

DeFoliart, Gene R. "They Ate What?" Food Insects Newsletter. November 1997. Volume 4, Issue 3.

The Diptera Site. Systematic Entomology Laboratory, United States Department of Agriculture, and Department of Entomology, National Museum of National History, Smithsonian Institution. (online) http://www.2.sel.barc.usda.gov/Diptera/flies.htm

The DK Science Encyclopedia. New York: DK Publishing, 1998.

Editors of Consumer Guide. *The Home Remedies Handbook*. Lincolnwood, Ill. : Publications International, Ltd., 1993.

Elfman, Eric. *Almanac of the Gross, Disgusting, and Totally Repulsive*. New York: Random House, 1994.

Ellis, Richard. *Monsters of the Sea*. New York: Doubleday, 1995.

Encarta Encyclopedia (online) http://encarta.msn.com/EncartaHome.asp

Ernst, Carl H., and George R. Zug. *Snakes in Question: The Smithsonian Answer Book*. Washington and London: Smithsonian Institution Press, 1996.

Evans, Arthur V., and Charles L. Bellamy. *An Inordinate Fondness for Beetles*. New York: Henry Holt and Company, 1996.

Facklam, Howard, and Margery Facklam. *Bacteria*. New York: Twenty-First Century Books, 1994.

Facklam, Howard, and Margery Facklam. *Viruses*. New York: Twenty-First Century Books, 1994.

Fountain, Henry. "These Bacteria Are So Big, the Microscope's Optional." *New York Times*, April 20, 1999.

Gies, Joseph, and Frances Gies. *Life in a Medieval City*. New York: Harper Perennial, 1981.

Greene, Henry W. *Snakes: The Evolution of Mystery in Nature*. Berkeley, Calif.: University of California Press, 1997.

Grolier Encyclopedia

Guinness, Alma E. (editor). *ABC's of the Human Body*. Pleasantville, N.Y.: Reader's Digest, 1987.

Hanski, Ilkka A., and Yves Cambefort. *Dung Beetle Ecology*. Princeton, N.J.: Princeton University Press, 1981.

Hanson, Jeanne K. *The Beastly Book: 100 of the World's Most Dangerous Creatures*.

The Happy D Ranch Worm Farm newsletter
"The History of Halloween." (online) http://www.interscape.net/homeroom/specialdays/halloween.ntml

"Indians, Tar Pits and Tar Mines" (online)
http://www.sjgs.com/tarpits_hist.html

Jayaraman, Prakash. "The La Brea Tar Pits." (online)
www.jayarama@scf.usc.edu

Knight, Margaret. *Fashion Through the Ages: From Overcoats to Petticoats*. New York: Viking Press, 1998.

Knutson, Roger M. *Furtive Fauna: A Field Guide to the Creatures Who Live on You*. Berkeley, Calif.: Ten Speed Press, 1996.

Larson, David E. (editor). *Mayo Clinic Family Health Book*, 2d ed. New York: William Morrow and Company, 1996.

Lyman, Francesca. *Inside the Dzanga Sangha Rain Forest*. New York: Workman Publishing, 1998.

Lyons, Albert S., and R. Joseph Petrucelli, II. *Medicine: An Illustrated History*. New York: Abradale Press, 1986.

Lyons, Ron. "Scarab Beetles and Cultural Entomology." (online)
http://www.rlyons@ucsd.edu

MacQuitty, Miranda. *Amazing Bugs (Inside Guides)*. New York: DK Publishing, 1996.

Marieb, Elaine N. *Human Anatomy and Physiology*, 2d ed. Redwood City, Calif.: Benjamin Cummings Science Books, 1997.

McCarthy, Colin, and Nick Arnold. *Reptile (Eyewitness Books)*. New York: Alfred A. Knopf, 1991.

Mertus, John. "Earthworms." (online)
http://www.mertus.org/gardening/worms.html

Montagne, Prosper. *Larousse Gastronomique*. New York: Crown Publishers, 1988.

The New Good Housekeeping Family Health and Medical Guide. New York: Hearst Books, 1988.

Nuland, Sherwin B. "Medical Fads: Bran, Midwives and Leeches," *New York Times*, June 25, 1995.

Parker, Steven. *The Body Atlas*. New York: DK Publishing, 1993.

Parker, Steven. *How the Body Works*. New York: Reader's Digest, 1999.

Perrins, Christopher. *Birds: Their Life, Their Ways, Their World*. Pleasantville, N.Y.: Reader's Digest, 1979.

Preston, Richard. *The Hot Zone*. New York: Random House, 1994.

Putnam, James. *Mummy (Eyewitness Books)*. New York: Alfred A. Knopf, 1993.

"Rat City: Seat Treatment." *New York Magazine*. May 4, 1998, p.25.

Reichl, Ruth. "The Vanishing Haute Cuisine" *New York Times*, June 12, 1997, p.C1.

Ring, Malvin E. *Dentistry: An Illustrated History*. New York: Abradale Press, 1992.

Royt, Elizabeth. "Holy Chiroptera, Batman!" *Outside*, October 1995.

Sawyer, Roy T. *Leech Biology and Behaviour*. Vols. 1 and 2. Oxford: Clarendon Press, 1984.

Sholz, Floyd. *Birds of Prey*. Mechanicsburg, Penn.: Stackpole Books, 1993.

Solomon, Charmaine. *The Complete Asian Cookbook*. New York: Charles E. Tuttle, 1991.

Stein, Sara Bonnett. *The Body Book*. New York: Workman Publishing, 1992.

Stein, Sara Bonnett. *The Science Book*. New York: Workman Publishing, 1983.

Wernert, Susan J. (editor). *Reader's Digest North American Wildlife*. Pleasantville, N.Y.: Reader's Digest, 1986.

Whitfield, Philip (editor). *Macmillan Illustrated Animal Encyclopedia*. New York: Macmillan, 1984.

Wollard, Kathy. "Nitty-Gritty on Quicksand." *New York Newsday*, August 18, 1998.

Worm Digest Web Site (online) http://www.wormdigest.org

Yoon, Carol Kaesuk. "Within Nests, Egret Chicks Are Natural Born Killers." *New York Times*, August 6, 1996, p.C1.

Young, Mark C. (editor). *The Guinness Book of World Records*. New York: Bantam Books, 1998.

Zimmerman, O.T., and Irvin Lavine. *DDT: Killer of Killers*. Dover, N.H.: Industrial Research Service, 1946.

Universities, Museums, and Research Foundations

California Department of Food and Agriculture, Sacramento, Calif.

The Exploratorium, San Francisco, Calif.

Florida Agricultural Information Retrieval System, Tampa, Fla.

The Franklin Institute, Philadelphia, Penn.

Health Services Agency, Environmental Health Department, Washington, D.C.

Iowa State University Food Safety Project, Ames, Iowa.

The Liberty Science Center, Newark, N.J.

Museum of Natural History, New York, N.Y.

Museum of Science, Boston, Mass.

The National Aquarium, Baltimore, Md.

The National Zoo, Washington, D.C.

The San Joaquin Geological Society, Bakersfield, Calif.

Sea Grant National Media Relations Office, Washington, D.C.

The University of Michigan Museum of Zoology, Ann Arbor, Mich.

PHOTO CREDITS

FRONT MATTER AND INTRODUCTION

page ii: *top*, Paul A. Zahl/Photo Researchers; **page iv:** *top*, Paul A. Zahl/Photo Researchers; *bottom*, Harold Lloyd, Trust/Archive Photos; **page vii:** Walt Anderson/Visuals Unlimited; **page viii:** Lambert/Archive Photos; **page ix:** Sean Ellis/Stone; **page x:** *top left*, Stephen Dalton/NHPA; *bottom left*, The Stock Market/LWA-Dann Tardif; *bottom right*, Gregory G. Dimijian/Photo Researchers; **page xi:** *left*, Barry E. Parker/Bruce Coleman Inc.; *top right*, Stephen Dalton/NHPA; *bottom right*, Reuters/Natalie Behring/Archive Photos.

ACNE—BURPING

page 1: The Advertising Archives; **page 3:** National Medical Slide/Custom Medical Stock Photo; **page 5:** *left*, Raymond A. Mendez/Animals Animals; *right*, Paul A. Zahl/Photo Researchers; **page 6:** Scott Camazine/CDC/Photo Researchers; **page 7:** *left*, CNRI/Science Photo Library/Photo Researchers; *right*, D. M. Phillips/Visuals Unlimited; **page 10:** *top*, CNRI/Science Photo Library/Photo Researchers; *middle* Scott Camazine/CDC/Photo Researchers; *bottom*, Dr. Karl Loupatmann/Science Photo Library/Photo Researchers; *right*, Mark Clarke/Science Photo Library/Photo Researchers; **page 12:** *top*, Michael Fogden/DRK; *right*, Stephen Dalton/NHPA; *bottom*, Stephen J. Krasemann/DRK; **page 13:** *top left & right*, Stephen Dalton/NHPA; **page 14:** Merlin D. Tuttle, Bat Conservation International/Photo Researchers; **page 16:** Gregory K. Scott/Photo Researchers; **page 17:** *left*, Stephen J. Krasemann/DRK; *top right*, Lewis S. Maxwell/National Audubon Society/Photo Researchers; *bottom right*, Anthony Bannister/NHPA; **page 18:** Don Fawcett/ E. Shelton/Photo Researchers; **page 19:** J. Gerard Smith/Photo Researchers; **page 21:** CORBIS/Bettmann; **page 22:** Archive Photos; **page 23:** CORBIS/Bettmann-UPI.

CANNIBALS—EYE GUNK

page 27: Photofest; **page 28:** American Stock/Archive Photos; **page 30:** James P. Rowan/DRK; **page 32:** AP/World Wide Photos; **page 33:** *alligator*, Renee Lynn/Photo Researchers; *caiman*, Lawrence Naylor/Photo Researchers; *crocodile*, Gerard Lacz/Animals Animals; *gavial*, Zig Leszczynski/Animals Animals; *bottom*,

Walt Anderson/Visuals Unlimited; **page 37:** *left*, CORBIS/ Bettmann-UPI; *right*, Custom Medical Stock Photo; **page 39:** CORBIS/Bettmann-UPI; **page 42:** Chip Simmons/FPG; **page 43:** Imapress/Archive Photos; **page 44:** Reuters/Luciano Mellace/ Archive Photos; **page 45:** Barry Runk/Grant Heilman, Inc.; **page 46:** *top*, Barry E. Parker/Bruce Coleman Inc.; **page 46-47:** Fred McConnaughey/Photo Researchers; **page 48:** Norbert Wu/DRK; **page 49:** Steinhart Aquarium/Photo Researchers.

FARTS—JELLYFISH

page 51: *top*, Science Photo Library/Photo Researchers; *right*, N. Durrell McKenna/Photo Researchers; **page 54:** CORBIS/ Bettmann; **page 55:** SuperStock; **page 56:** Geri Bauer Photographics, Inc.; **page 58:** Stephen Dalton/Photo Researchers; **page 62:** SuperStock; **page 63:** Dr. P. Marazzi/Science Photo Library/Photo Researchers; **page 64:** Lambert/Archive Photos; **page 65:** James Watt/Animals Animals; **page 66:** Tom McHugh/Steinhart Aquarium/Photo Researchers; **page 67:** *top*, Paul Silver/Bruce Coleman Inc.; *middle*, Hal Beral/Visuals Unlimited; *bottom*, Columbia Pictures/Archive Photos; **page 68:** CORBIS/Bettmann; **page 69:** The Granger Collection, New York; **page 70:** *top right*, SuperStock; *left*, CORBIS/Bettmann; *bottom right*, George Holton/Photo Researchers; **page 71:** Michael Lustbader/Photo Researchers; **page 73:** *left*, Gregory G. Dimijian/Photo Researchers; *right*, Gregory G. Dimijian/Photo Researchers; **page 75:** CORBIS/Bettmann-Reuters; **page 76:** Reuters/Claro Cortes/Archive Photos; **page 79:** CORBIS/ Bettmann; **page 80:** Dr. Tony Brain/Science Photo Library/Photo Researchers; **page 81:** CORBIS/Reuters; **page 82:** *left*, Gianni Tortoli/Photo Researchers; *right*, A. Blank/Bruce Coleman Inc.; **page 83:** Bill Bachman/Photo Researchers; **page 84:** CORBIS/Bettmann-Reuters; **page 86:** Beth Davidow/Visuals Unlimited; **page 87:** Runk/Schoenberger/Grant Heilman, Inc.

LEECHES—NAKED MOLE RATS

page 89: Reuters/A. Elsner/Archive Photos; **page 90:** Geoff Tompkinson/Science Photo Library/Photo Researchers; **page 91:** Jack K. Clark/The Image Works; **page 93:** Wayne Lynch/DRK; **page 94:** Len & Des Bartlett/Bruce Coleman Inc.; **page 95:** Tom

Brakefield/Bruce Coleman Inc.; **page 96:** Stephen Dalton/Photo Researchers; **page 98:** E. R. Degginger/Photo Researchers; **page 100:** Index Stock Imagery; **page 102:** *left*, AP/Wide World Photos; *right*, Andrew Syred/Science Photo Library/Photo Researchers; **page 103:** Rapho/Photo Researchers; **page 105:** *top left*, Jack K. Clark/The Image Works; *bottom left*, Science Photo Library/Custom Medical Stock Photo; *right*, SuperStock; **page 106:** Runk/Schoenberger/Grant Heilman, Inc.; **page 107:** Archive Photos; **page 109:** *left*, Archive Photos; *right*, J&L Waldman/Bruce Coleman Inc.; **page 110:** Archive Photos; **page 111:** Photofest; **page 112:** CORBIS/Bettmann; **page 114:** R. Andrew Odum/Peter Arnold, Inc.; *left*; John Visser/Bruce Coleman Inc.; *right*, Raymond A. Mendez/Animals Animals.

PARASITES—RAUNCHY RECIPES

page 115: Oliver Meek/Photo Researchers; **page 116:** *top left*, J. H. Robinson/Photo Researchers; *bottom left*, Gregory G. Dimijian/Photo Researchers; *right*, Science Photo Library/Photo Researchers; **page 117:** Eric Pears/FPG; **page 119:** A. Farnsworth/The Image Works; **page 120:** The Stock Market/Chuck Savage; **page 122:** The Stock Market/Mugshots; **page 124:** *left*, Archive Photos; *right*, SIU/Visuals Unlimited; **page 126:** Photofest; **page 128:** Dr P. Marazzi/ Science Photo Library/Photo Researchers; **page 129:** *top*, The Granger Collection, New York; *bottom*, H. & K. Ammann/Bruce Coleman Inc.; **page 130:** *left*, Tom McHugh/Photo Researchers; *right*, CORBIS/Bettmann; **page 133:** Photofest.

SCABS—SPITTING

page 134: Esbin-Anderson/The Image Works; **page 135:** F. Jackson/Bruce Coleman Inc.; **page 137:** CORBIS/Reuters; **page 138:** Austin J. Stevens/Animals Animals; **page 140:** *left*, CORBIS/Bettmann-UPI; *right*, Index Stock Imagery; **page 141:** *left*, Doug Perrine/DRK; **page 141:** *right*, A. Flowers & L. Newman/Photo Researchers; **page 142:** Mark Stouffer/Animals Animals; **page 143:** Index

Stock Imagery; **page 145:** Biophoto Associates/Photo Researchers; **page 146:** Dr. P. Marazzi/Science Photo Library/Photo Researchers; **page 147:** Biophoto Associates/Photo Researchers; **page 148:** George Holz/The Image Works; **page 149:** Tom Ulrich/Visuals Unlimited; **page 153:** Runk/Schoenberger/Grant Heilman, Inc.; **page 156:** SuperStock; **page 157:** *left*, Jim Meeli/Visuals Unlimited; *right*, Erwin & Peggy Bauer/Animals Animals; **page 158:** *left*, Francois Gohier/Photo Researchers; *right*, David M. Schleser/Photo Researchers; **page 159:** *right*, Michel Luquet/Jacana/Photo Researchers; *left*, Wade W. Thornton/Photo Researchers; **page 160:** The Stock Market/LWA-Dann Tardif; **page 161:** CORBIS/Bettmann-UPI; **page 163:** Simon D. Pollard/Photo Researchers; **page 166:** Jim Bockowski/Animals Animals; **page 167:** Joe McDonald/DRK.

TAR PITS—X-PERIMENTS

page 171: John D. Cunningham/Visuals Unlimited; **page 173:** J. H. Robinson/Photo Researchers; **page 174:** J. Marshall/The Image Works; **page 175:** CORBIS/Bettmann-UPI; **page 178:** CORBIS/NASA/Roger Ressmeyer; **page 181:** *left*, N. Et Perennou/Photo Researchers; *right*, Ed Degginger/Bruce Coleman Inc.; **page 183:** Compost/Visaoe/Peter Arnold, Inc.; **page 185:** *left*, Barry Dowsett/Science Photo Library/Photo Researchers; *center left*, Chris Bjornberg/Photo Researchers; *center right*, Barry Dowsett/Science Photo Library/Photo Researchers; *right*, EM Unit, University of Southampton/Science Photo Library/Photo Researchers; **page 186:** CORBIS/Bettmann-UPI; **page 189:** Mark Clark/Science Photo Library/Photo Researchers; **page 192:** John Bavosi/Science Photo Library/Custom Medical Stock Photo; **page 194:** *top*, John Gerlach/Visuals Unlimited; *bottom*, John D. Cunningham/Visuals Unlimited; **page 197:** Tony Stone Images/Sean Ellis; **page 198:** The Kobal Collection; **page 199:** Index Stock Imagery; **page 200:** *left*, Lambert/Archive Photos; **page 201:** Michael Fogden/Bruce Coleman Inc.; **page 202:** Simon D. Pollard/Photo Researchers.

INDEX

(Page numbers in *italic* refer to illustrations.)